7.95

BREADS
by Sharon Tyler Herbst

Sharon Tyler Herbst

Sharon Tyler Herbst was born at noon on Thanksgiving day and, appropriate for one arriving on a day of feasting, has loved the world of food and cooking ever since. With parents who encouraged her natural talents—and the freedom to innovate and experiment—the kitchen was always an exciting place for her.

After college, Sharon apprenticed in the kitchens of a popular Denver restaurant where she met her husband, Ron. Later, in California, Sharon put her journalism major to work as a free-lance copywriter, editor and short-story writer. She currently writes articles for several popular food publications. Sharon is actively involved with the International Association of Cooking Schools. She has studied with many cooking luminaries, including Julia Child, James Beard and Jacques Pepin. She and Ron enjoy traveling throughout the world. They often plan their itineraries according to the region's cuisine and are always searching for new and exciting food ideas.

As a popular cooking teacher in her home and in cooking schools, Sharon delights in sharing her enthusiasm, talent and knowledge. She encourages her students to have fun and to be creative in the kitchen. A spontaneous and creative cook, Sharon loves to develop new recipes. Her efforts have won prizes in 10 professional cooking contests over the past 9 years! Family and friends look forward to samples from the Herbst kitchen whenever Sharon is testing for a class or cookbook.

In this book, Sharon dispels the *yeast mystique* that so often inhibits would-be bakers. She shows how fun and easy it is for anyone to make his or her own homemade bread. She guides both novice and experienced bakers through a delightful selection of classic and exciting new breads. You'll love the raves you receive when you serve your very own homemade bread!

Contents

Bread Basics 4

White-Flour Yeast Breads 18

Whole-Grain & Rye Breads 35

Sweet Yeast Breads & Coffeecakes 58

Batter Breads 74

Little Yeast Breads 86

Little Quick Breads 107

Savory Quick Breads 118

Sweet Quick Breads & Coffeecakes 128

Festive & Holiday Breads 140

Griddle & Fried Breads 160

Index 173

ANOTHER BEST-SELLING VOLUME FROM HPBOOKS®

Publishers: Bill and Helen Fisher; Executive Editor: Rick Bailey;
Editorial Director: Helen Fisher; Editor: Carroll Latham;
Art Director: Don Burton; Book Design: Paul Fitzgerald;
Food Stylist: Mable Hoffman; Photography: George de Gennaro Studios

Published by HPBooks®
P.O. Box 5367, Tucson, AZ 85703
602/888-2150
ISBN 0-89586-219-0
Library of Congress Catalog Card Number 83-81845
© 1983 Fisher Publishing, Inc. Printed in the U.S.A.

COVER PHOTO: Clockwise from top left: Classic French Bread, page 23;
Sunflower-Seed & Yogurt Bread, page 48; Honey Butter, page 46; and Dilly-Rye
Bread, page 53.

Bread Basics

There are few things in the food world that warm hearts and bring on smiles more quickly than a loaf of freshly baked homemade bread. Perhaps, it's the glowing satisfaction and sense of accomplishment you get from baking and serving it to admiring family or guests.

No doubt about it—home breadmaking is on the "rise!" Perhaps it's popular because there's something special about baking bread that appeals to all the senses and positive emotions. You're first aware of the delicious, earthy aroma of yeast as it dissolves and begins to grow or *ferment.* Next comes the warm and responsive feel of the dough as you pummel and knead it—a perfect way to work off pent-up aggressions. Soon the dough begins to rise—slowly the first time, more vigorously the second. This gives you a sense of wonder and excitement. Before long the dough is puffy and rounded, ready for the oven. Soon after, comes one of life's greatest pleasures—the soul-warming fragrance of baking bread, wafting its delicious promise throughout the house.

While the bread cools, you experience the mouth-watering anticipation of that first bite of wholesome, home-baked goodness. Finally, you hear the crackling as your knife cuts the crispy, golden-brown crust to reveal a bread so tender and delicious it doesn't even need butter!

For some unknown reason, the difficulty and "mystery" of baking bread has long been exaggerated. Nonsense! Making bread is a fun, exciting and creative process. There's absolutely no mystery about it! The simple fact is that anyone can make bread—even a beginner. Using bread-kneading aids, such as food processors and heavy-duty mixers with dough hooks, makes breadmaking faster and easier than ever. If you know the basics, can read a recipe and have an oven, you can easily bake perfectly delicious bread.

One of my aims is to dissolve the "yeast mystique" that has intimidated would-be bakers for decades. The truth is, once you learn a few details about yeast, you'll find it's simple and fun to make bread. Once you're charmed by the wonders of yeast, you'll be a breadmaker for life. Learn and remember this basic breadmaking formula: Use the best ingredients you can afford; know the fundamental breadmaking techniques; have the necessary equipment on hand; and start with a good recipe. Now, relax and have fun making your own bread!

You may prefer moist quick breads, biscuits and muffins that take only about an hour from start to finish. Or, your favorites may be tender yeast breads, rolls or coffeecakes that require a slightly longer time. You'll find a wide selection of each in the pages that follow.

Nothing enhances a slice of freshly baked bread better than a layer of creamy butter. But sometimes your mood or the occasion demands a little more flavor than plain butter. I have created an exciting group of flavored spreads and butters. Look for these recipes throughout the book.

Every household has its share of leftover bread but it doesn't have to end up as bird food! There are all manner of delicious ways to use these leftovers and such recipes can be found in several chapters. Keep in mind, recipes aren't written in stone—they're simply blueprints. After you've had a little practice, begin to improvise. Part of the magic and excitement of breadmaking is adding your personal touch to each loaf!

If you're already an experienced baker, you'll want to start trying some of these recipes immediately. If you're a beginner or have never had any "luck" baking bread, take a few minutes to read *Bread Talk,* page 9. Come on, it won't take long! Breadmaking should be an adventure—not a trauma. Once you know a few basics, you'll discover how easy it is to bake bread.

Breadmaking is an exhilarating experience—one of the most positive personal statements you can make. And there's nothing more rewarding than baking a beautiful, delicious loaf of homemade bread and sharing it with someone you love!

Ingredients

FLOUR

The most commonly used flour in breadmaking today is made from wheat, which contains a protein called *gluten*. When dough is kneaded, gluten forms the elastic network that holds in the gas created by fermenting yeast. Gas bubbles cause gluten to stretch and expand, making the dough rise. The less gluten in the flour, the weaker the elasticity of the dough. Without a strong elastic network, gas bubbles will escape into the air rather than leavening the bread.

Look on the flour-package label under *Nutritional Information,* to select a high-protein, good gluten-developing flour. Flours with 12 to 14 grams of protein per cup are best for yeast breads; those with 9 to 11 grams are better for quick breads and pie crusts.

Characteristics of flour vary greatly, making it impossible to give a precise amount of flour for each recipe. Flour absorbs less liquid during hot, humid months than in dry weather because it has already absorbed some moisture from the atmosphere. Your best guideline is to *add only enough flour to keep the dough from being too sticky to work with.* A dough that is slightly *tacky but not sticky* to the touch will yield a much nicer loaf than one that is dry.

Sifting flour isn't necessary. Recipes in this book use the *stir and spoon* method. Simply stir the flour to loosen it. Then spoon it into your measuring cup and level it off with a straight-edged knife or metal spatula. Don't shake or pack the flour down into the cup before leveling.

Store flour in air-tight containers. *All-purpose* and *bread flours* can be kept at room temperature up to 6 months. Temperatures above 75F (25C) and high humidity invite bugs and mold. Flours containing part of the grain's germ, such as whole-wheat flour, turn rancid quickly because of the oil in the germ. Store these flours, tightly wrapped, in the refrigerator or freezer and use as soon as possible. Always bring chilled flours to room temperature before using.

Flour grinding is done with steel or stone rollers that break the wheat kernels, then grind the pieces to a fine flour. Most commercial flour is *steel-ground* and is available in all supermarkets.

Stone-ground flour is available at health-food stores and some supermarkets. Many people feel that stone-ground flour is more nutritious than steel-ground flour. However, it is coarser than steel-ground flour. If you use all stone-ground flour in a recipe and a medium-weight, even-textured loaf is desired, it's necessary to use about 1-1/2 times the yeast normally used.

All-purpose flour is made from a blend of high-gluten hard wheat and low-gluten soft wheat. It's a fine-textured flour milled from the inner part of the wheat kernel and contains neither the *germ*—the sprouting part—nor the *bran*—the outer shell. By law, in the United States, all flours not containing wheat germ must have niacin, riboflavin and thiamin added. Most all-purpose and bread flours are labeled *enriched,* indicating these nutrients have been added.

All-purpose flour comes *bleached* and *unbleached.* They can be used interchangeably. Flour may be bleached chemically or naturally. As it ages, flour becomes lighter in color. All-purpose flour is suitable for most baking, including quick and yeast breads, biscuits, muffins, cookies and cakes.

Bread flour is readily available in most supermarkets. It is a specially formulated flour high in protein—usually about 14 grams per cup. Bread flour is 99.8% unbleached flour with a small amount of malted barley flour—to improve yeast activity—and ascorbic acid (vitamin C) or potassium bromate to make the gluten more elastic and improve the dough's gas retention. I like to use bread flour because it gives a hearty loaf with a firm crumb.

Whole-wheat flour has a higher fat content than all-purpose flour because it is milled from the whole kernel and contains the germ. Purchase whole-wheat flour in small quantities. Store it in the refrigerator or freezer to prevent it from becoming rancid. Breads made with all whole-wheat flour are heavy and compact. The addition of some all-purpose or bread flour provides a better gluten structure, higher volume and finer texture.

Whole-wheat pastry flour is made from finely milled soft wheat and contains very little gluten. It's not recommended for yeast breads, with the exception of Whole-Wheat Croissants, page 102. However, it makes excellent biscuits, quick breads and pastries. It can generally be found in health-food stores. *White pastry flour* is usually sold as cake flour.

Hard-wheat flour, ground from hard spring wheat, is high in protein. It is ideal for yeast breads and can be used in any recipe calling for *bread flour.* It is available in health-food stores.

Rye flour has a very low gluten content and won't produce a satisfactory loaf of bread without the addition of a higher-protein flour. The same is true of oat, corn, rice, barley and buckwheat flours. Rye flour is heavier than all-purpose or whole-wheat flour. It produces a sticky dough requiring patience and extra kneading. *Pumpernickel flour* is a dark, coarsely ground rye flour. *Medium rye flour* is available in most supermarkets; *light* and *dark rye flours* are usually found in health-food stores.

Self-rising flour has salt and leavening added to it. It may be substituted for all-purpose flour if you omit salt in yeast breads and baking powder and salt in quick breads.

SPECIAL FLOURS, MEALS & GRAINS

Bran is referred to in the recipes as *unprocessed bran flakes.* Unprocessed bran is the outer layer of the wheat kernel and is used to add flavor and texture to breads. Store it in the refrigerator or freezer. Do not substitute bran "cereal" for unprocessed bran flakes.

Buckwheat flour can be made at home by processing buckwheat groats in a blender. Buckwheat groats and commercial buckwheat flour can be found in health-food stores and some supermarkets.

Cornmeal is coarsely ground yellow or white corn. It gives a crunchy, grainy texture and slightly sweet flavor to bread.

Cracked wheat is made by cutting whole-wheat kernels into fragments rather than grinding them into flour. It gives bread a chewy texture and a nutty, whole-grain flavor.

Gluten flour is wheat flour treated to remove most of the starch, leaving a high gluten content. It is used mainly as an additive in dough using flour with little or no gluten—such as rye flour—and in dietetic breads. Store gluten flour in the refrigerator.

Oats, a grain rich in minerals and protein, are usually rolled or steel-cut. Regular rolled oats—also called *oat flakes*—are made by rolling each grain into a flake. Quick oats are first cut into thirds, then rolled into flakes. Regular or quick-cooking rolled oats—not instant oatmeal—are used in these recipes. You can make your own oat flour by processing rolled oats in a blender or wheat grinder.

Rice flour is milled from both white and brown rice. It has no gluten and is therefore added to breads mainly for its hearty flavor. *Oriental sweet rice flour* is a thickening agent and should not be used in baking.

Rye flakes, like oatmeal, are flakes from the whole kernel. They add a coarse chewiness and pleasantly bitter flavor to bread.

Soy flour, made from soybeans, is extremely high in vitamins, minerals and protein. Soy flour creates a very brown crust, so oven heat should be reduced by 25F (15C). It has a strong, musty flavor. It is generally added to bread as an enrichment rather than being used as the main flour.

Triticale flour is a modern hybrid of wheat and rye with an even higher protein content than wheat flour. Triticale flour should be refrigerated. It is generally available at health-food stores.

Wheat berries are the entire wheat kernels. They're usually available in health-food stores or storage-food outlets that sell food for home storage. The berries must be softened before using either by soaking overnight in warm water to cover, or by sprouting, page 38.

If you have a wheat grinder, you can grind wheat berries into flour or make cracked wheat. Wheat berries contribute a wonderfully chewy texture and wholesome nutty flavor to bread.

Wheat flakes look like oatmeal and are made from whole berries. They add a lightly sweet flavor and chewy texture to bread.

Wheat germ is the flaky embryo of the wheat kernel and is rich in vitamins, iron, protein and fat. It is sold raw or toasted and should be kept refrigerated. Wheat germ gives a nutty, slightly sweet flavor.

LEAVENING AGENTS

Simply stated, leaveners are what make your bread rise.

Yeast is a living organism that thrives on the natural sugar in starch. When combined with moisture and warmth, yeast begins to ferment, converting the flour's starchy nutrients into alcohol and carbon dioxide. Gas bubbles trapped in the elastic gluten mesh make the dough rise. Oven heat kills the yeast and evaporates the alcohol. It causes the gas to expand in a final burst of energy called *oven-spring,* and raises the dough.

Active dry yeast is packaged in 1/4-ounce envelopes. *Compressed fresh yeast* is packaged in .06-ounce cakes. One package of dry yeast is equal to 1 scant tablespoon dry yeast or 1 cake compressed yeast. Active dry yeast was used in these recipes.

Active dry yeast comes in two forms—regular and quick-rising. They may be used interchangeably. Quick-rising is a new strain of yeast that rises bread in half the time of regular dry yeast. All active dry yeast has been dehydrated. Its cells are alive, but dormant. The cells become active again when mixed with a warm liquid. Dry yeast should be stored in a cool, dry place, but can be kept in the refrigerator or freezer. Properly stored, it is reliable when used by the expiration date stamped on the envelope. Bulk dry yeast, available at health-food stores and storage-food outlets, is a bit more risky to use because you don't know how old it is or how it was stored. The best way to check any questionable yeast is to *proof* it, page 9.

Compressed fresh yeast is moist and extremely perishable. It must be refrigerated and used within one to two weeks or by the date indicated on the package. It can be frozen, but should be defrosted at room temperature and used immediately. *Always* proof compressed yeast.

The temperature of liquid in which yeast is dissolved is very important. Too much heat will kill it—too little will slow its growth. Dissolve dry yeast in liquids at 105F to 115F (40C to 45C), compressed yeast at 95F (35C). Don't guess! Until you're experienced, use a thermometer for accurate readings of warm liquids.

Generally, 1 package or cake of yeast is used to raise 4 to 5 cups of flour. Extra yeast may be used to speed the rising, but too much produces a porous texture and yeasty flavor. Too little yeast creates a heavy, dense loaf. Doughs rich in butter, eggs, sweeteners, fruits or nuts often require double the amount of yeast.

Sourdough starter is a homemade leavening agent. Basically, it's a mixture of flour and liquid into which yeast spores have been introduced. It's extremely temperamental but, at its best, produces a tangy, slightly sour loaf.

Salt-rising bread uses a starter made with water or milk, cornmeal, sugar and salt. No yeast is added. A salt-rising starter is even more temperamental than sourdough and demands an initial incubation temperature of about 95F (35C) for 12 to 24 hours.

Baking soda or *bicarbonate of soda,* when combined with a liquid acid such as buttermilk, yogurt or molasses, produces carbon dioxide. Because baking soda reacts immediately when moistened, it should always be mixed with dry ingredients in the recipe before adding any liquid.

Baking powder contains baking soda, an acid such as cream of tartar and a moisture-absorber such as cornstarch. When mixed with liquid, baking powder releases carbon dioxide, as fermenting yeast does, but with a different flavor and texture. *Single-acting* baking powder immediately releases its gas into the batter. More commonly used *double-acting* baking powder releases some gas when it becomes wet and again when the batter is exposed to heat. Double-acting baking powder is used in these recipes.

Baking powder is perishable and should be kept in a cool, dry place. Always check the date on the bottom of the can when you buy it. If you're unsure of your baking powder's integrity, combine 1 teaspoon baking powder with 1/3 cup hot water. If it bubbles enthusiastically, use it.

Too much baking powder or baking soda gives bread a crumbly, dry texture and bitter flavor. It can also make the batter overrise, causing the bread to fall. Too little baking powder or baking soda gives bread a heavy, gummy texture.

LIQUIDS

Liquids moisten dry ingredients and hold the bread together. Water and milk are the two most commonly used liquids. Many other liquids bring their own characteristics to bread.

Water creates a crisp crust and brings out the wheat flavor. If your water has a high mineral content, use bottled water to prevent an off-flavor.

Potato water is water in which peeled potatoes have been boiled. It gives good flavor and a smooth crumb. Because of the added starch, the dough rises faster than with other liquids.

Milk products, including milk, buttermilk, yogurt and sour cream, give the bread a creamy tan color and produce a fine texture and a soft, brown crust. Breads made with milk stay fresher longer than those made with water.

With modern pasteurization, scalding milk isn't necessary. The only time scalding is mandatory is when you're using raw, unpasteurized milk. Raw milk contains an organism that breaks down the gluten structure. Nonfat-milk powder and evaporated milk produce a rich dough. Add milk powder to the dry ingredients or dissolve it in warm water.

Eggs give bread a rich, moist crumb, a creamy-yellow color and a brown crust.

Fruit and vegetable juices add flavor and body. Baking soda is added to quick breads made with fruit juices to neutralize their natural acid.

Syrups, such as molasses, honey and maple syrup, give a moist crumb and dark crust.

Vegetable and meat broths add flavor and create a lightly crisp crust. If the broth is salted, reduce the amount of salt called for in the recipe.

Beer, wine, cider and liquors give bread a smooth grain and distinctive flavor. The quality and flavor of the liquid will be reflected in your bread, so don't bake with anything you wouldn't drink! And don't worry about any alcohol—it evaporates as bread bakes.

Tea and coffee provide flavor, a richly colored crumb and a dark, crisp crust.

OTHER ADDITIONS

Sugar adds flavor and tenderness to bread, helps brown the crust and creates a nicely textured loaf. It's also a food for yeast. Many classic yeast breads, such as French and Italian, do not use sugar. The yeast gets its energy from starch in the flour. Breads without sugar take longer to rise. Too much sugar overpowers the leavening action of the yeast and inhibits rising; too much in quick bread produces a soggy loaf with a thick crust. If you want to substitute a syrup sweetener for dry sugar, reduce the liquid by 1/4 cup for each 1/2 cup syrup added.

Salt intensifies flavor. Saltless bread tastes bland and flat. Unless absolutely necessary, don't leave it out entirely. Salt also stabilizes the fermentation of yeast and strengthens the gluten. Too much salt will prevent yeast from fermenting; too little lets yeast grow unchecked.

Fats include butter, margarine, oil, lard, shortening and bacon fat or other meat drippings. They can generally be used interchangeably. Fat increases the bread's tenderness and keeps it soft and moist. In yeast breads, it lubricates the gluten strands, making them more elastic. Yeast breads made without fat are very chewy and tend to dry out quickly. Too little fat in quick breads creates a dry, coarsely grained loaf. Too much fat produces an oily bread with a crumbly texture.

Unsalted butter was used in these recipes for its sweet flavor and because it gives the cook more control over the final flavor. If you use salted butter or margarine, reduce the amount of salt called for. Unsalted margarine can be substituted for unsalted butter. However, unsalted butter is a must for delicate pastries, such as croissants and Danish pastry.

Eggs add to the liquid content of bread, but they also contribute flavor, structure, fat and leavening power. Recipes in this book were made with large, Grade AA or Grade A eggs. One large egg equals about 1/4 cup liquid. For a richer dough, substitute 2 egg yolks for 1 whole egg. If cutting a recipe in half that calls for 5 eggs, use 2 whole eggs and 1 egg yolk.

Dried or fresh fruits, vegetables, nuts, cheese, seeds, spices, herbs, flavoring extracts and *cocoa* all add flavor and personality to bread. In yeast breads, cheese, dried fruits and nuts are usually kneaded into the dough after the first rise. Lightly flour them before adding to dough to keep them separate. Herbs, spices and cocoa are added to dry ingredients, and flavoring extracts to liquid ingredients.

Techniques for Making Yeast Doughs

Proofing Yeast—This simply means testing the yeast to be sure it's alive. Because of the reliability of today's active dry yeast, proofing isn't always necessary. However, because it gives yeast a *head start,* proofing is done in these recipes. If you prefer not to proof the yeast, after it is dissolved, immediately continue making your bread. However, if the expiration date on the package has passed or if you're unsure of your yeast, proof it before using. Because of its perishability, compressed fresh yeast should always be proofed. For more information on yeast, see page 7.

To proof yeast: Dissolve the yeast and 1 teaspoon sugar in the warm liquid called for in the recipe. Let the mixture stand 5 to 10 minutes. If the mixture begins to swell and foam, the yeast is alive. If you see no activity, discard the mixture and begin again with new yeast. There's absolutely no way to revive dead yeast!

Mixing and Kneading—After dissolving and proofing the yeast, add the remaining ingredients as directed in the recipe, using 2 to 3 cups flour. Beat 2 to 3 minutes with an electric mixer or, beat 200 to 300 strokes by hand. This initial beating stimulates development of the gluten and shortens kneading time. In *batter breads*—yeast breads that are not kneaded—the mixture is beaten 4 minutes or 400 strokes.

After beating, stir in enough remaining flour to make a soft dough. Turn out dough onto a lightly floured surface. Use a paper towel to rub any dry particles out of the bowl in which the dough was mixed. Grease the bowl and use it for the first rise of the dough.

The height of your work surface is critical for successful kneading. If the table or countertop is too high, you lose leverage and power—too low and you're sure to finish with a tired back. The ideal height lets you fully extend your arms downward, palms resting on the surface.

Kneading is important because it strengthens and stretches the *gluten strands,* so they can form the mesh that holds in gas bubbles produced by the yeast. Everyone has his or her own style of kneading. Any way you do it is fine, as long as the end result is smooth, elastic dough.

How to Make Yeast Dough

1/Proof yeast by adding warm liquid and sugar. If it swells and foams, use the mixture to leaven bread.

2/Beat 2 to 3 minutes with electric mixer or, beat 200 to 300 strokes by hand.

Basically, kneading is a push-fold-turn action. To begin, dust your hands with flour. Firmly press down on the dough with the heels of both hands, pushing away from you. Fold the dough and give it a slight turn. Repeat pushing, folding and turning for the time specified in each recipe. Be careful not to tear the dough or it will break the gluten strands. Establish your own pace and develop a rhythm. Lean into the dough and let your body weight help. To give your wrists a rest, you can pick up the dough and slam it down hard on the work surface several times. It's great fun and a wonderful way to work off tension!

Too much flour on the work surface may result in a heavy dough. The amount of flour to use depends on the flour's basic characteristics and the humidity and temperature of the day. The more humidity, the more flour needed. If the dough is extremely soft and sticky when you begin to knead, use a *pastry scraper*. Add a little more flour to the work surface. Gradually knead flour into the dough with the scraper until the dough is smooth, tender and elastic. If you knead too much flour into the dough, use an atomizer to mist it lightly with warm water. Gradually knead in enough water to make the dough pliable.

If layers of flour and dough build up on the palms of your hands, rub your palms together over a sink or wastebasket. These particles should not be kneaded back into the dough. If you're interrupted while kneading, place a bowl over the dough until you can continue. This will prevent the dough from drying. Don't leave your dough longer than 15 to 20 minutes.

Properly kneaded dough is smooth and elastic. Press on the dough with your fingers, making shallow indentations. If the dough springs back, it's been kneaded enough. Another indication is when tiny blisters form on the dough's surface. After making bread a few times, you'll know when the dough has been kneaded enough by the way it *feels*.

Using a *heavy-duty mixer* with one or two *dough hooks* conserves time and energy when mixing and kneading dough. Kneading by machine takes two-thirds to three-fourths as long as by hand. You'll miss out on the pleasure of plunging your fingers into the warm, resilient dough, but it does save time! Simply add the ingredients to the yeast mixture in the bowl, according to the recipe. Then begin kneading with the mixer, following manufacturer's directions. Finish the last few minutes of kneading by hand. Machines can't tell you the exact moment when the dough feels right.

Many breads can be mixed and kneaded in a large-capacity *food processor* with a strong motor. Smaller food processors can handle doughs using only about 3 cups of flour. For most bread recipes, this means you have to mix the dough in a separate bowl. Then, knead half of it at a time in the food processor. Larger food processors usually handle dough with up to 6 cups of flour. Consult the manufacturer's booklet to be sure your food processor can be used to knead dough.

To use your food processor, combine yeast, 1 teaspoon sugar and the warm liquid in a 2-cup liquid measuring cup. Stir to dissolve, then set aside until foamy. Meanwhile, combine dry ingredients in the food-processor bowl fitted with the metal blade or plastic dough blade. Process dry ingredients 5 seconds to blend. Stir other liquid ingredients into the yeast mixture. With the processor running, slowly pour the yeast mixture into the work bowl. Process until the mixture comes away from the sides of the work bowl. Process about 30 seconds longer. Let the dough stand 2 to 3 minutes to absorb the liquid completely. With the processor running, add more flour, if necessary, to make a dough that forms a ball. Process about 30 seconds longer or until smooth. Knead 1 to 2 minutes by hand.

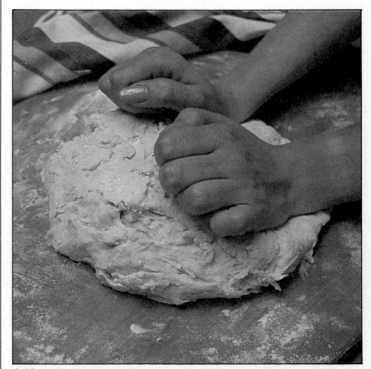

3/Knead dough with a push-fold-turn motion until smooth and elastic.

The *sponge method* adds flavor and texture to breads and reduces kneading and rising times. Almost any yeast-bread recipe can be adapted to this method. Simply stir yeast into warm liquid until dissolved. Add remaining liquid except eggs, butter, oil or shortening. Add as much as 1/4 cup sugar—but no more than what is called for in the recipe—and enough flour to make a stiff *batter*. Beat with an electric mixer at least 3 minutes to help develop the gluten. Tightly cover with plastic wrap. Let rise in a warm place, free from drafts, until the mixture foams and bubbles to twice its original bulk. This will take at least 30 minutes. If a tangy flavor is desired, let the mixture stand overnight. Stir down the sponge and add remaining ingredients. Follow recipe directions for kneading and rising.

The *Rapidmix method*® was developed by the Fleischmann's Yeast test kitchens. Although no recipes using this method are included in this book, most breads can be adapted to it. In a large bowl, blend active dry yeast, other dry ingredients and about a third of the flour. Heat the liquids—except eggs—until very warm (120F to 130F, 50C to 55C). Stir warm liquid into the dry ingredients, then beat at medium speed about 2 minutes. Add eggs, if they are called for; beat 3

minutes longer. Stir in enough remaining flour to make a soft dough. Turn out dough onto a lightly floured surface; knead as directed.

Betty Crocker Kitchens developed the *Can-Do Quick method*® that combines yeast with baking powder. Most plain yeast breads can be adapted to this method. For a basic recipe using 5 to 6 cups flour and 2 cups liquid, use 2 (1/4-ounce) packages active dry yeast and 2 teaspoons baking powder. Dissolve yeast as recipe directs. Add baking powder with remaining ingredients. Knead the dough as directed. Shape into loaves; place in greased pans. Brush melted butter over tops of loaves. Cover with buttered waxed paper. Set in a warm place to rise until doubled in bulk. Bake in a preheated 400F (205C) oven 30 to 40 minutes or until loaf tests done, page 14.

Setting Dough to Rise—Now you're ready to place the dough in a bowl for the first rising. Shape the dough into a ball. Place it smooth-side down in the prepared bowl, then turn it right-side up to coat all surfaces. This light coating of grease keeps the dough moist and prevents it from forming a skin that will inhibit the dough's expansion. Cover with a slightly damp towel and set the bowl in a warm place, free from drafts. Drafts cause dough to rise slowly and unevenly.

During the rising time, the yeast continues to grow, giving off gas that gently and slowly expands the dough. Rising time varies, depending on temperature of ingredients, amount of yeast used and where the dough is set to rise. The first rising will take 1 to 1-1/2 hours in a warm place; at normal room temperature, 1-1/2 to 2 hours; and 8 to 12 hours in the refrigerator. Dough rises faster the second and third times.

Ideally, dough should rise at 80F to 85F (25C to 30C), but will rise at 100F (45C) without killing the yeast. It rises nicely inside a gas oven warmed only by the pilot light. Or, let rise in an electric oven heated at 200F (95C) for 1 minute and then turned off. Always check the temperature with an oven thermometer to be sure it's not too hot. If your washer or dryer have been recently used and are warm, dough can be placed on them to rise. The room will be warm and humid—yeast's favorite atmosphere. You can also set the dough over a pan of hot water in a closed oven. Or, bring 2 cups of water to a boil in your microwave oven to create a warm, moist atmosphere. Turn off the power; set the dough in the microwave oven and close the door.

4/Shape dough into a ball. Place smooth-side down in greased bowl, then turn right-side up to coat all sides.

Dough should rise to double its original bulk. To test it after the first rising, poke 2 fingers about 1/2 inch deep into the dough. If the indentations stay after your fingers are removed, the dough is ready. Batter breads are ready when the batter has doubled in bulk and is bubbly and spongy.

Micro-rise method lets dough rise in a microwave oven at 10% power in 1/4 to 1/3 the regular time. However, any form of quick rising means the dough won't have as much time to develop its full flavor. You *must* have a microwave oven with 10% power. If your power level doesn't go that low, or your microwave oven only has "low, medium and high" settings, forget micro-rising or the end result will be a baked lump of dough. *To micro-rise dough for two standard-size loaves:* Set a cup of hot water at a back corner of your microwave oven. Place the dough in a large, greased, *glass* bowl. Cover with plastic wrap, then a damp towel. Set the power level at 10%; turn on for 8 minutes. Let the dough rest 5 minutes. Repeat at 10% power 5 to 8 minutes longer or until the dough has doubled in bulk. Doughs enriched with butter, fruits and nuts will take longer to rise than plain doughs. The second rising—after the dough is shaped into loaves—will take 8 to 10 minutes, but the loaves must be in glass baking dishes. Refer to your microwave owner's guide for specific information on rising bread in your microwave oven.

Quick-rise method can be used if you're really in a hurry. Knead the dough as usual. Cover and let rest in a warm place 20 minutes. Knead 30 seconds; shape into loaves and place in greased pans. Let rise, then bake as directed.

Coolrise ® is a two-day rising method developed by the Robin Hood Flour test kitchens. Use it only for basic white and wheat loaves that do not contain weighty ingredients such as fruits and nuts. Knead the dough as directed. Cover and let rest in a warm place 20 minutes. Knead 30 seconds; shape into loaves and place in greased pans. Lightly brush the tops of loaves with vegetable oil to prevent a dry crust from forming. Cover loosely with waxed paper. Place each pan in a plas-

5/To test after first rising, poke 2 fingers into dough, about 1/2 inch deep. If indentations stay, dough has raised long enough.

6/Punch down dough by pressing down center with your fist. Pull dough from side of bowl to center.

tic bag large enough for the dough to expand without bursting the bag. Refrigerate 2 to 24 hours. Remove loaves from the plastic bags. Slash the tops of loaves as desired, page 14. Let stand at room temperature 15 minutes while the oven preheats to 400F (205C). Bake 35 to 45 minutes or until the bread tests done, page 14.

Punching Down and Shaping—Now comes the fun part! Give the dough a good "sock" in the middle with your fist. This is called "punching down the dough." The air will release like a sigh as the dough collapses. On a lightly floured surface, gently knead about 30 seconds, to remove air bubbles. At this time, the dough can be returned to the greased bowl and let rise again before shaping, if desired. *Texture of the final loaf will become progressively finer each time it rises.* Or, after returning dough to the bowl, cover tightly and refrigerate up to 2 days. It will continue to rise in the refrigerator and should be punched down once a day. Remove from the refrigerator at least 3 hours before shaping.

Baking-pan materials affect the way your bread bakes. In general, dull metals are better heat conductors than shiny metals. Pans with a dark surface—including teflon-coated—absorb and hold heat, creating an even, crunchy, dark-brown crust. Bright metal finishes, such as aluminum, reflect heat and make bread soft and pale. Glass, ceramic and clay containers also retain heat well and produce beautiful, deep golden-brown crusts. *Reduce oven temperatures 25F (15C) when using glass bakeware.*

To shape, divide dough as directed. Cover and let rest 10 minutes. This makes the dough easier to handle for final shaping and gives you time to grease required baking pans or sheets. Shape as directed and place in pans or on baking sheets. Shape dough into an oblong to fit pan. Pull sides of dough to bottom; pinch to seal. Or, pat or roll out dough to a rectangle. Roll or fold to fit pan; pinch edges to seal. Cover with a dry towel. Let rise in a warm place, free from drafts, until doubled in bulk.

7/Shape dough to fit pan. Pull dough sides to bottom; pinch to seal.

8/For free-form loaf, shape dough into a round ball, tapered oblong or braid, page 73.

Slashing and Topping—After the dough rises, slash loaf tops with a sharp knife, razor blade or metal food-processor blade. Make slashes 1/4 to 1/2 inch deep. You can also use pointed scissors to clip loaf tops. Slashing the loaves not only gives a professional look, but lets excess gas escape during baking, preventing ragged splitting. Brush loaf tops with a glaze as directed in each recipe. Or, choose your own glaze from *The Upper Crust,* opposite. If the recipe calls for them, sprinkle loaves with seeds or grains before baking.

Baking and Cooling—Place baking pans, about 4 inches apart, near the center of the middle shelf in a preheated oven. Resist peeking during the first 15 to 20 minutes. You can lose up to 25% oven heat by opening the door. It's not unusual for a loaf to increase in size by one-third during the first 15 minutes of baking. This dramatic rise is known as *oven-spring* and will continue until the interior temperature of the bread reaches 140F (60C), when the yeast is killed.

Bread may also be started in a cold oven if you're in a hurry and trying to speed the last few minutes of rising time. However, it should not be used to replace the entire second rise. When the dough has almost doubled, place the loaves in a cold oven. Set the temperature 25F (15C) higher than called for in the recipe. Bake five minutes less than the time called for in the recipe before testing for doneness. The crust on a loaf started in a cold oven will be thicker and firmer.

To test bread for doneness: Cover your hands with hot pads or oven mitts. Turn the baked loaf out onto your covered hand and lightly tap the bottom with your fingertips. When done, bread sounds hollow. If the bottom of your loaf isn't browned or quite as firm as you desire, place it directly on the oven rack and bake five minutes longer. Place the bread top-side up on a rack to cool. For best texture, let your yeast breads cool two to three hours before slicing. If you absolutely can't wait and don't mind a doughy crumb, wait 30 minutes, then enjoy!

9/Cut 1/4- to 1/2-inch-deep slashes in tops of loaves with a sharp knife, razor blade, metal food-processor blade or pointed scissors.

10/Brush loaf tops with a glaze as directed in each recipe. Or, choose your own glaze from *The Upper Crust,* opposite.

The Upper Crust

You can slash the tops of unbaked loaves before or after brushing them with a glaze and sprinkling with seeds and nuts. Slashing before they are glazed gives a uniformly colored and garnished crust. If you brush them with glaze first, then slash them, it creates a crust with textural contrast and an attractive two-tone effect. The slashes will be a lighter color and free of seeds or nuts.

Whether you like your crust tender, crisp or chewy, you can achieve what you want with a few simple techniques.

Before baking, brush the tops of your loaves with:

Water for a crisp crust. Brush again 10 minutes before baking time is complete or, spray with an atomizer. For a lightly salted crust, dissolve 1/2 teaspoon salt in 1/4 cup water. Placing a pan of hot water on the oven shelf below the bread while baking will also create steam for a crisper crust. Remove the water 10 minutes before baking time is over to let crust dry.

Egg Glaze for shine and holding seeds in place. Egg yolks give a dark-brown crust; egg whites a shiny crust; whole eggs give shine and color. Mix 1 whole egg with 1 tablespoon cold water; 1 egg yolk or egg white with 2 teaspoons cold water.

Milk or Melted Butter for a soft, tender crust.

Honey, Molasses or Maple-Syrup Glaze for a soft, shiny and slightly sweet crust. Any syrupy sweetener can be combined with water or melted butter to create a crust glaze. Usually, 1 teaspoon honey, molasses or maple syrup is mixed with 2 to 3 teaspoons water or melted butter until thoroughly combined before brushing on tops of loaves. Undiluted syrupy sweeteners may also be used for more concentrated flavor and sheen.

Cornstarch Wash for a chewy crust. In a small saucepan, dissolve 1/2 teaspoon cornstarch in 1/3 cup cold water. Bring mixture to a boil; cook 30 seconds, stirring constantly. Cool to warm before brushing on tops of loaves.

Dutch-Crunch Topping for a crackled, flour-crunchy crust. Dissolve 3 (1/4-ounce) packages active dry yeast and 1 teaspoon sugar in 3/4 cup warm water (110F, 45C). Let stand until foamy, 5 to 10 minutes. Add 1 tablespoon sugar, 1 teaspoon salt, 1 tablespoon vegetable oil and 1 cup rice flour—not Oriental sweet rice flour. Beat until smooth. Cover and let rise in a warm place until bubbly and doubled in bulk, about 30 minutes. Spread over tops of loaves or rolls before second rising.

High-Altitude Adjustments

At altitudes above 3,500 feet, flour tends to be drier and absorbs more liquid. Slightly more liquid or less flour may be required for dough to reach the proper consistency.

Dough rises faster at higher altitudes. No recipe adjustment is suggested for yeast doughs. But, the dough develops a fuller flavor when it rises twice before the final shaping and rising. Increase the baking temperature by 25F (15C). This sets the crust faster so the bread cannot rise too much during the first 10 to 15 minutes of baking.

When using baking powder and baking soda, reduce each by 1/8 to 1/4 teaspoon. Generally, 1 teaspoon baking powder or 1/2 teaspoon baking soda per cup of flour is enough for high-altitude quick breads. Decrease sugar in sweet quick breads by 1 to 2 tablespoons per cup of flour to prevent a porous crumb with a thick crust.

What Went Wrong?

Problem	Cause	Solution
Yeast Breads:		
Bread rose up and over sides of pan.	Pan was too small.	Do not fill pans more than 1/2 to 2/3 full.
Crust is too pale.	Oven temperature too low.	Place pan higher in oven.
Crust too dark.	Oven too hot. Too much sugar in dough.	Place a tent of foil over top after lightly browned. Use amount of sugar stated in recipe.
Bread is crumbly and dry.	Not enough flour for liquid. Not enough kneading.	Follow recipe directions. Knead for longer time.
Top crust separates from rest of loaf.	Crust dried during rising. Loaf improperly shaped.	Cover rising dough with slightly damp towel. Knead excess air from dough after punching down. Use greater care in shaping.
Bread rose unevenly.	Oven temperature too low. Loaf improperly shaped.	Use an oven thermometer to determine oven temperature. Use greater care in shaping.
Pale bottom and side crusts.	Baked in shiny aluminum pans that deflect heat.	Remove from pans; bake directly on oven rack 5 minutes or until crust is nicely browned.
Large holes in bread.	Too much yeast. Overkneading. Inadequate punch down. Too long a rising time.	Reduce yeast 1 teaspoon. Knead only recommended time. Knead out excess air before shaping. Reduce rising time.
Loaf has crack on one side. (Doesn't affect flavor. Call loaf *country* or *peasant*, because of rugged appearance.)	Bread expanded after crust formed.	Slash top of loaf before baking.
Free-form loaf is flat.	Dough too soft.	Add extra flour for a firmer dough.
Bread is dense and soggy.	Too much liquid; not enough kneading.	Follow recipe directions for liquid and kneading.
Has nice crumb, but is slightly gummy.	Underbaked.	Test loaf for doneness before cooling.
One side higher than the other.	Uneven baking.	All ovens have hot spots. Rotate pans front to back; bottom shelf to top shelf.

What Went Wrong?

Problem	Cause	Solution
Bread is flat and compact.	Rose too long in pans, then collapsed in oven heat.	Let rise a shorter time in pans.
Crust too thick and tough.	Oven temperature too low.	Raise oven temperature 25F (15C). Test doneness sooner.
Dense, close-textured crumb.	Not enough yeast. Too much salt. Insufficient rising time.	Add 1 to 3 teaspoons yeast. Measure salt carefully. Let dough rise until doubled in bulk or as directed.
Porous texture. Strong yeast flavor	Too much yeast.	Use less yeast or as recipe directs.
Bread is chewy and dry.	Too little fat.	Use 2 tablespoons fat per loaf of bread.

Quick Breads:

Soggy and sunken in middle.	Too much liquid or sugar. Too little baking powder or baking soda.	Follow recipe directions.
Crack in top of loaf.	Characteristic of quick breads. Caused by escaping steam and gas.	Leave as is or, line pan with waxed paper, letting paper extend 3 inches over top. This deflects heat from top of loaf.
Dry crumb with bulge in center.	Not enough liquid. Not enough shortening.	Follow recipe directions.
Coarse, crumbly texture and bitter aftertaste.	Too much baking soda or baking powder.	Reduce baking soda or baking powder. See recipe directions. Make altitude adjustments.
Bread is greasy with crisp edges.	Too much shortening.	Measure shortening correctly.
Crust is thick, porous and too brown.	Too much sugar.	Reduce sugar slightly.
Breads, muffins or biscuits are tough.	Overhandling of batter or dough.	Stir ingredients together *only* until dry ingredients are moistened. Never beat batter or dough.

White-Flour Yeast Breads

Don't let the title of this chapter mislead you. It doesn't promise an ordinary assortment of uninteresting loaves lacking flavor and character. Far from it! White flour—I use unbleached bread flour or all-purpose flour—forms the foundation for a variety of flavors with the possibility of all kinds of additions. Add whatever you choose—mushrooms, garlic, butter, cheese, potatoes, shredded wheat. You name it! Before you know it, you'll be creating delicious, full-flavor breads that are *anything* but ordinary!

No one ever called a *brioche* "ordinary." *Au contraire!* Buttery-rich and finely textured, this regal French member of the bread family is fit for the highest royalty. I fell in love with this buttery delight in Paris, where Petites Brioches are served with deliciously thick black coffee for *petit déjeuner*—breakfast. The classic Brioche has a fluted base and a jaunty topknot that makes it easy to recognize.

Another delightfully different bread is cheese-filled Khachapuri from the Georgian Republic of Russia. There, hawkers sell miniature, simplified versions on the streets to passersby who eat it on the run. Khachapuri is best served at room temperature and is therefore ideal for special picnics. Slice thick wedges to serve with marinated artichokes and mushrooms, cherry tomatoes, fresh fruit and a chilled bottle of wine. What a delightful way to spend a lazy summer afternoon!

Living just across the majestic Golden Gate Bridge, with the city of San Francisco sparkling in full view, is it any wonder I have a passion for tangy San Francisco Sourdough Bread? How can such simple beginnings as water and flour produce such delicious flavor? Early American frontier families knew the value of a good sourdough starter and carried crocks of it with them on long treks. It was a legacy to be treasured and passed on to family and friends throughout the years. Why should we be any different?

Basic White Bread

Photos on pages 22 and 98.

Use your imagination to vary this tasty white bread.

1 (1/4-oz.) pkg. active dry yeast
   (1 tablespoon)
1 teaspoon sugar
1/4 cup warm water (110F, 45C)
2 tablespoons sugar
1 tablespoon salt

1-3/4 cups milk, room temperature
1/4 cup butter, melted
6 to 6-1/2 cups all-purpose or bread flour
1 egg white blended with
   1 tablespoon water for glaze

In large bowl of electric mixer, dissolve yeast and 1 teaspoon sugar in water. Let stand until foamy, 5 to 10 minutes. Add 2 tablespoons sugar, salt, milk, butter and 1-1/2 cups flour. Beat at medium speed with electric mixer 2 minutes or, beat 200 vigorous strokes by hand. Stir in enough remaining flour to make a soft dough. Turn out dough onto a lightly floured surface. Clean and grease bowl. **Knead dough** 8 to 10 minutes or until smooth and elastic. Place dough in greased bowl, turning to coat all sides. Cover with a slightly damp towel. Let rise in a warm place, free from drafts, until doubled in bulk, about 1 hour. Grease 2 (8" x 4") loaf pans. **Punch down dough;** knead 30 seconds. Divide dough in half. Shape into loaves and place in prepared pans. Cover with a dry towel. Let rise until doubled in bulk, about 1 hour. **Preheat oven** to 375F (190C). Slash tops of loaves. Brush with egg-white glaze. Bake 35 to 40 minutes or until bread sounds hollow when tapped on bottom. Remove from pans. Cool on racks. Makes 2 loaves.

Variations

Substitute fruit juice, vegetable juice, beer or bouillon for milk.

Monkey Bread: Generously grease a 10-cup tube or Bundt pan. After first rising, divide dough in half. Roll out each half until 1/4 inch thick. Cut in diamond shapes, about 3 inches long. Dip each piece in melted butter. Arrange in prepared pan in an overlapping pattern, making 3 or 4 layers. For sweet Monkey Bread, make a mixture of 1 cup packed brown sugar, 1 teaspoon ground cinnamon, 1 cup chopped walnuts or pecans and 1/2 cup raisins. Sprinkle evenly over each layer. Cover with a dry towel. Let rise as above. Bake in preheated 375F (190C) oven, 45 to 55 minutes or until bread sounds hollow when tapped on top. Carefully turn out onto a rack. Cool at least 20 minutes; serve warm. Makes 1 large loaf.

Nut or Fruit Bread: Increase 2 tablespoons sugar to 1/2 to 3/4 cup. Add 1-1/2 cups finely chopped nuts or dried fruit and 1 to 2 teaspoons spices of your choice with first addition of flour. Add 1 tablespoon freshly grated lemon peel or orange peel for citrus bread.

Seeded Bread: Add 1 tablespoon caraway seeds, 1/4 cup poppy seeds or 1/3 cup toasted sesame seeds with first addition of flour. Sprinkle same seeds over top of unbaked loaf.

Herb Bread: Add 2 to 4 teaspoons dried herbs or 1 to 3 tablespoons minced fresh herbs with first addition of flour. If desired, add 1 tablespoon dried minced onion or 1/4 cup minced fresh onion.

Salt-Free Diet Bread: Omit salt; decrease 2 tablespoons sugar to 1 teaspoon; decrease butter to 2 tablespoons.

Butter-Top Bread: Prepare as directed through second rising. Brush tops of loaves with melted butter. Make a 1/2-inch-deep slash down center of each loaf. Drizzle 1 teaspoon melted butter in center of each slash.

Saffron Bread: Dissolve 1/4 teaspoon powdered saffron in 1 tablespoon hot water. With first addition of flour, add saffron mixture.

Brioche   Photo on page 22.

This classic, butter-rich "Queen" of breads makes any occasion special!

1 (1/4-oz.) pkg. active dry yeast (1 tablespoon)	2 eggs, room temperature
1/4 teaspoon sugar	1 egg yolk, room temperature
1/4 cup warm water (110F, 45C)	3/4 cup butter, cut in 12 pieces, brought to room temperature
2 cups all-purpose flour	1 egg yolk blended with
2 tablespoons sugar	1 teaspoon cream for glaze
1 teaspoon salt	

In large bowl of electric mixer, dissolve yeast and 1/4 teaspoon sugar in water. Let stand until foamy, 5 to 10 minutes. Add flour, 2 tablespoons sugar, salt, 2 eggs, 1 egg yolk and butter. Beat at medium speed with electric mixer 4 to 6 minutes until shiny and pliable. Dough will be soft and sticky. If your mixer can't beat dough, beat vigorously with a wooden spoon, 10 to 15 minutes. Or grasp dough with your hands, lift about 12 inches above bowl, then slap back down hard into bowl. Repeat 12 to 15 times or until shiny and pliable. Cover bowl tightly with plastic wrap and a slightly damp towel. Let rise in a warm place, free from drafts, until light, spongy and tripled in bulk, about 3 hours. **Stir down dough;** beat 1 minute. Cover tightly with plastic wrap; refrigerate overnight or at least 6 hours. Remove dough from refrigerator. Punch down and shape as desired. Makes 1 large loaf or 16 rolls.

Brioche à Tête: Generously grease a fluted, 7- or 8-inch brioche mold or a 1-1/2-quart casserole or soufflé dish. Pinch off a piece of dough the size of an extra-large egg; set aside. Shape remaining dough into a smooth ball. Place seam-side down in prepared mold or dish. Butter your thumb and a 12-inch square of waxed paper. Press your thumb into center of dough ball, making an indentation about 3/4 inch deep. Shape reserved dough like a teardrop. Pressing lightly, insert small end into depression made by your thumb. Loosely cover with buttered waxed paper. Let rise until doubled in bulk, 1-1/2 to 2 hours. **Preheat oven** to 425F (220C). Gently brush brioche with egg-yolk glaze. Bake 5 minutes. Reduce heat to 375F (190C). Bake 35 minutes longer or until a wooden pick inserted in center comes out clean. Turn out onto a rack; cool, top-side up, 20 minutes. Serve warm. Makes 1 loaf.

Petites Brioches: Generously grease 16 individual brioche tins or muffin cups. Divide dough in half; cover and return 1 portion to refrigerator. Divide remaining dough into 8 pieces. Pinch off about one-fifth of each piece. Shape each small piece like a teardrop; refrigerate. Shape larger pieces into smooth balls. Place 1 ball into each prepared brioche tin or muffin cup. Butter your little finger or handle of a wooden spoon and a 15-inch length of waxed paper. Press your finger or spoon handle into center of each ball, making a depression about 3/8 inch deep. Pressing lightly, insert reserved teardrop-shape pieces, small-ends down. Repeat with remaining dough. Place filled individual tins on a baking sheet. Lightly cover filled tins or cups with buttered waxed paper. Let rise until doubled in bulk, about 1-1/2 hours. Gently brush brioches with egg-yolk glaze. Let stand 5 minutes. **Preheat oven** to 450F (230C). Bake 5 minutes. Reduce heat to 350F (175C). Bake 6 to 7 minutes longer or until a wooden pick inserted in center comes out clean. Serve warm. Makes 16 individual brioches.

Variations

Brioche au Fromage: After first rising, stir in 1 cup (4 ounces) shredded Gruyère cheese. If desired, add 2 tablespoons each of minced fresh parsley and basil.
Lemon-Pecan Brioche: Increase salt to 1-1/2 teaspoons. Add freshly grated peel from 1 large lemon and 1/4 teaspoon ground cinnamon. After first rising, stir in 1 cup finely chopped pecans.

How to Make Brioche

1/Butter your thumb. Press your buttered thumb into center of dough ball, making an indentation about 3/4 inch deep.

2/Shape reserved dough like a teardrop. Pressing lightly, insert small end into depression made by your thumb.

Shredded-Wheat Bread

Toasty shredded-wheat flavor and a crisp crust make this a favorite for sandwiches!

4 large shredded-wheat biscuits
1/3 cup packed brown sugar
1 tablespoon salt
2 cups milk, room temperature
2 (1/4-oz.) pkgs. active dry yeast
   (2 tablespoons)

1 teaspoon granulated sugar
1/2 cup warm water (110F, 45C)
1/4 cup butter, melted
1/3 cup wheat germ
5-1/2 to 6 cups all-purpose or bread flour

Finely crumble 1 shredded-wheat biscuit into a small bowl; set aside. In large bowl of electric mixer, crumble remaining 3 shredded-wheat biscuits. Stir in brown sugar, salt and milk; let stand 10 minutes. In a small bowl, dissolve yeast and granulated sugar in water. Let stand until foamy, 5 to 10 minutes. Add yeast mixture to shredded-wheat mixture. Stir in butter, wheat germ and 2-1/2 to 3 cups flour. Beat at medium speed with electric mixer 2 minutes or, beat 200 vigorous strokes by hand. Stir in enough remaining flour to make a soft dough. Turn out dough onto a lightly floured surface. Clean and grease bowl. **Knead dough** 8 to 10 minutes or until smooth and elastic. Place dough in greased bowl, turning to coat all sides. Cover with a slightly damp towel. Let rise in a warm place, free from drafts, until doubled in bulk, about 1 hour. Generously grease 2 (9" x 5") loaf pans or 2 (2-quart) casserole dishes. Sprinkle 2 tablespoons reserved shredded-wheat crumbs over bottom and sides of each pan. **Punch down dough;** knead 30 seconds. Divide dough in half. Shape into loaves; place in prepared pans. Sprinkle 1 tablespoon shredded-wheat crumbs over top of each loaf. Press crumbs firmly into surface. Cover with a dry towel. Let rise until doubled in bulk, about 45 minutes. Slash tops of loaves as desired. **Place bread in cold oven.** Set oven temperature at 400F (205C). Bake 30 to 35 minutes or until bread sounds hollow when tapped on bottom. Remove from pans. Cool on racks. Makes 2 loaves.

Classic French Bread   Photos on cover and opposite.

An overnight sponge and lots of kneading are necessary—but, ooh-la-la, the flavor!

2 (1/4-oz.) pkgs. active dry yeast
  (2 tablespoons)
2-1/2 cups warm water (110F, 45C)
7-1/2 to 8 cups all-purpose or bread flour

1 tablespoon salt
1 egg white blended with
  1 tablespoon water for glaze

In large bowl of electric mixer, dissolve yeast in 2-1/2 cups water. Add 2-1/2 to 3 cups flour; stir 1 minute. Batter will have consistency of soft pudding. Cover bowl tightly with plastic wrap. Let rise in a warm place, free from drafts, overnight or at least 8 hours. The longer the sponge ferments, the better the flavor will be. Stir in salt and 1 to 1-1/2 cups of remaining flour. Beat at medium speed with electric mixer 6 minutes or, beat 600 vigorous strokes by hand. Stir in enough remaining flour to make a soft dough. Turn out dough onto a lightly floured surface. Clean and lightly flour bowl. **Knead dough** 15 to 20 minutes or until smooth and elastic. Place dough in floured bowl; dust surface lightly with flour. Cover with a slightly damp towel. Let rise in a warm place, free from drafts, until tripled in bulk, about 1-1/2 hours. Grease 2 large baking sheets or 4 French-bread pans. **Punch down dough;** knead 2 minutes. Cover and let rest 10 minutes. **For oblong loaves,** divide dough into 3 or 4 pieces, depending on desired thickness of loaves. On a lightly floured surface, shape each piece into a smooth log, gently tapering ends. **For round loaves,** divide dough in half. Shape each half into a smooth ball. Place shaped dough on prepared baking sheets. Cover with a dry towel. Let rise until doubled in bulk, about 1 hour. Adjust oven racks to 2 lowest positions. Place a shallow roasting pan on lowest shelf. Pour in 2 cups boiling water. **Preheat oven** 15 minutes to 425F (220C). Slash tops of oblong loaves with 5 diagonal slashes each. Slash tops of each round loaf with 3 horizontal slashes and 3 vertical slashes, in a tic-tac-toe design. Brush loaves with cold water. Bake 15 minutes. Brush loaves with egg-white glaze. Bake 10 minutes longer. Brush again with egg-white glaze. Remove roasting pan from oven. Bake loaves 10 to 15 minutes longer, for a total of 35 to 40 minutes, or until bread sounds hollow when tapped on bottom. Remove from pans. Place loaves directly on oven rack; bake 5 minutes longer. Cool on racks. Makes 2 to 4 loaves.

Variation
Wheat French Bread: Substitute 1/2 cup wheat germ and 1/2 cup whole-wheat flour for 1 cup all-purpose or bread flour in sponge mixture.

Melba Toast

Quick, easy and super-crispy!

1 lb. leftover bread

Preheat oven to 250F (120C). Cut crusts from bread, if desired. Cut bread into 1/8-inch slices or slice as thinly as possible. Place slices on an ungreased baking sheet. Turning once, bake 20 to 30 minutes or until toast is crisp and dry. Store in a medium container with an airtight lid. Store 2 months at room temperature, 4 months in a refrigerator or 6 months in a freezer. Makes about 14 ounces toast.

Top to bottom: Classic French Bread, above; Basic White Bread, page 19; Brioche, pages 20-21; and San Francisco Sourdough Bread, page 25.

Basic Sourdough Starter

A starter is the "mother" of all sourdough breads—refrigerate between uses.

1 (1/4-oz.) pkg. active dry yeast (1 tablespoon)	**2 cups warm water (110F, 45C)**
2 tablespoons sugar or honey	**1/3 cup nonfat-milk powder**
	2 cups all-purpose or bread flour

In a large, nonmetal container or bowl, dissolve yeast and sugar or honey in water. Let stand until foamy, 5 to 10 minutes. With a wooden or plastic spoon, stir in milk powder and flour. Small lumps in batter will be dissolved by fermentation process. Cover container with 2 to 3 layers of cheesecloth; secure with an elastic band. Set in a warm place free from drafts. Stir mixture several times each day. Let stand 3 to 5 days until starter has a pleasant sour aroma and is full of bubbles.

Note: If starter turns orange or pink, undesirable bacteria have invaded it. Mixture must be discarded.

Variations

Potato Starter: Substitute 2 cups warm water in which peeled potatoes have been cooked for 2 cups warm water.
Whole-Wheat Starter: Substitute 2 cups whole-wheat flour for 2 cups all-purpose or bread flour. Substitute honey for sugar.
Rye Starter: Substitute 2 cups rye flour for 2 cups all-purpose or bread flour.

Working with Sourdough

- Sourdough starter should be made several days before you plan to bake to allow proper fermentation for the characteristically tangy flavor.
- Always use glass or plastic containers and plastic or wooden spoons when working with sourdough starters. Metal containers and utensils produce an undesirable flavor.
- Containers for mixing starters should be large enough to allow mixture to double in bulk.
- Starters should ferment in a warm place (80F to 90F, 25C to 30C).
- Clear liquid that rises to the top of the starter should be stirred back into it several times a day.
- If your starter turns orange or pink and develops an unpleasantly acrid odor, undesirable bacteria have invaded it and the mixture must be discarded.
- To use starter, remove amount called for in recipe; bring to room temperature before preparing *sponge.*
- Once starter is made, it may be refrigerated indefinitely, as long as it is replenished every 2 weeks.
- To replenish starter, add equal amounts of flour and water. For instance, if you use 1 cup starter, replenish by adding 1 cup flour and 1 cup water. Cover and let stand in a warm place overnight. Cover and refrigerate.
- If refrigerated starter isn't used for 2 to 3 weeks, remove 1/2 cup and discard, or give it to a friend. Replenish as directed above.
- Freshly fed starter may be frozen up to 2 months. Thaw at room temperature. Let stand in a warm place overnight until active and bubbly.
- It's a good idea to wash your starter container occasionally to remove any caked-on residue.
- Share your starter with friends to start them on the road to sourdough success!

San Francisco Sourdough Bread   Photo on page 22.

You'll think you hear cable cars clanging when you bite into this tangy loaf.

Sponge, see below	Cornmeal, if desired
2-1/2 teaspoons salt	1 egg white blended with
4-3/4 to 5-1/4 cups all-purpose or	1 tablespoon water for glaze
bread flour	

Sponge:

1-1/2 cups warm water (110F, 45C)	1 cup Basic Sourdough Starter, opposite
1 teaspoon sugar	2 cups all-purpose or bread flour
1/3 cup nonfat-milk powder	

Prepare Sponge. When sponge is fermented and bubbly, add salt and enough flour to make a soft dough. Turn out dough onto a lightly floured surface. Clean and grease bowl, set aside. **Knead dough** 10 to 12 minutes or until smooth and elastic. Place dough in greased bowl, turning to coat all sides. Cover with a slightly damp towel. Let rise in a warm place, free from drafts, until doubled in bulk, 1-1/2 to 2 hours. Grease 2 large baking sheets or 2 (2-quart) casserole dishes. If desired, lightly sprinkle cornmeal over baking sheets or bottoms of dishes. **Punch down dough;** knead 30 seconds. Divide dough in half. Shape into narrow oblong loaves with tapered ends for baking sheets or round loaves for casserole dishes. Place on prepared baking sheets or in prepared dishes. Cover with a dry towel. Let rise until doubled in bulk, about 1-1/2 hours. Adjust oven racks to 2 lowest positions. Place a shallow roasting pan on lowest shelf; pour in 2 cups boiling water. **Preheat oven** to 425F (220C). Slash tops of oblong loaves diagonally and round loaves in 3 slashes horizontally and 3 slashes vertically, in tic-tac-toe designs. Brush slashed loaves with egg-white glaze. Bake 15 minutes; brush again with egg-white glaze. Remove roasting pan from oven. Bake loaves 15 to 20 minutes longer or until bread sounds hollow when tapped on bottom. Brush loaves a third time with egg-white glaze, 5 minutes before removing from oven. Remove from dishes or baking sheets. Cool on racks. Makes 2 loaves.

Sponge:
In a large nonmetal bowl, combine all ingredients. Cover with a double layer of cheesecloth; secure with an elastic band. Let stand and ferment in a warm place, free from drafts, 24 to 48 hours, depending on sourness desired. Stir once or twice a day with a wooden or plastic spoon.

Variations

Quick Sourdough Bread: For Sponge, dissolve 1 (1/4-ounce) package active dry yeast and sugar in warm water. Let stand until foamy, 5 to 10 minutes. Stir in remaining sponge ingredients. Cover and let stand 8 hours or overnight. Proceed as directed above. Rising times will be shorter.
Sourdough-Wheat Bread: Substitute 1 cup Whole-Wheat Starter, opposite, for 1 cup Basic Sourdough Starter. Substitute 2 cups whole-wheat flour for 2 cups all-purpose or bread flour. Add 1 cup cracked wheat to Sponge. After Sponge has fermented, stir in 1/4 cup honey, 2 tablespoons melted butter and 1/2 cup toasted wheat germ. After brushing raised loaves with egg-white glaze, sprinkle additional wheat germ over tops of loaves.
Sourdough-Rye Bread: Substitute 1 cup Rye Starter, opposite, for 1 cup Basic Sourdough Starter in Sponge. After Sponge has fermented, substitute 1 cup rye flour for 1 cup all-purpose or bread flour. Stir in 1/4 cup dark molasses, 1 tablespoon freshly grated orange peel, 1 tablespoon vegetable oil, 1 tablespoon caraway seeds and 1 cup rye flakes, if desired. After brushing raised loaves with egg-white glaze, sprinkle additional caraway seeds or rye flakes over tops of loaves.

How to Make Butterflake Bread

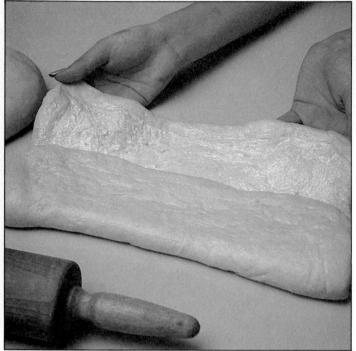

1/Fold unbuttered third over center third of buttered dough. Fold remaining third over top.

2/Cut dough crosswise into 12 (1-inch) slices. Arrange slices, cut-side down and side by side, in prepared pan.

Butterflake Bread   Photo on page 98.

Inspired by butterflake rolls, this rich, pull-apart bread won't need additional butter.

2 (1/4-oz.) pkgs. active dry yeast (2 tablespoons)	3 eggs, room temperature
1 teaspoon sugar	1/2 cup butter, melted
3/4 cup warm water (110F, 45C)	4-1/2 to 5 cups all-purpose flour
1/4 cup sugar	1/4 cup butter, softened
1-1/2 teaspoons salt	1 tablespoon butter, melted
	4 teaspoons sesame seeds

In large bowl of electric mixer, dissolve yeast and 1 teaspoon sugar in water. Let stand until foamy, 5 to 10 minutes. Add 1/4 cup sugar, salt, eggs, 1/2 cup melted butter and 1-1/2 to 2 cups flour. Beat at medium speed with electric mixer 2 minutes or, beat 200 vigorous strokes by hand. Stir in enough remaining flour to make a soft dough. Turn out dough onto a lightly floured surface. Clean and grease bowl. **Knead dough** 5 minutes or until smooth. Place dough in greased bowl, turning to coat all sides. Cover with a slightly damp towel. Let rise in a warm place, free from drafts, until doubled in bulk, about 1 hour. Grease 2 (8" x 4") loaf pans. **Punch down dough;** knead 30 seconds. Divide dough in half. Pat or roll out 1 piece of dough to a 12-inch square. Spread 2 tablespoons softened butter over two-thirds of rolled-out dough. Fold unbuttered third over center; fold remaining third over top, making a 12" x 4" rectangle. Cut dough crosswise into 12 (1-inch) slices. Arrange slices, cut-side down and side by side, in prepared pan. Repeat with remaining dough. Brush with 1 tablespoon melted butter; sprinkle with sesame seeds. Butter a 15-inch length of waxed paper. Place over loaves. Let rise until doubled in bulk, 45 to 60 minutes. **Preheat oven** to 400F (205C). Bake 30 to 35 minutes or until bread sounds hollow on bottom. Cool on racks about 25 minutes. Serve warm. Makes 2 loaves.

Mama's Egg Bread

Wonderfully rich—perfect for all kinds of sandwiches.

2 (1/4-oz.) pkgs. active dry yeast
  (2 tablespoons)
1 teaspoon sugar
1/2 cup warm water (110F, 45C)
4 eggs, room temperature
2 egg yolks, room temperature
1/3 cup butter, melted
1/4 cup honey

2 teaspoons salt
1/2 cup nonfat-milk powder
4-3/4 to 5-1/4 cups all-purpose or
  bread flour
1 egg white blended with 1 teaspoon honey
  and 1 teaspoon water for glaze
6 teaspoons sesame seeds

In large bowl of electric mixer, dissolve yeast and sugar in 1/2 cup water. Let stand until foamy, 5 to 10 minutes. Add eggs, egg yolks, butter, 1/4 cup honey, salt, milk powder and 2 to 2-1/2 cups flour. Beat at medium speed with electric mixer 2 minutes or, beat 200 vigorous strokes by hand. Stir in enough remaining flour to make a soft dough. Turn out dough onto a lightly floured surface. Clean and grease bowl. **Knead dough** 8 to 10 minutes or until smooth and elastic. Place dough in greased bowl, turning to coat all sides. Cover with a slightly damp towel. Let rise in a warm place, free from drafts, until doubled in bulk, about 1-1/2 hours. Grease 2 (9" x 5") loaf pans or 2 (2-quart) casserole dishes. Sprinkle 2 teaspoons sesame seeds over bottom and sides of each pan. **Punch down dough;** knead 30 seconds. Divide dough in half. Shape into loaves; place in prepared pans. Cover with a dry towel. Let rise until doubled in bulk, about 1 hour. **Preheat oven** to 350F (175C). Slash tops of loaves as desired. Brush with egg-white glaze. Sprinkle 1 teaspoon sesame seeds over each loaf. Bake 30 to 35 minutes or until bread sounds hollow when tapped on bottom. Remove from pans. Cool on racks. Makes 2 loaves.

Peasant French Bread

This quickly made loaf boasts a crispy crust and chewy texture.

1 (1/4-oz.) pkg. active dry yeast
  (1 tablespoon)
1 tablespoon sugar
2 cups warm water (110F, 45C)

1 tablespoon salt
5-1/2 to 6 cups all-purpose or bread flour
1/4 cup water blended with
  1/4 teaspoon salt for glaze

In large bowl of electric mixer, dissolve yeast and sugar in 2 cups water. Let stand until foamy, 5 to 10 minutes. Add 1 tablespoon salt and 2 to 2-1/2 cups flour. Beat at medium speed with electric mixer 2 minutes or, beat 200 vigorous strokes by hand. Stir in enough remaining flour to make a soft dough. Turn out dough onto a lightly floured surface. Clean and grease bowl. **Knead dough** 10 to 12 minutes or until smooth and elastic. Place dough in greased bowl, turning to coat all sides. Cover with a slightly damp towel. Let rise in a warm place, free from drafts, until doubled in bulk, 1 to 1-1/2 hours. Grease 1 or 2 baking sheets. **Punch down dough;** knead 30 seconds. Divide dough in half. Shape into round or oval loaves; place on prepared baking sheets. Cover with a dry towel. Let rise until doubled in bulk, about 45 minutes. Slash tops of loaves as desired. Brush with salt-water glaze. Adjust oven racks to 2 lowest positions. Place a shallow roasting pan on lowest shelf. Pour in 2 cups boiling water. **Place bread in cold oven.** Set oven temperature at 400F (205C). Bake 20 minutes; brush again with salt-water glaze. Bake 10 to 20 minutes longer or until bread sounds hollow when tapped on bottom. Cool on racks. Makes 2 loaves.

Potatoes-au-Gratin Bread

Bits of Cheddar cheese dot this moist bread. It's even better the second day.

2 (1/4-oz.) pkgs. active dry yeast (2 tablespoons)	1 tablespoon salt
2 tablespoons sugar	1/8 teaspoon red (cayenne) pepper
1/2 cup warm water (110F, 45C)	4 to 5 cups all-purpose or bread flour
1 cup half and half	2 cups shredded peeled or unpeeled potatoes
3 tablespoons butter, melted	1 cup shredded Cheddar cheese (4 oz.)
	2 tablespoons butter, melted

In large bowl of electric mixer, dissolve yeast and sugar in water. Let stand until foamy, 5 to 10 minutes. Add half and half, 3 tablespoons butter, salt, red pepper and 2 to 2-1/2 cups flour. Beat at medium speed with electric mixer 2 minutes or, beat 200 vigorous strokes by hand. Stir in potatoes and enough remaining flour to make a soft dough. Turn out dough onto a lightly floured surface. Clean and grease bowl. **Knead dough** 8 to 10 minutes or until smooth and elastic. Because of starch in potatoes, dough will feel slightly sticky. Place dough in greased bowl, turning to coat all sides. Cover with a slightly damp towel. Let rise in a warm place, free from drafts, until doubled in bulk, about 1 hour. Grease and flour 2 round 9-inch cake pans or 2 (1-1/2-quart) casserole dishes. **Punch down dough.** Roll or pat to a rectangle, 1/2 inch thick. Sprinkle cheese over dough. Knead cheese into dough until evenly distributed. Divide dough in half. Shape into 2 round loaves; place in prepared pans. Butter 2 (12-inch) squares of waxed paper. Place over loaves. Let rise until doubled in bulk, about 45 minutes. **Preheat oven** to 400F (205C). Slash tops of loaves as desired. Brush each loaf with 1 tablespoon melted butter. Bake 35 to 40 minutes or until bread sounds hollow when tapped on bottom. Remove from pans. Cool on racks. Makes 2 loaves.

Roquefort Baguettes

Toast rounds of this fragrant bread and spread with pâté for a delightful appetizer!

1 (1/4-oz.) pkg. active dry yeast (1 tablespoon)	1/4 teaspoon white pepper
1 tablespoon sugar	3 to 3-1/2 cups all-purpose or bread flour
3/4 cup warm water (110F, 45C)	4 oz. Roquefort or Bleu cheese, crumbled
3 tablespoons butter, melted	1 egg white blended with
1 teaspoon salt	2 teaspoons water for glaze

In large bowl of electric mixer, dissolve yeast and sugar in 3/4 cup water. Let stand until foamy, 5 to 10 minutes. Add butter, salt, white pepper and 1 to 1-1/2 cups flour. Beat at medium speed with electric mixer 2 minutes or, beat 200 vigorous strokes by hand. Stir in cheese and enough remaining flour to make a soft dough. Turn out dough onto a lightly floured surface. Clean and grease bowl. **Knead dough** 4 to 6 minutes or until smooth. Dough will be soft. Place dough in greased bowl, turning to coat all sides. Cover with a slightly damp towel. Let rise in a warm place, free from drafts, until doubled in bulk, about 1 hour. Grease 2 baking sheets. **Punch down dough;** knead 30 seconds. Divide dough into 3 equal pieces. Shape each piece into a 12-inch rope or baguette, slightly tapered at ends. Place 2 baguettes on 1 prepared baking sheet, about 4 inches apart. Place 1 baguette on remaining baking sheet. Cover with a dry towel. Let rise until doubled in bulk, 30 to 45 minutes. **Preheat oven** to 375F (190C). Slash tops of loaves as desired. Brush with egg-white glaze. Bake 20 to 30 minutes or until bread sounds hollow when tapped on bottom. Cool on racks. Makes 3 baguettes.

Potatoes-au-Gratin Bread

Khachapuri   Photo on page 152.

Pronounced "kha-cha-poor-ee." Serve this turban-shape Russian loaf with soup or salad.

1 (1/4-oz.) pkg. active dry yeast
   (1 tablespoon)
1 teaspoon sugar
1/4 cup warm water (110F, 45C)
3/4 cup milk, room temperature
2 tablespoons sugar
1/2 cup butter, melted

1 teaspoon salt
3 to 3-1/2 cups all-purpose or
   bread flour
Cheese Filling, see below
1 egg white blended with
   1 tablespoon water for glaze

Cheese Filling:

8 oz. Muenster cheese, shredded
8 oz. Jarlsberg or Swiss cheese, shredded
8 oz. white Cheddar cheese or 4 oz. each,
   Muenster and Swiss cheese, shredded

2 eggs, slightly beaten
2 tablespoons finely chopped fresh parsley
1/4 teaspoon white pepper

In large bowl of electric mixer, dissolve yeast and 1 teaspoon sugar in 1/4 cup water. Let stand until foamy, 5 to 10 minutes. Add milk, 2 tablespoons sugar, butter, salt and 1-1/2 to 2 cups flour. Beat at medium speed with electric mixer 2 minutes or, beat 200 vigorous strokes by hand. Stir in enough remaining flour to make a soft dough. Turn out dough onto a lightly floured surface. Clean and grease bowl. **Knead dough** 4 to 6 minutes or until smooth. Dough will be soft. Place dough in greased bowl, turning to coat all sides. Cover with a slightly damp towel. Let rise in a warm place, free from drafts, until doubled in bulk, about 1 hour. Prepare Cheese Filling; cover and refrigerate. Grease a 9-inch springform pan or round 8- or 9-inch cake pan. **Punch down dough;** knead 30 seconds. Shape into a smooth ball. On a lightly floured surface, roll out dough to a 20-inch circle. Gently ease dough into prepared pan, letting excess hang over edge. Spoon Cheese Filling on center of dough, making a smooth mound. Bring dough up over filling, folding to make 8 to 12 evenly spaced pleats. Bring ends of pleats to center top. Twist and pinch ends together to make a rough knob. Butter a 12-inch square of waxed paper. Place over loaf. Let rise until doubled in bulk, about 45 minutes. **Preheat oven** to 375F (190C). Brush loaf with egg-white glaze. Bake 40 to 50 minutes or until deep golden brown. Remove bread from pan. Place bread directly on oven rack during final 5 minutes of baking, to brown bottom crust. Cool on a rack 45 minutes before cutting into wedges or, serve at room temperature. Makes 1 loaf.

Cheese Filling:
Combine all ingredients in a large bowl.

 Cheese is easier to grate if it's cold. Add cheese to the dough after the first rising to retain distinctive color and shape of cheese shreds.

How to Make Khachapuri

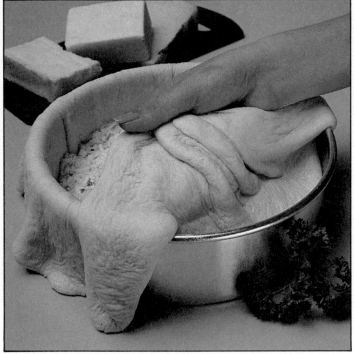

1/Bring side dough up over filling, folding to make 8 to 12 evenly spaced pleats.

2/Bring ends of pleats to center top. Twist and pinch ends together to make a rough knob.

Garlic-Cheese Bread

Garlicky good and scented with Parmesan cheese—perfect with Italian food!

1 (1/4-oz.) pkg. active dry yeast
  (1 tablespoon)
2 teaspoons sugar
1/3 cup warm water (110F, 45C)
1 cup milk, room temperature
2 tablespoons olive oil
1 egg, room temperature

2 to 3 large garlic cloves, crushed
2 teaspoons salt
4-1/4 to 4-3/4 cups all-purpose or
  bread flour
1-2/3 cups grated Parmesan cheese (5 oz.)
1/4 cup butter, melted

In large bowl of electric mixer, dissolve yeast and sugar in water. Let stand until foamy, 5 to 10 minutes. Add milk, olive oil, egg, garlic, salt and 2 to 2-1/2 cups flour. Beat at medium speed with electric mixer 2 minutes or, beat 200 vigorous strokes by hand. Stir in 1 cup cheese and enough remaining flour to make a soft dough. Turn out dough onto a lightly floured surface. Clean and grease bowl. **Knead dough** 6 to 8 minutes or until smooth and elastic. Place dough in greased bowl, turning to coat all sides. Cover with a slightly damp towel. Let rise in a warm place, free from drafts, until doubled in bulk, about 1-1/2 hours. Grease 2 (9" x 5") loaf pans. **Punch down dough;** knead 30 seconds. Divide dough in half, divide each half into 6 equal pieces. Roll each piece into a smooth ball. Roll balls in melted butter, then in remaining cheese. Arrange 6 coated balls, zig-zag fashion, in each prepared pan. Drizzle with any remaining butter; sprinkle with cheese left from coating dough. Butter a 15-inch length of waxed paper. Place over loaves. Let rise until doubled in bulk, about 1 hour. **Preheat oven** to 375F (190C). Bake 30 to 35 minutes or until bread sounds hollow when tapped on top. Carefully remove from pans. Cool on racks. Makes 2 loaves.

Herbed Mushroom Bread

Savory mushroom-shape loaves with the nutty flavor of mushrooms.

1/4 cup butter
1/2 lb. mushrooms, trimmed, minced
1/2 cup minced shallots or green onions
2 (1/4-oz.) pkgs. active dry yeast
   (2 tablespoons)
2 tablespoons sugar
1-1/2 cups warm water (110F, 45C)
2 eggs, room temperature
2-1/2 teaspoons salt

1/4 teaspoon ground pepper
1/8 teaspoon ground thyme
1/2 teaspoon dried leaf rosemary, crushed
1/4 teaspoon ground sage
6-1/4 to 6-3/4 cups all-purpose or
   bread flour
1 egg yolk blended with
   1 teaspoon cream for glaze

Melt butter in a large skillet. Add mushrooms and green onions. Stir occasionally over medium heat until all liquid has evaporated, 10 to 15 minutes. Cool to room temperature. In large bowl of electric mixer, dissolve yeast and sugar in water. Let stand until foamy, 5 to 10 minutes. Add eggs, salt, pepper, thyme, rosemary, sage and 2-1/2 to 3 cups flour. Beat at medium speed with electric mixer 2 minutes or, beat 200 vigorous strokes by hand. Stir in cooled mushroom mixture, including any butter in skillet. Stir in enough remaining flour to make a soft dough. Turn out dough onto a lightly floured surface. Clean and grease bowl. **Knead dough** 8 to 10 minutes or until smooth and elastic. Place dough in greased bowl, turning to coat all sides. Cover with a slightly damp towel. Let rise in a warm place, free from drafts, until doubled in bulk, about 1 hour. Grease 2 (1-1/2-quart) soufflé or casserole dishes or, if making mushroom shapes, 2 large baking sheets. **Punch down dough;** knead 30 seconds. Divide dough in half. Shape into round loaves; place in prepared dishes. Or, shape into 2 mushroom-shape loaves. **To make mushroom shapes:** Divide dough in half. Pinch a 2-inch ball from each half. Shape each large piece of dough to resemble side view of a mushroom top, about 7 inches wide and 5 inches tall. Place on prepared baking sheets. Shape small pieces of dough to resemble fat stems, about 1 inch thick and 2-1/2 inches long. Thin stems will burn while baking. Place 1 end of each stem at center bottom and 1/4 inch under each larger piece. Pinch undersides to seal. Curve stem slightly. Cover with a dry towel. Let rise until doubled in bulk, about 45 minutes. **Preheat oven** to 375F (190C). Slash tops of round loaves as desired. Do not slash mushroom-shape loaves. Brush loaves with egg-yolk glaze. Bake 30 to 35 minutes or until bread sounds hollow when tapped on bottom. Remove from dishes or baking sheets. Cool on racks. Makes 2 loaves.

Speedy Breadsticks

Easy, crisp breadsticks for everything from soup to snacks!

3 slices leftover bread,
   1/2 inch thick
1/2 to 3/4 cup butter, melted

Coarse salt, crushed dried herbs or
   garlic salt, if desired

Preheat oven to 400F (205C). Cut crusts from bread, if desired. Cut each slice into 1/2-inch strips. Dip quickly in and out of melted butter. Arrange on an ungreased baking sheet, 1 inch apart. Sprinkle coarse salt, herbs or garlic salt over strips, if desired. Turning once, bake 6 to 10 minutes or until lightly browned on all sides. Makes about 24 to 30 breadsticks.

Swiss Onion Bread

Onion filling in an onion-and-Swiss-cheese bread—for onion lovers only!

2 (1/4-oz.) pkgs. active dry yeast
   (2 tablespoons)
1 teaspoon sugar
1-1/2 cups warm water (110F, 45C)
1/4 cup sugar
1/2 cup butter, melted
1 egg, room temperature
2 teaspoons salt
1/4 teaspoon dry mustard

1/2 cup finely chopped onion or
   2 tablespoons dried minced onion
6-3/4 to 7-1/4 cups all-purpose or
   bread flour
3/4 cup shredded Swiss cheese (3 oz.)
Onion-Poppy Filling, see below
1 egg yolk blended with
   2 teaspoons water for glaze
Poppy seeds for garnish

Onion-Poppy Filling:
3 tablespoons butter
3/4 cup finely chopped onion
1 tablespoon poppy seeds

1 teaspoon paprika
1/2 teaspoon salt
1/4 cup shredded Swiss cheese (1 oz.)

In large bowl of electric mixer, dissolve yeast and 1 teaspoon sugar in 1-1/2 cups water. Let stand until foamy, 5 to 10 minutes. Add 1/4 cup sugar, butter, egg, salt, dry mustard, onion and 2-1/2 to 3 cups flour. Beat at medium speed with electric mixer 2 minutes or, beat 200 vigorous strokes by hand. Stir in cheese and enough remaining flour to make a soft dough. Turn out dough onto a lightly floured surface. Clean and grease bowl. **Knead dough** 8 to 10 minutes or until smooth and elastic. Place dough in greased bowl, turning to coat all sides. Cover with a slightly damp towel. Let rise in a warm place, free from drafts, until doubled in bulk, 45 to 60 minutes. Prepare Onion-Poppy Filling. Grease 2 large baking sheets. **Punch down dough;** knead 30 seconds. Divide dough in half. Roll out half of dough to an 18" x 10" rectangle. Cut in half lengthwise. Spread each 18" x 5" rectangle with about 2 tablespoons filling, to within 1/2 inch of edges. Beginning on a long side, tightly roll up each rectangle, jelly-roll fashion. Pinch seams and ends to seal. Repeat with remaining dough. Lay 2 rolls, seam-side down, side by side on 1 prepared baking sheet. Twist together 4 or 5 times, keeping seam-sides down. Pinch ends together; tuck under and pinch again. Repeat with remaining dough. Cover with a dry towel. Let rise until doubled in bulk, about 45 minutes. **Preheat oven** to 375F (190C). Brush with egg-yolk glaze; sprinkle poppy seeds in creases of twists. Bake 30 to 35 minutes or until bread sounds hollow when tapped on bottom. Cool on racks. Makes 2 loaves.

Onion-Poppy Filling:
Melt butter in a small skillet over medium heat. Add onion, poppy seeds and paprika. Cook 3 minutes or until onion begins to soften. Cool to room temperature. Stir in salt and cheese.

Variation
Grease 2 round 8-inch cake pans. Divide dough in half. Roll out each half to a 22" x 10" rectangle. Spread each rectangle with half the filling. Beginning on a long side, roll up tightly, jelly-roll fashion. Stretching slightly, arrange rolls, seam-side down, in spirals in prepared pans. Bake as directed above.

 Cooked food to be added to bread dough will cool more rapidly if transferred from skillet to a bowl or plate and stirred occasionally.

Pita Bread

Fill this Middle-Eastern pocket bread with your favorite salad or sandwich filling.

1 (1/4-oz.) pkg. active dry yeast
   (1 tablespoon)
1/2 teaspoon sugar
1-1/2 cups warm water (110F, 45C)
2 teaspoons salt

2 tablespoon vegetable oil
4-1/2 to 5 cups all-purpose or bread flour
Sesame seeds, if desired
Cornmeal

In large bowl of electric mixer, dissolve yeast and sugar in water. Let stand until foamy, 5 to 10 minutes. Add salt, oil and 2 to 2-1/2 cups flour. Beat at medium speed 2 minutes or, beat 200 vigorous strokes by hand. Stir in enough remaining flour to make a soft dough. Turn out dough onto a lightly floured surface. **Knead dough** 8 to 10 minutes or until smooth and elastic. Roll dough between your hands and work surface, making a 12-inch rope. Cut into 12 equal pieces. Shape each piece into a smooth ball, pulling sides of dough to center bottom of ball. Pinch dough at bottom to seal. Cover with a dry towel; let stand 10 minutes. Roll out each ball to a 6-inch round. If desired, sprinkle with sesame seeds; lightly press seeds into surface of dough. Place rounds about 1 inch apart on a lightly floured surface. Cover with dry towels. Let rise in a warm place, free from drafts, until almost doubled in bulk, about 30 minutes. Arrange an oven shelf at lowest position and another in center of oven. **Preheat oven** 15 minutes at 500F (260C). Lightly sprinkle 2 large baking sheets with cornmeal. Using a spatula, gently transfer 3 or 4 rounds to each prepared baking sheet. Set 1 baking sheet aside; place remaining baking sheet on lower shelf of oven. Bake 3 to 4 minutes or until puffed. Move baking sheet with puffed pita to upper oven shelf. Place reserved baking sheet on bottom shelf. Work quickly to avoid loss of oven heat. Bake pitas on top shelf 2 to 4 minutes longer or until lightly browned. Remove from oven. Continue baking pitas and rotating placement in oven until all pita rounds are baked. Cool pitas on racks, 3 to 4 minutes, before stacking in a plastic bag to soften. Serve warm or, cool completely and store in plastic bags. Serve pita within 1 to 2 days or, wrap airtight and store in freezer. Use frozen pita within 3 months. Leave in plastic bags; thaw in refrigerator. Makes 12 pita bread rounds.

Variation

Pita Petals: Preheat oven to 350F (175C). Separate cooled, baked pita around edge. Pull apart horizontally, making 2 pita rounds. Lightly brush insides with melted butter. Cut each into 8 wedges. Bake 8 to 10 minutes or until golden brown and crisp. Serve warm. Or, cool on a rack, then store in an airtight container up to 4 days at room temperature.

Serving suggestions: Cut pita in half crosswise. Fill each half with salad, cold cuts, cheese, avocado, bacon and alfalfa sprouts. Use Pita Petals for dipping.

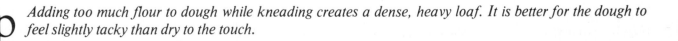

Tip   *Adding too much flour to dough while kneading creates a dense, heavy loaf. It is better for the dough to feel slightly tacky than dry to the touch.*

Whole-Grain & Rye Breads

There's nothing quite like biting into a slice of whole-grain bread, full-flavored and chewy with texture. Some of my best childhood memories are of my sister Tia and I gathering ingredients for mother's weekly breadbaking. The anticipation was unbearable! I knew that in a few hours, loaves of honey or molasses-scented goodness would emerge piping-hot from the oven, tempting little girls to scorch their fingers.

Many whole-grain breads have "roots" in early America. Squaw Bread, with its hearty combination of rye and wheat flours, is supposed to have originated with the American Indian. And legend says that Anadama Bread was created by a New England farmer plagued by a lazy wife who served him the same cornmeal and molasses gruel, day after day. Finally, in desperation, the disgusted farmer grabbed the bowl of gruel, tossed in some flour and yeast, and began stirring like crazy, all the while muttering angrily, "Anna, damn 'er!" And so the irritated but inspired farmer is credited with creating the delicious bread whose name was later changed by polite society to Anadama.

Flash forward a few hundred years and we have Triticale Bread. Triticale flour is a modern hybrid of rye and wheat with a higher protein content than either, and a hearty flavor. My recipe adds nutrients with nonfat-milk powder and the natural sweetening of honey and molasses. You may have to be persistent in your search for triticale flour. Most health-food stores stock it or will special-order it for you. It's worth the search!

We often think of rye breads as coming from "the old country." Certainly, Russian Black Bread evokes visions of Russian peasants tromping in from the snow to be served thick slices of dense, brownish-black bread slathered with homemade butter. The addition of blackened caramel, unsweetened chocolate and powdered coffee not only adds rich color, but give this Russian classic its robust flavor.

Cracked-Wheat Bread

Cracked wheat gives this bread a soul-satisfying flavor and chewiness.

2 cups boiling water
2 cups cracked wheat
2 (1/4-oz.) pkgs. active dry yeast
   (2 tablespoons)
2 teaspoons sugar
1/2 cup warm water (110F, 45C)

1 tablespoon salt
2 tablespoons vegetable oil
4-1/2 to 5 cups all-purpose or bread flour
1 egg white blended with
   1 tablespoon water for glaze

In large bowl of electric mixer, combine 2 cups water and cracked wheat. Cool to room temperature. In a small bowl, dissolve yeast and sugar in 1/2 cup water. Let stand until foamy, 5 to 10 minutes. Add to wheat mixture. Add salt, oil and 1 cup flour. Beat at medium speed with electric mixer 2 minutes or, beat 200 vigorous strokes by hand. Stir in enough remaining flour to make a soft dough. Turn out dough onto a lightly floured surface. Clean and grease bowl; set aside. **Knead dough** 10 to 12 minutes or until smooth and elastic. Place dough in greased bowl, turning to coat all sides. Cover with a slightly damp towel. Let rise in a warm place, free from drafts, until doubled in bulk, about 1 hour. Grease 2 (8" x 4") loaf pans or 2 (1-1/2-quart) casserole dishes; set aside. **Punch down dough;** knead 30 seconds. Divide dough in half; shape into loaves. Place in prepared pans. Cover with a dry towel. Let rise until doubled in bulk, about 45 minutes. **Preheat oven** to 400F (205C). Slash tops of loaves as desired; brush with egg-white glaze. Bake 20 minutes; brush again with egg-white glaze. Bake 10 to 15 minutes longer or until bread sounds hollow when tapped on bottom. Remove from pans. Cool on racks. Makes 2 loaves.

Triticale Bread

Triticale flour is a hybrid of wheat and rye with a wonderful flavor.

2 (1/4-oz.) pkgs. active dry yeast
   (2 tablespoons)
2 tablespoons molasses
2 cups warm water (110F, 45C)
1/3 cup honey
1/3 cup vegetable oil
1 egg, room temperature

1/2 cup nonfat-milk powder
2 teaspoons salt
4 cups triticale flour
4 to 4-1/2 cups all-purpose or bread flour
1 egg white blended with
   2 teaspoons honey for glaze

In large bowl of electric mixer, dissolve yeast and molasses in water. Let stand until foamy, 5 to 10 minutes. Add honey, oil, egg, milk powder, salt, 1-1/2 cups triticale flour and 2 to 2-1/2 cups all-purpose or bread flour. Beat at medium speed with electric mixer 2 minutes or, beat 200 vigorous strokes by hand. Stir in remaining 2-1/2 cups triticale flour and enough remaining all-purpose or bread flour to make a soft dough. Turn out dough onto a lightly floured surface. Clean and grease bowl; set aside. **Knead dough** 8 to 10 minutes or until smooth and elastic. Place dough in greased bowl, turning to coat all sides. Cover with a slightly damp towel. Let rise in a warm place, free from drafts, until doubled in bulk, about 1 hour. Grease 2 (9" x 5") loaf pans; set aside. **Punch down dough;** knead 30 seconds. Divide dough in half; shape into loaves. Place in prepared pans. Cover with a dry towel. Let rise until doubled in bulk, about 45 minutes. **Preheat oven** to 350F (175C). Slash tops of loaves; brush with egg-white glaze. Bake 35 to 40 minutes or until bread sounds hollow when tapped on bottom. Remove from pans. Cool on racks. Makes 2 loaves.

Malted Multi-Grain Bread

This power-packed bread will energize your day.

1 cup wheat flakes
1 cup rye flakes
1/4 cup butter, cut in 4 pieces
1/3 cup malt syrup or honey
2 cups hot water (200F, 95C)
2 (1/4-oz.) pkgs. active dry yeast
  (2 tablespoons)
1 teaspoon malt syrup or honey
1/3 cup warm water (110F, 45C)
1 cup nonfat-milk powder

1 tablespoon salt
1/2 cup unprocessed bran flakes
1/2 cup wheat germ
4-3/4 to 5-1/4 cups all-purpose or
  bread flour
1-1/2 cups whole-wheat flour
1 egg white blended with
  2 teaspoons water for glaze
Wheat or rye flakes for garnish

In large bowl of electric mixer, combine 1 cup wheat flakes, 1 cup rye flakes, butter, 1/3 cup malt syrup or honey and 2 cups water. Stir to combine; cool to room temperature. Dissolve yeast and 1 teaspoon malt syrup or honey in 1/3 cup water. Let stand until foamy, 5 to 10 minutes. Stir into wheat-flakes mixture. Add milk powder, salt, bran flakes, wheat germ and 1 to 1-1/2 cups all-purpose or bread flour. Beat at medium speed with electric mixer 2 minutes or, beat 200 vigorous strokes by hand. Stir in whole-wheat flour and enough remaining all-purpose or bread flour to make a soft dough. Turn out dough onto a lightly floured surface. Clean and grease bowl; set aside. **Knead dough** 10 to 12 minutes or until smooth and elastic. Place dough in greased bowl, turning to coat all sides. Cover with a slightly damp towel. Let rise in a warm place, free from drafts, until doubled in bulk, about 1 hour. Grease 2 (9" x 5") loaf pans or 2 (2-quart) casserole dishes; set aside. **Punch down dough;** knead 30 seconds. Divide dough in half; shape into loaves. Place in prepared pans. Cover with a dry towel. Let rise until doubled in bulk, about 45 minutes. **Preheat oven** to 375F (190C). Brush tops of loaves with egg-white glaze; sprinkle with wheat or rye flakes. Slash tops as desired. Bake 30 to 35 minutes or until bread sounds hollow when tapped on bottom. Remove from pans. Cool on racks. Makes 2 loaves.

Variations

Substitute 2 cups regular rolled oats for wheat flakes and rye flakes.

Add 1-1/2 cups raisins along with whole-wheat flour.

Note: Malt syrup is available in health-food stores.

Add nutrients to any bread with the Cornell Enrichment Formula. Before measuring flour, spoon 1 tablespoon soy flour, 1 tablespoon nonfat-milk powder and 1 teaspoon wheat germ into measuring cup. Spoon in flour and level off. Repeat for each cup of flour used in recipe.

Sprouted Wheat-Berry Bread

One of my favorite whole-grain breads. Wheat sprouts add a delicious nutty flavor.

2 to 2-1/2 cups Wheat-Berry Sprouts,
   see below
2 (1/4-oz.) pkgs. active dry yeast
   (2 tablespoons)
1 tablespoon brown sugar
2 cups warm water (110F, 45C)
2/3 cup nonfat-milk powder
3 tablespoons honey
2 tablespoons molasses

1 tablespoon salt
1/4 cup vegetable oil
3-1/2 cups whole-wheat flour
4-3/4 to 5-1/4 cups all-purpose or
   bread flour
1/2 cup wheat germ
1 teaspoon honey blended with
   2 teaspoons water for glaze

Wheat-Berry Sprouts:
1/2 cup wheat berries (whole-wheat kernels)
Warm water (110F, 45C)

Prepare Wheat-Berry Sprouts 2 to 4 days before beginning bread. In large bowl of electric mixer, dissolve yeast and brown sugar in 2 cups water. Let stand until foamy, 5 to 10 minutes. Add milk powder, 3 tablespoons honey, molasses, salt, oil, 1 cup whole-wheat flour and 2-1/2 to 3 cups all-purpose or bread flour. Beat at medium speed with electric mixer 2 minutes or, beat 200 vigorous strokes by hand. Stir in Wheat-Berry Sprouts, remaining whole-wheat flour, wheat germ and enough remaining all-purpose or bread flour to make a soft dough. Turn out dough onto a lightly floured surface. Clean and grease bowl; set aside. **Knead dough** 10 to 12 minutes or until smooth and elastic. Place dough in greased bowl, turning to coat all sides. Cover with a slightly damp towel. Let rise in a warm place, free from drafts, until doubled in bulk, 1 to 1-1/2 hours. Grease 2 (9" x 5") loaf pans or 2 (2-quart) casserole dishes; set aside. **Punch down dough;** knead 30 seconds. Divide dough in half; shape into loaves. Place in prepared pans. Cover with a dry towel. Let rise until doubled in bulk, 45 to 60 minutes. **Preheat oven** to 375F (190C). Slash tops of loaves as desired; brush with honey glaze. Bake 25 minutes; brush again with honey glaze. Bake 5 to 10 minutes longer or until bread sounds hollow when tapped on bottom. Remove from pans. Cool on racks. Makes 2 loaves.

Wheat-Berry Sprouts:
Place wheat berries in a large glass jar or square casserole dish. Add water to cover. Cover container with a double layer of cheesecloth; secure with an elastic band. Place container in a warm, dark place (about 70F, 20C). Let stand 12 hours or overnight. Drain off water. Rinse berries with fresh warm water; drain. Turn jar sideways and gently shake berries to distribute evenly or, spread evenly over bottom of casserole dish. Set container in a warm, dark place. Repeat rinsing and draining 2 or 3 times a day for 2 to 4 days or until sprouts are about 3/4-inch long. Thoroughly drain sprouts on paper towels before using in bread. If wheat-berry sprouts tangle, coarsely chop before adding to bread.

Tip *Wheat germ, bran flakes and shelled nuts should be tightly wrapped and stored in the freezer to prevent rancidity. Warm to room temperature before adding to breads.*

How to Make Sprouted Wheat-Berry Bread

1/Repeat rinsing and draining wheat berries 2 or 3 times a day for 2 to 4 days.

2/Thoroughly drain sprouts on paper towels before using in bread. If sprouts tangle, chop coarsely.

All-Wheat Bread

Using 100% whole-wheat flour gives a whole-grain flavor that's especially delicious toasted.

2 (1/4-oz.) pkgs. active dry yeast
  (2 tablespoons)
1 teaspoon malt syrup or honey
1/2 cup warm water (110F, 45C)
1 cup cottage cheese (8 oz.),
  room temperature
1/4 cup malt syrup or honey
2 tablespoons molasses

5 to 5-1/5 cups whole-wheat flour
1/4 cup vegetable oil
2 eggs, slightly beaten, room temperature
2-1/2 teaspoons salt
1/2 cup wheat germ, if desired
3 tablespoons wheat germ, if desired
2 teaspoons malt syrup or honey mixed with
  1 tablespoon water for glaze

In large bowl of electric mixer, dissolve yeast and 1 teaspoon malt syrup or honey in 1/2 cup water. Let stand until foamy, 5 to 10 minutes. Add cottage cheese, 1/4 cup malt syrup or honey, molasses and 1 to 1-1/2 cups flour. Beat at medium speed with electric mixer 2 minutes or, beat 200 vigorous strokes by hand. Scrape down bowl. Cover tightly with plastic wrap. Let stand in a warm place, free from drafts, until bubbly and *tripled,* 45 to 60 minutes. Stir in oil, eggs, salt, 1/2 cup wheat germ, if desired, and enough remaining flour to make a soft dough. Turn out dough onto a lightly floured surface. Clean and grease bowl. **Knead dough** 10 to 12 minutes or until smooth and elastic. Place dough in greased bowl, turning to coat all sides. Cover with a slightly damp towel. Let rise until *tripled,* about 1 hour. Grease 2 (8" x 4") loaf pans. Sprinkle bottom and sides of each with 1 tablespoon wheat germ, if desired. **Punch down dough;** knead 30 seconds. Shape dough into 2 loaves. Place in prepared pans. Cover with a dry towel. Let rise until doubled, about 45 minutes. Slash tops of loaves as desired. Brush with malt-syrup or honey glaze. Sprinkle remaining 1 tablespoon wheat germ over loaves, if desired. **Place bread in cold oven.** Set oven temperature at 375F (190C). Bake 30 to 35 minutes or until bread sounds hollow when tapped on bottom. Remove from pans. Cool on racks. Makes 2 loaves.

High-Rise Cornbread

This yeast cornbread is wonderful with soups—toasted and spread with Honey Butter, page 46.

1 cup milk
2 tablespoons butter
2 teaspoons salt
3/4 cup yellow cornmeal
1/4 cup honey
2 (1/4-oz.) pkgs. active dry yeast
   (2 tablespoons)

1 tablespoon brown sugar
1/2 cup warm water (110F, 45C)
2 eggs, room temperature
4-3/4 to 5-1/4 cups all-purpose or
   bread flour
1 tablespoon butter, melted
3 tablespoons yellow cornmeal

In a small saucepan, combine milk, 2 tablespoons butter and salt. Over medium heat, bring to a simmer. Butter may not melt. Remove from heat. Slowly whisk in 3/4 cup cornmeal, stirring until smooth. Stir in honey; set aside to cool. In large bowl of electric mixer, dissolve yeast and brown sugar in water. Let stand until foamy, 5 to 10 minutes. Add eggs, cooled cornmeal mixture and 1 to 1-1/2 cups flour. Beat at medium speed with electric mixer 2 minutes or, beat 200 vigorous strokes by hand. Stir in enough remaining flour to make a soft dough. Turn out dough onto a lightly floured surface. Clean and grease bowl; set aside. **Knead dough** 8 to 10 minutes or until smooth and elastic. Place dough in greased bowl, turning to coat all sides. Cover with a slightly damp towel. Let rise in a warm place, free from drafts, until doubled in bulk, about 1 hour. Grease 2 (9'' x 5'') loaf pans or 2 (2-quart) casserole dishes. Sprinkle 1 tablespoon cornmeal over bottom and sides of each pan; set aside. **Punch down dough;** knead 30 seconds. Divide dough in half; shape into loaves. Place in prepared pans. Cover with a dry towel. Let rise until doubled in bulk, 30 to 45 minutes. **Preheat oven** to 375F (190C). Slash tops of loaves as desired. Brush with melted butter; sprinkle with remaining cornmeal. Bake 30 to 35 minutes or until bread sounds hollow when tapped on bottom. Remove from pans. Cool on racks. Makes 2 loaves.

Fried Bread

One of my childhood favorites. Fry sweet doughs for breakfast and savory doughs for dinner!

High-Rise Cornbread, above;
   Basic White Bread, page 19;
   Buttermilk-Wheat Bread, page 43;
   Basic Sweet Yeast Dough, page 59;
   or other yeast dough

Peanut oil or vegetable oil for frying
Sugar, if desired
1/4 cup sugar blended with
   1 teaspoon cinnamon, if desired
Honey and jam

Prepare any of above bread doughs through first rising. Pinch off egg-size pieces of dough. Flatten between palms of your hands until 1/2 inch thick. Or, roll out dough with a rolling pin until 1/2 inch thick; use a floured cutter to cut into any shape desired. Cover dough pieces with a dry towel. Let stand 20 minutes. Pour oil 2 inches deep in a large deep skillet, 4-quart saucepan or deep-fat fryer. Heat oil to 370F (190C) or until a 1-inch cube of bread turns golden brown in 50 seconds. Fry bread pieces, a few at a time, until crisp and evenly browned on both sides, 1 to 2 minutes. Use a slotted spoon to remove fried breads from oil. Drain on paper towels. If desired, roll in sugar or cinnamon-sugar. Serve hot with plenty of honey and jam. Makes 30 to 40 fried breads.

Anadama Bread

An early American bread, rich with molasses and cornmeal.

1 cup yellow cornmeal	1 teaspoon sugar
2 teaspoons salt	1/4 cup warm water (110F, 45C)
1 cup water	5-1/2 to 6 cups all-purpose or bread flour
1 cup milk	1 tablespoon yellow cornmeal
1/4 cup butter	1 tablespoon butter, melted
1/2 cup dark molasses	
1 (1/4-oz.) pkg. active dry yeast	
(1 tablespoon)	

In large bowl of electric mixer, combine 1 cup cornmeal and salt; set aside. In a medium saucepan, combine 1 cup water, milk and 1/4 cup butter. Bring to a boil over medium heat. Slowly pour hot mixture over cornmeal mixture, whisking constantly until smooth. Stir in molasses; set aside to cool. In a small bowl, dissolve yeast and sugar in 1/4 cup water. Let stand until foamy, 5 to 10 minutes. Stir yeast mixture and 2 to 2-1/2 cups flour into cornmeal mixture. Beat at medium speed with electric mixer 2 minutes or, beat 200 vigorous strokes by hand. Stir in enough remaining flour to make a soft dough. Turn out dough onto a lightly floured surface. Clean and grease bowl; set aside. **Knead dough** 10 to 12 minutes or until smooth and elastic. Place dough in greased bowl, turning to coat all sides. Cover with a slightly damp towel. Let rise in a warm place, free from drafts, until doubled in bulk, about 1-1/2 hours. Grease 2 (8" x 4") loaf pans or 2 (1-1/2-quart) casserole dishes. Sprinkle 1/2 tablespoon cornmeal over bottom of each pan; set aside. **Punch down dough;** knead 30 seconds. Divide dough in half; shape into round or oblong loaves. Place in prepared pans. Cover with a dry towel. Let rise until doubled in bulk, 45 to 60 minutes. **Preheat oven** to 375F (190C). Bake 35 to 40 minutes or until bread sounds hollow when tapped on bottom. Remove from pans. Brush melted butter over tops. Cool on racks. Makes 2 loaves.

Variations

Raisin Anadama Bread: Stir in 1 cup raisins with second addition of flour, before kneading.
Cheddar Anadama Bread: After first rising, knead in 1 cup (4 ounces) shredded Cheddar cheese. Shape into loaves.

Tip *The amount of flour required in a recipe may vary from day to day, depending on humidity, temperature and brand of flour. For perfect end results, learn to judge the dough by feel rather than rely on the amount of flour called for in a recipe.*

Squaw Bread

Honey and ground raisins sweeten this hearty early American loaf.

2 (1/4-oz.) pkgs. active dry yeast
  (2 tablespoons)
1 teaspoon honey
1/2 cup warm water (110F, 45C)
1/4 cup honey
1/3 cup raisins
1/4 cup packed brown sugar

1-3/4 cups milk, room temperature
1/3 cup butter, melted
1 tablespoon salt
1-1/2 cups medium rye flour
2-1/2 cups all-purpose or bread flour
2-1/2 to 3 cups whole-wheat flour
Cornmeal

In large bowl of electric mixer, dissolve yeast and 1 teaspoon honey in water. Let stand until foamy, 5 to 10 minutes. In a blender or food processor fitted with a metal blade, combine 1/4 cup honey, raisins, brown sugar and 1/2 cup milk. Process 30 to 45 seconds or until raisins are ground. To yeast mixture, add raisin mixture, remaining milk, butter, salt, 1 cup rye flour, 1 cup all-purpose or bread flour and 1 cup whole-wheat flour. Beat at medium speed with electric mixer 2 minutes or, beat 200 vigorous strokes by hand. Stir in remaining rye flour, remaining all-purpose or bread flour and enough remaining whole-wheat flour to make a soft dough. Turn out dough onto a lightly floured surface. Clean and grease bowl; set aside. **Knead dough** 10 to 12 minutes or until smooth and elastic. Place dough in greased bowl, turning to coat all sides. Cover with a slightly damp towel. Let rise in a warm place, free from drafts, until doubled in bulk, about 1-1/2 hours. Grease 2 (2-quart) soufflé or casserole dishes or 2 large baking sheets. Sprinkle lightly with cornmeal; set aside. **Punch down dough;** knead 30 seconds. Divide dough in half for 2 large loaves or, divide in quarters for 4 small loaves. Shape into round loaves; place in prepared pans or on prepared baking sheets. Cover with a dry towel. Let rise until doubled in bulk, about 1 hour. **Preheat oven** to 375F (190C). Bake 35 to 40 minutes for large loaves and 25 to 30 minutes for small loaves. Or, bake until bread sounds hollow when tapped on bottom. Remove from pans. Cool on racks. Makes 2 large or 4 small loaves.

Homemade Butter

The food processor makes homemade butter easy and fun—try it unsalted for a real treat!

2 cups cold whipping cream

1/4 teaspoon salt, if desired

Chill food processor bowl and metal blade in freezer, 15 minutes. Pour cream into work bowl fitted with metal blade. Add salt, if desired. Process 2 minutes; scrape down sides of bowl. Continue to process until solids separate from liquid, 3 to 5 minutes. Pour off liquid; store in refrigerator. Use liquid to make pastries or soups. Remove butter from work bowl. Squeeze with your hands to remove any liquid. Or, place in a fine strainer; press with a rubber spatula to remove liquid. Spoon or pipe into a pretty glass bowl. Cover and refrigerate. Let stand at room temperature 30 minutes before serving. Makes about 6 ounces butter and 1 cup liquid.

Variation

Blender Butter: Pour 1 cup whipping cream into a chilled blender. Blend at high speed 15 seconds or until cream coats blades. Add 1/2 cup ice water. Blend at high speed 2 to 3 minutes or until butter separates from liquid. Drain off liquid. Squeeze to remove moisture.

Buttermilk-Wheat Bread

An old-fashioned favorite full of nutrients and good flavor.

2 cups buttermilk
3 tablespoons butter
1/4 cup honey or maple syrup
1 tablespoon salt
1 cup cracked wheat
2 (1/4-oz.) pkgs. active dry yeast
 (2 tablespoons)
1 teaspoon brown sugar

1/2 cup warm water (110F, 45C)
1/2 teaspoon baking soda
3-1/4 to 3-3/4 cups all-purpose or
 bread flour
3 cups whole-wheat flour
1/2 cup toasted wheat germ
Melted butter

In a medium saucepan, combine buttermilk, 3 tablespoons butter, honey and salt. Bring to a simmer over medium heat. Butter may not melt. Remove from heat; stir in cracked wheat. Set aside until cool or, to cool faster, pour into a large bowl; stir often until cooled. In large bowl of electric mixer, dissolve yeast and brown sugar in water. Let stand until foamy, 5 to 10 minutes. Add cooled cracked-wheat mixture, baking soda and 1 to 1-1/2 cups all-purpose or bread flour. Beat at medium speed with electric mixer 2 minutes or, beat 200 vigorous strokes by hand. Stir in whole-wheat flour, wheat germ and enough remaining all-purpose or bread flour to make a soft dough. Turn out dough onto a lightly floured surface. Clean and grease bowl; set aside. **Knead dough** 8 to 10 minutes or until smooth and elastic. Place dough in greased bowl, turning to coat all sides. Cover with a slightly damp towel. Let rise in a warm place, free from drafts, until doubled in bulk, about 1 hour. Grease 2 (8" x 4" or 9" x 5") loaf pans; set aside. **Punch down dough;** knead 30 seconds. Divide dough in half; shape into loaves. Place in prepared pans. Cover with a dry towel. Let rise until doubled in bulk, about 45 minutes. **Preheat oven** to 375F (190C). Slash tops of loaves as desired; brush with melted butter. Bake 30 to 35 minutes or until bread sounds hollow when tapped on bottom. Brush again with melted butter. Remove from pans. Cool on racks. Makes 2 loaves.

Variation

Substitute 1/2 cup buttermilk powder, added to dry ingredients, and 2 cups water, added to other liquids, for 2 cups fluid buttermilk.

Creamy Maple Spread

The perfect partner to wheat loaves.

1 (3-oz.) pkg. cream cheese,
 room temperature
1/2 cup butter, room temperature

Pinch of salt
1/2 teaspoon vanilla extract
1/4 cup pure maple syrup

In small bowl of electric mixer, combine cream cheese, butter, salt and vanilla. Beat until smooth and fluffy. Beating constantly, slowly add maple syrup. Beat until thoroughly blended. Spoon into a small serving dish. Cover and refrigerate. Let stand at room temperature 20 to 30 minutes before serving. Makes about 1 cup.

Shown on the following pages, clockwise from center top: Whole-Earth Date Bread, page 46; Molasses-Bran Bread, page 49; Grandma's Oatmeal Bread, page 47; Potato-Chive Rolls, page 96; and Classic Croissants, pages 100-103.

Whole-Earth Date Bread   Photo on pages 44 and 45.

Toast slices of this nutritious loaf and serve it with Honey Butter, below.

1-1/2 cups finely chopped dates
5 to 5-1/2 cups all-purpose or bread flour
2 (1/4-oz.) pkgs. active dry yeast
  (2 tablespoons)
2 teaspoons brown sugar
2 cups warm water (110F, 45C)
1/3 cup honey
1/4 cup butter, melted
1/2 cup nonfat-milk powder

1 tablespoon salt
1-1/2 cups whole-wheat flour
1/2 cup medium rye flour
1/2 cup wheat germ
1/2 cup unprocessed bran flakes
1/4 cup toasted sesame seeds
1 teaspoon honey blended with
  1 tablespoon milk for glaze
4 teaspoons sesame seeds

In a small bowl, combine dates with 1/2 cup all-purpose or bread flour. Toss to coat and separate; set aside. In large bowl of electric mixer, dissolve yeast and brown sugar in water. Let stand until foamy, 5 to 10 minutes. Add honey, butter, milk powder, salt, whole-wheat flour and 1-1/2 to 2 cups all-purpose or bread flour. Beat at medium speed with electric mixer 2 minutes or, beat 200 vigorous strokes by hand. Stir in rye flour, wheat germ, bran flakes, 1/4 cup sesame seeds, date mixture and enough remaining all-purpose or bread flour to make a soft dough. Turn out dough onto a lightly floured surface. Clean and grease bowl; set aside. **Knead dough** 8 to 10 minutes or until smooth and elastic. Place dough in greased bowl, turning to coat all sides. Cover with a slightly damp towel. Let rise in a warm place, free from drafts, until doubled in bulk, about 1-1/2 hours. Grease 2 (8" x 4" or 9" x 5") loaf pans; set aside. **Punch down dough;** knead 30 seconds. Divide dough in half; shape into loaves. Place in prepared pans. Cover with a dry towel. Let rise until doubled in bulk, about 45 minutes. **Preheat oven** to 375F (190C). Slash tops of loaves as desired; brush with honey glaze. Sprinkle 2 teaspoons sesame seeds over each unbaked loaf. Bake 30 to 35 minutes or until bread sounds hollow when tapped on bottom. Remove from pans. Cool on racks. Makes 2 loaves.

Honey Butter   Photo on cover.

Naturally sweetened with honey, this creamy spread is delicious on almost any bread!

1/2 cup butter, room temperature
1/3 cup honey

1/4 teaspoon vanilla extract

In small bowl of electric mixer or a food processor fitted with a metal blade, process all ingredients until creamy. Spoon into a small serving bowl. Cover and refrigerate. Let stand at room temperature 20 minutes before serving. Makes about 3/4 cup.

Variations
Cinnamon-Honey Butter: Add 1/2 to 3/4 teaspoon ground cinnamon.
Honey-Berry Butter: Blot 1/2 cup minced fresh blueberries or strawberries on paper towels. Fold into honey butter.
Citrus-Honey Butter: Increase butter to 2/3 cup. Add 2 tablespoons lemon or orange juice and 2 teaspoons grated lemon or orange peel.

Grandma's Oatmeal Bread   Photo on pages 44 and 45.

Serve this delicious, chewy and wholesome bread with Cinnamon-Honey Butter, opposite.

2-1/2 cups regular or quick-cooking
   rolled oats
2 tablespoons dark molasses
1/3 cup honey
1/3 cup butter, cut in 5 pieces,
   brought to room temperature
1 tablespoon salt
1/2 teaspoon ground ginger
1/2 teaspoon ground cinnamon
1-1/2 cups milk

2 (1/4-oz.) pkgs. active dry yeast
   (2 tablespoons)
1 teaspoon sugar
1/3 cup warm water (110F, 45C)
4-1/2 to 5 cups all-purpose or bread flour
6 tablespoons regular or
   quick-cooking rolled oats
1 teaspoon dark molasses blended with
   2 teaspoons water for glaze

In large bowl of electric mixer, combine 2-1/2 cups oats, 2 tablespoons molasses, honey, butter, salt, ginger and cinnamon; set aside. In a small saucepan, bring milk to a simmer over medium heat. Pour over oat mixture; stir to combine. Let stand 10 to 15 minutes or until cool. In a small bowl, dissolve yeast and sugar in 1/3 cup water. Let stand until foamy, 5 to 10 minutes. Add to cooled oat mixture. Add 1 to 1-1/2 cups flour. Beat at medium speed with electric mixer 2 minutes or, beat 200 vigorous strokes by hand. Stir in enough remaining flour to make a soft dough. Turn out dough onto a lightly floured surface. Clean and grease bowl; set aside. **Knead dough** 10 to 12 minutes or until smooth and elastic. Place dough in greased bowl, turning to coat all sides. Cover with a slightly damp towel. Let rise in a warm place, free from drafts, until doubled in bulk, about 1 hour. Generously grease 2 (8" x 4") loaf pans or 2 (1-1/2-quart) casserole dishes. Sprinkle 2 tablespoons oats over bottom and sides of each pan; set aside. **Punch down dough;** knead 30 seconds. Divide dough in half; shape into loaves. Place in prepared pans. Cover with a dry towel. Let rise until doubled in bulk, about 45 minutes. **Preheat oven** to 375F (190C). Brush tops of loaves with molasses glaze; sprinkle 1 tablespoon oats over top of each loaf. Slash tops of loaves as desired. Bake 40 to 45 minutes or until bread sounds hollow when tapped on bottom. Remove from pans. Cool on racks. Makes 2 loaves.

Variations

Wheat & Oatmeal Bread: Substitute 1-1/2 cups whole-wheat flour for 1-1/2 cups all-purpose or bread flour.
Oatmeal Bread with Raisins or Nuts: Add 1 cup chopped nuts or 1 cup raisins. Or, add 1/2 cup nuts and 1/2 cup raisins before kneading.

Tip *Toast seeds and nuts in a skillet over medium heat, stirring often, until golden brown. Oven-toast at 350F (175C), stirring occasionally, for 15 minutes or until golden brown.*

Sunflower-Seed & Yogurt Bread   Photo on cover.

Makes wonderful avocado, tomato and alfalfa-sprout sandwiches.

1-3/4 cups raw hulled sunflower seeds,
   toasted
2 (1/4-oz.) pkgs. active dry yeast
   (2 tablespoons)
1 teaspoon sugar
1 cup warm water (110F, 45C)
1/4 cup honey
1/4 cup vegetable oil
1 cup plain yogurt (8 oz.), room temperature

1 egg, room temperature
1 egg yolk
2 teaspoons salt
5 to 5-1/2 cups all-purpose or bread flour
1-1/2 cups whole-wheat flour
5 to 6 tablespoons raw hulled
   sunflower seeds
1 egg white blended with
   2 teaspoons water for glaze

In a blender or food processor fitted with metal blade, grind 1/2 cup sunflower seeds until very fine; set aside. In large bowl of electric mixer, dissolve yeast and sugar in 1 cup water. Let stand until foamy, 5 to 10 minutes. Add honey, oil, yogurt, egg, egg yolk, salt and 2-1/2 to 3 cups all-purpose or bread flour. Beat at medium speed with electric mixer 2 minutes or, beat 200 vigorous strokes by hand. Stir in whole-wheat flour, ground sunflower seeds, reserved 1-1/4 cups whole sunflower seeds and enough remaining all-purpose or bread flour to make a soft dough. Turn out dough onto a lightly floured surface. Clean and grease bowl; set aside. **Knead dough** 8 to 10 minutes or until smooth and elastic. Place dough in greased bowl, turning to coat all sides. Cover with a slightly damp towel. Let rise in a warm place, free from drafts, until doubled in bulk, about 1 hour. Generously grease 2 (8" x 4" or 9" x 5") loaf pans. Sprinkle 2 tablespoons sunflower seeds over bottom and sides of each pan; set aside. **Punch down dough;** knead 30 seconds. Divide dough in half; shape into loaves. Place in prepared pans. Cover with a dry towel. Let rise until doubled in bulk, 30 to 45 minutes. **Preheat oven** to 375F (190C). Slash tops of loaves as desired. Brush with egg-white glaze. Sprinkle about 2 teaspoons sunflower seeds over each unbaked loaf. Bake 30 to 35 minutes or until bread sounds hollow when tapped on bottom. Remove from pans. Cool on racks. Makes 2 loaves.

Molasses Butter

Subtly sweet and lightly laced with molasses—perfect for whole-grain breads!

1 cup butter, room temperature
2 tablespoons brown sugar
2 tablespoons molasses

1 teaspoon vanilla extract
Pinch of salt

In small bowl of electric mixer, cream butter and brown sugar until fluffy. Beating constantly, slowly add molasses and vanilla. Beat until thoroughly blended. Spoon into a small serving dish. Cover and refrigerate. Let stand at room temperature 20 to 30 minutes before serving. Makes about 1-1/4 cups.

Variation

Maple Butter: Substitute 3 tablespoons pure maple syrup for molasses. Stir in 2 tablespoons toasted finely chopped pecans, if desired.

How to Make Molasses-Bran Bread

1/With pointed scissors, cut diagonal notches in a zig-zag pattern in tops of loaves, every 1-1/2 inches.

2/Bake 30 to 35 minutes or until bread sounds hollow when tapped on bottom. Cool on racks.

Molasses-Bran Bread   Photo on pages 44-45 and 98.

Serve this wholesome bread with Molasses Butter, opposite.

2 (1/4-oz.) pkgs. active dry yeast
  (2 tablespoons)
1 tablespoon brown sugar
2-1/3 cups warm water (110F, 45C)
2/3 cup nonfat-milk powder
1/2 cup dark molasses or honey
1/3 cup butter, melted
2-1/2 teaspoons salt

3/4 teaspoon ground ginger
6-3/4 to 7-1/4 cups all-purpose or
  bread flour
1-1/4 cups unprocessed bran flakes
1 cup whole-wheat flour
1 teaspoon dark molasses blended with
  1 tablespoon melted butter for glaze
Unprocessed bran flakes, if desired

In large bowl of electric mixer, dissolve yeast and brown sugar in water. Let stand until foamy, 5 to 10 minutes. Add milk powder, 1/2 cup molasses or honey, 1/3 cup butter, salt, ginger and 4 to 4-1/2 cups all-purpose or bread flour. Beat at medium speed with electric mixer 2 minutes or, beat 200 vigorous strokes by hand. Stir in 1-1/4 cups bran flakes, whole-wheat flour and enough remaining all-purpose or bread flour to make a soft dough. Turn out dough onto a lightly floured surface. Clean and grease bowl; set aside. **Knead dough** 8 to 10 minutes or until smooth and elastic. Place dough in greased bowl, turning to coat all sides. Cover with a slightly damp towel. Let rise in a warm place, free from drafts, until doubled in bulk, about 1 hour. Grease 2 large baking sheets; set aside. **Punch down dough;** knead 30 seconds. Divide dough in half; shape into oval loaves. Place on prepared baking sheets. With pointed scissors, cut diagonal notches in a zig-zag pattern in tops of loaves, every 1-1/2 inches. Cover with a dry towel. Let rise until doubled in bulk, 45 to 60 minutes. **Preheat oven** to 375F (190C). Brush with molasses glaze. If desired, sprinkle with additional bran flakes. Bake 30 to 35 minutes or until bread sounds hollow when tapped on bottom. Remove from pans. Cool on racks. Makes 2 loaves.

Pizza Crisps

Sautéed in garlic-flavored oil and topped with melted cheese and tomato.

About 1/4 cup olive oil
1 garlic clove, crushed
8 slices leftover French or other
   firm bread, 1/2-inch thick
8 to 10 thin slices mozzarella or
   provolone cheese

2 firm, ripe tomatoes, thinly sliced,
   seeds removed
Salt and pepper, if desired
Freshly minced basil or oregano,
   if desired

Preheat oven to 375F (190C). If slices are large, cut in half vertically; set aside. In a small bowl, combine olive oil and garlic; let stand 15 minutes. Lightly brush both sides of bread slices with oil mixture. Place a large skillet over medium-high heat. Add bread slices; sauté on both sides until golden brown. Blot on paper towels. Arrange sautéed bread slices, 1-1/2 inches apart, on an ungreased baking sheet. Top each slice with a single layer of sliced cheese and a tomato slice. Sprinkle with salt and pepper. Bake until cheese melts, about 3 minutes. Sprinkle with basil or oregano, if desired. Serve hot. Makes 4 to 8 servings.

Wheaty Carrot-Raisin Bread

Carrots, raisins and wheat germ give this beautiful loaf its nutritious down-to-earth goodness.

2 (1/4-oz.) pkgs. active dry yeast
   (2 tablespoons)
1 tablespoon molasses
1 cup warm water (110F, 45C)
1/4 cup honey
2 eggs, room temperature
1/4 cup vegetable oil
1 teaspoon vanilla extract
2 teaspoons salt
1/2 teaspoon ground ginger
1/2 teaspoon ground nutmeg

1/3 cup nonfat-milk powder
4-3/4 to 5-1/4 cups all-purpose or
   bread flour
1 cup whole-wheat flour
1/2 cup wheat germ
1-1/2 cups shredded carrots, blotted dry
1 cup raisins
3/4 cup chopped walnuts, if desired
1 egg yolk blended with
   2 teaspoons water for glaze

In large bowl of electric mixer, dissolve yeast and molasses in 1 cup water. Let stand until foamy, 5 to 10 minutes. Add honey, eggs, oil, vanilla, salt, ginger, nutmeg, milk powder and 2-1/2 to 3 cups all-purpose or bread flour. Beat at medium speed with electric mixer 2 minutes or, beat 200 vigorous strokes by hand. Stir in whole-wheat flour, wheat germ, carrots, raisins, nuts, if desired. Add enough remaining all-purpose or bread flour to make a soft dough. Turn out dough onto a lightly floured surface. Clean and grease bowl; set aside. **Knead dough** 8 to 10 minutes or until smooth and elastic. Place dough in greased bowl, turning to coat all sides. Cover with a slightly damp towel. Let rise in a warm place, free from drafts, until doubled in bulk, about 1-1/2 hours. Grease 2 (8" x 4") loaf pans or 2 (1-1/2-quart) casserole dishes; set aside. **Punch down dough;** knead 30 seconds. Divide dough in half; shape into loaves. Place in prepared pans. Cover with a dry towel. Let rise until doubled in bulk, about 1 hour. **Preheat oven** to 375F (190C). Slash tops of loaves as desired; brush with egg-yolk glaze. Bake 35 to 40 minutes or until bread sounds hollow when tapped on bottom. Remove from pans. Cool on racks. Makes 2 loaves.

Russian Black Bread

A dark, chewy loaf—wonderful for sandwiches and with hearty soups.

1/2 cup granulated sugar
2 cups boiling water
1/4 cup vinegar
1/4 cup butter
1-1/2 oz. unsweetened chocolate,
   cut in 6 pieces
3 (1/4-oz.) pkgs. active dry yeast
   (3 tablespoons)
2 tablespoons brown sugar
1/2 cup warm water (110F, 45C)
3 cups medium or dark rye flour

1 cup whole-bran cereal
1/2 cup wheat germ
1 tablespoon instant-coffee granules
1 tablespoon salt
2 teaspoons caraway seeds, crushed
1/2 teaspoon fennel seeds, crushed
1 teaspoon onion powder
4 to 4-1/2 cups all-purpose or bread flour
1 teaspoon dark molasses blended with
   a pinch of salt and
   1 tablespoon water for glaze

In a large, heavy saucepan, stir granulated sugar over medium-high heat until melted. Continue to stir until sugar smokes and is almost black. Slowly and carefully stir in 2 cups boiling water. This will cause mixture to smoke and sugar to lump and harden. Continue cooking and stirring until sugar is completely dissolved. Stir in vinegar, butter and chocolate. Set aside to cool, stirring occasionally to dissolve chocolate. In large bowl of electric mixer, dissolve yeast and brown sugar in 1/2 cup water. Let stand until foamy, 5 to 10 minutes. Add 1 cup rye flour, bran cereal, wheat germ, coffee granules, salt, caraway seeds, fennel seeds, onion powder and 2 to 2-1/2 cups all-purpose or bread flour. Beat at medium speed with electric mixer 2 minutes or, beat 200 vigorous strokes by hand. Stir in remaining rye flour and enough of remaining all-purpose or bread flour to make a stiff dough. Turn out onto a lightly floured surface. Clean and grease bowl; set aside. **Knead dough** 10 to 12 minutes or until smooth and elastic. Place dough in greased bowl, turning to coat all sides. Cover with a slightly damp towel. Let rise in a warm place, free from drafts, until doubled in bulk, about 1 hour. Grease 2 medium baking sheets or 2 round 8-inch cake pans; set aside. **Punch down dough;** knead 2 minutes. Divide dough in half; cover and let rest 10 minutes. Shape into 2 round loaves. Place on prepared baking sheets or in prepared pans. Cover with a dry towel. Let rise until doubled in bulk, about 1 hour. **Preheat oven** to 375F (190C). Slash tops of loaves as desired; brush with molasses glaze. Bake 30 to 35 minutes; brush again with molasses glaze. Bake 10 minutes longer or until bread sounds hollow when tapped on bottom. Remove from pans. Cool on racks. Makes 2 loaves.

Kaymak

A Yugoslavian cheese spread—delicious with hearty ryes and other dark loaves!

1 (8-oz.) pkg. cream cheese,
   room temperature
1/2 cup butter, room temperature

1/2 cup feta cheese (2 oz.),
   room temperature

In small bowl of electric mixer, beat all ingredients until light and fluffy. Spoon into a small serving dish. Cover and refrigerate. Let stand at room temperature 20 to 30 minutes before serving. Makes about 2 cups.

Dilly-Rye Bread   Photo on cover.

Dill gives this light rye bread a scent of summer.

2 (1/4-oz.) pkgs. active dry yeast
   (2 tablespoons)
2 tablespoons sugar
1/2 cup warm water (110F, 45C)
1 (16-oz.) carton cottage cheese (2 cups),
   room temperature
1/4 cup butter, melted
4 eggs, room temperature
1 tablespoon salt

4 teaspoons dill weed or dill seeds or
   2-1/2 tablespoons minced fresh dill
2 cups medium rye flour
5 to 5-1/2 cups all-purpose or bread flour
1 egg white blended with
   1 tablespoon water for glaze
1 to 2 teaspoons dill weed or
   dill seeds for garnish

In large bowl of electric mixer, dissolve yeast and sugar in 1/2 cup water. Let stand until foamy, 5 to 10 minutes. Add cottage cheese, butter, eggs, salt, 4 teaspoons dill weed or dill seeds or 1-1/2 tablespoons fresh dill, rye flour and 1/2 to 1 cup all-purpose or bread flour. Beat at medium speed with electric mixer 2 minutes or, beat 200 vigorous strokes by hand. Stir in enough remaining all-purpose or bread flour to make a soft dough. Turn out dough onto a lightly floured surface. Clean and grease bowl; set aside. **Knead dough** 8 to 10 minutes or until smooth and elastic. Place dough in greased bowl, turning to coat all sides. Cover with a slightly damp towel. Let rise in a warm place, free from drafts, until doubled in bulk, about 1 hour. Grease 2 (9" x 5") loaf pans or 2 (2-quart) casserole dishes; set aside. **Punch down dough;** knead 30 seconds. Divide dough in half; shape into loaves. Place in prepared pans. Cover with a dry towel. Let rise until doubled in bulk, about 45 minutes. **Preheat oven** to 375F (190C). Slash tops of loaves as desired. Brush with egg-white glaze; sprinkle with dill weed or dill seeds. Bake 30 to 35 minutes or until bread sounds hollow when tapped on bottom. Remove from pans. Cool on racks. Makes 2 loaves.

Variation

Cheesy-Dill Rye Bread: After first rising, knead in 1 cup (4 ounces) shredded Cheddar or Swiss cheese. Shape as directed.

Sesame Butter

The nutty flavor of toasted sesame seeds will make this savory spread a favorite.

1/2 cup finely ground toasted sesame seeds
2/3 cup butter, room temperature

1/4 teaspoon salt, if desired

In a medium bowl, combine all ingredients. Stir with a spoon until blended. Spoon into a small serving bowl. Cover and refrigerate. Let stand at room temperature 20 to 30 minutes before serving. Makes about 1 cup.

Variation

Sunflower-Seed Butter: Substitute 2/3 cup finely ground, toasted, hulled raw sunflower seeds for sesame seeds.

Swedish Limpa   Photo on page 152.

A wonderful Scandinavian legacy—heady with orange peel, fennel and anise.

2 (1/4-oz.) pkgs. active dry yeast
  (2 tablespoons)
1 teaspoon brown sugar
1 cup warm water (110F, 45C)
1-1/2 cups milk, room temperature
1/4 cup packed brown sugar
1/4 cup molasses
1/4 cup butter, melted
2 teaspoons anise seeds, crushed

2 teaspoons fennel seeds, crushed
1/2 teaspoon ground cardamom
1 tablespoon salt
Grated peel of 2 medium oranges
3 cups medium rye flour
6 to 6-1/2 cups all-purpose or
  bread flour
1 egg white blended with
  2 teaspoons water for glaze

In large bowl of electric mixer, dissolve yeast and 1 teaspoon brown sugar in 1 cup water. Let stand until foamy, 5 to 10 minutes. Add milk, 1/4 cup brown sugar, molasses, butter, anise seeds, fennel seeds, cardamom, salt, orange peel, 1 cup rye flour and 2-1/2 to 3 cups all-purpose or bread flour. Beat at medium speed with electric mixer 2 minutes or, beat 200 vigorous strokes by hand. Stir in remaining rye flour and enough remaining all-purpose or bread flour to make a soft dough. Turn out dough onto a lightly floured surface. Clean and grease bowl; set aside. **Knead dough** 10 to 12 minutes or until smooth and elastic. Dough will be slightly sticky. Place dough in greased bowl, turning to coat all sides. Cover with a slightly damp towel. Let rise in a warm place, free from drafts, until doubled in bulk, about 1 hour. Grease 2 large baking sheets; set aside. **Punch down dough;** knead 2 minutes. Divide dough in half. Shape into 2 round balls about 6 inches in diameter. Place on prepared baking sheets. Use end of a wooden-spoon handle to press 12 indentations, 1/2 inch deep, in tops of loaves. Cover with a dry towel. Let rise until doubled in bulk, about 45 minutes. **Preheat oven** to 375F (190C). Brush tops of loaves with egg-white glaze. Bake 30 to 40 minutes or until bread sounds hollow when tapped on bottom. Remove from pans. Cool on racks. Makes 2 loaves.

Storing & Freezing Baked Bread

   Bread must be completely cooled before storing or freezing. If breads will be used within 3 to 4 days, wrap them airtight in foil or heavy plastic. Store them in a dry place at room temperature. The traditional bread box is an ideal place. Bread can also be stored in the refrigerator up to 7 days. If bread contains meat, it must be refrigerated. Croissants and Danish pastries should be refrigerated because of their high butter content. Breads enriched with eggs, butter, fruits and nuts will keep longer than plain breads because of the added fat and moisture content. Breads with little or no fat, such as French bread, will keep only 1 or 2 days.

   To freeze baked bread: Bread freezes well if wrapped airtight in heavy foil and sealed in a plastic bag. Label each package with the contents and date frozen. If you can't use a loaf of bread within 3 to 4 days, consider freezing half. Most yeast breads can be frozen up to 3 months and quick breads up to 6 months. Add icings or glazes to coffeecakes and sweet breads after thawing.

   To use frozen bread: Thaw bread at room temperature. Reheat in a 350F to 375F (175C to 190C) oven. Heat loaves with soft crusts in the same foil in which they were frozen. Open the foil for hard-crusted loaves or, place loaves directly on oven rack. Heat rolls 8 to 12 minutes and loaves 15 to 25 minutes. Add icings and glazes after thawing.

Beer & Rye Bread

Molasses and dark beer add body and flavor to this delicious, hearty bread.

2 (1/4-oz.) pkgs. active dry yeast
  (2 tablespoons)
2 cups warm, flat dark beer (110F, 45C)
1/3 cup dark molasses
3 tablespoons butter, melted
2-1/2 teaspoons salt
1 tablespoon caraway seeds
1 tablespoon freshly grated orange peel

3/4 teaspoon cumin seeds, crushed
2 cups medium rye flour
4-1/2 to 5 cups all-purpose or bread flour
1/2 cup wheat germ
2 teaspoons yellow cornmeal
1 egg white blended with
  1 tablespoon water for glaze
1 to 2 teaspoons caraway seeds for garnish

In large bowl of electric mixer, dissolve yeast in beer. Let stand until foamy, 5 to 10 minutes. Add molasses, butter, salt, 1 tablespoon caraway seeds, orange peel, cumin seeds, 1 cup rye flour and 2 to 2-1/2 cups all-purpose or bread flour. Beat at medium speed with electric mixer 2 minutes or, beat 200 vigorous strokes by hand. Stir in wheat germ, remaining 1 cup rye flour and enough remaining all-purpose or bread flour to make a soft dough. Turn out dough onto a lightly floured surface. Clean and grease bowl; set aside. **Knead dough** 10 to 12 minutes or until smooth and elastic. Place dough in greased bowl, turning to coat all sides. Cover with a slightly damp towel. Let rise in a warm place, free from drafts, until doubled in bulk, about 1 hour. Grease 2 medium baking sheets or 2 (8" x 4") loaf pans. Sprinkle cornmeal over baking sheets or bottoms of loaf pans; set aside. **Punch down dough;** knead 30 seconds. Divide dough in half; shape into round or oblong loaves. Place on prepared baking sheets or in prepared pans. Cover with a dry towel. Let rise until doubled in bulk, about 45 minutes. Brush egg-white glaze over tops of loaves. Sprinkle 1/2 to 1 teaspoon caraway seeds over each loaf; slash as desired. **Place bread in cold oven.** Set oven temperature at 400F (205C). Bake 30 to 40 minutes or until bread sounds hollow when tapped on bottom. Remove from baking sheet or pans. Cool on racks. Makes 2 loaves.

Storing & Freezing Unbaked Dough

Although not usually recommended, unbaked dough can be frozen, if necessary. Freeze it before or after the first rise. For best results, don't freeze dough longer than 2 to 3 weeks.

To freeze dough before first rise: Knead dough. Cover and let rest 15 minutes. Lightly oil surface of dough. Wrap in heavy plastic wrap or freezer wrap. Freeze until solid. Then place dough in a second plastic bag or wrap airtight in heavy foil. Return to freezer.

Defrost at room temperature 6 to 7 hours. Unwrap dough and place in a large bowl. Cover and let rise. Punch down dough; shape into loaves and let rise again before baking.

To freeze after first rise: Punch down dough; knead 30 seconds to expel excess air. Line baking pans with plastic wrap large enough to extend 3 inches over edges of pan. Shape loaves; coat lightly with vegetable oil. Place loaves in lined pans. Fold plastic wrap loosely over dough. Freeze until solid. Remove dough from pan by lifting with edges of plastic wrap. Tightly seal plastic wrap around dough. Wrap frozen loaves airtight in heavy foil or a plastic bag. Return to freezer.

To defrost: Remove dough from wrappings. Place in same baking pan in which it was frozen. Cover lightly with a towel. Let stand at room temperature 5 to 6 hours. Let rise until doubled in bulk; bake as directed.

Oatmeal-Apple Bread

Lightly scented with molasses and studded with apples and nuts.

1/3 cup raisins
2 tablespoons rum or brandy
2 (1/4-oz.) pkgs. active dry yeast
 (2 tablespoons)
1 teaspoon granulated sugar
1/2 cup warm water (110F, 45C)
1/3 cup packed brown sugar
1-1/2 cups regular rolled oats
1 tablespoon salt
1/2 teaspoon ground cinnamon

1-1/3 cups unsweetened apple juice or
 apple cider
2 tablespoons molasses
1/4 cup butter, melted
5-1/2 to 6 cups all-purpose or bread flour
3/4 cup finely chopped unpeeled apple
1/2 cup chopped walnuts
1 egg white blended with
 1 tablespoon water for glaze

In a small bowl, combine raisins and rum or brandy. Cover; set aside 3 to 4 hours or overnight to soak. In large bowl of electric mixer, dissolve yeast and 1 teaspoon granulated sugar in 1/2 cup water. Let stand until foamy, 5 to 10 minutes. Add brown sugar, oats, salt, cinnamon, apple juice or cider, molasses, butter and 2 to 2-1/2 cups flour. Beat at medium speed with electric mixer 2 minutes or, beat 200 vigorous strokes by hand. Stir in raisins and rum or brandy, apple, nuts and enough remaining flour to make a soft dough. Turn out dough onto a lightly floured surface. Clean and grease bowl; set aside. **Knead dough** 8 to 10 minutes or until smooth and elastic. Place dough in greased bowl, turning to coat all sides. Cover with a slightly damp towel. Let rise in a warm place, free from drafts, until doubled in bulk, about 1 hour. Grease 2 (9" x 5") loaf pans or 2 (2-quart) casserole dishes; set aside. **Punch down dough;** knead 30 seconds. Divide dough in half; shape into loaves. Place in prepared pans. Cover with a dry towel. Let rise until doubled in bulk, about 45 minutes. **Preheat oven** to 375F (190C). Slash tops of loaves as desired; brush with egg-white glaze. Bake 35 to 40 minutes or until bread sounds hollow when tapped on bottom. Remove from pans. Cool on racks. Makes 2 loaves.

Toast Baskets

Wonderful edible containers for cream fillings, thick stews and scrambled eggs.

4 slices day-old bread, 2 inches thick
Melted butter

Preheat oven to 375F (190C). Cut crusts from bread. Use a serrated or sharp, pointed knife to scoop out center of bread slices, leaving 1/2-inch borders around edges and 1/2-inch-thick bottoms. Brush melted butter over baskets, inside and outside. Arrange on an ungreased baking sheet, 3 inches apart. Bake 10 to 15 minutes or until crisp and golden brown. Cool to room temperature. Makes 4 baskets.

Croutons

Use oven-crisped croutons for salads and soups. Try fried croutons for a crunchy surprise!

1/2 lb. leftover bread   **Salt, if desired**
1/4 cup butter, room temperature

Preheat oven to 300F (150C). Cut crusts from bread, if desired, Cut bread into 1/2-inch slices. Lightly butter both sides of bread. Cut slices into 1/2-inch cubes. Spread cubes on 2 ungreased large baking sheets. Stirring 2 to 3 times, bake 30 to 40 minutes or until crisp and golden brown. Lightly sprinkle salt over warm croutons, if desired. Cool to room temperature. Store in an air-tight container. Store 1 month at room temperature, 2 to 3 months in refrigerator or freezer. Makes about 7 ounces croutons.

Variations

Garlic Croutons: Blend 1 crushed garlic clove or 1/8 teaspoon garlic powder and 1/4 cup soft butter. Spread on bread as directed.

Cheese Croutons: In a large bowl, combine 1/2 cup (1-1/2 ounces) grated Parmesan cheese and 1/2 teaspoon each crumbled dried leaf oregano and dried leaf basil. Toss buttered bread cubes in cheese mixture before baking.

Fried Croutons: Pour olive oil 1/2 inch deep into a large skillet. Place over medium heat. When hot, add unbuttered bread cubes. Turning often, sauté until evenly browned. Use a slotted spoon to remove from skillet. Drain on paper towels. Sprinkle salt or garlic salt over warm croutons, if desired.

How to Make Toast Baskets

1/Remove crusts; cut bread into 2-inch slices. Remove center, leaving a 1/2-inch border around edge and a 1/2-inch base.

2/Brush baskets inside and out with melted butter. Bake until golden brown and crisp. Cool before filling.

Sweet Yeast Breads & Coffeecakes

For centuries, cooks have been serving sweetened yeast breads with coffee and tea—both to begin and end the day. With their pretty shapes and decorative glazes, sweet breads and coffeecakes always look so inviting! And homemade sweet breads deliver the taste that's promised by the appearance.

Sweet yeast doughs, often enriched with eggs and butter, are a delight to work with. Eggs supply extra protein, while butter relaxes the gluten and provides a softer crumb. Both create a rich flavor and pale, golden hue in the final bread.

One of the showiest sweet breads you can make is Viennese Striezel, as light and lovely as a Viennese waltz! This braided, three-tier spectacular is flavored with lemon peel and prolific with golden raisins. There is a secret to keeping the stacked braids in place. Make a depression in the bottom and second braid with the edge of your hand, then center the successive braids in place. For a festive look, tuck candied cherry halves randomly in the folds of the braids. Another European favorite is Polish Cheese Babka. Though there are dozens of babka variations, this one boasts a rich lemon-cheese filling and a crispy streusel crown. Either bread makes a beautiful edible centerpiece for a special brunch or tea!

Old-Fashioned Cinnamon Bread, my father's favorite, is special and different. It not only has a cinnamon-nut swirl, but the dough is spiced as well. The deliciously homey fragrance of this double-spiced bread is wonderful. I have a real-estate friend who claims if she could bottle its essence to spray around her open houses, she'd sell them on the first day!

Do you prefer breads sweetened lightly with fruit or nuts, or more boldly with chocolate or marzipan? Whatever your preference, you're sure to find a recipe here that appeals to you. If you have even the tiniest sweet tooth, you won't be able to resist these beautiful breads!

Basic Sweet Yeast Dough

Rich and easy sour-cream dough to use for dozens of breads, coffeecakes and rolls.

1 (1/4-oz.) pkg. active dry yeast (1 tablespoon)	1/3 cup butter, melted
1 teaspoon sugar	1/2 cup dairy sour cream, room temperature
1/4 cup warm water (110F, 45C)	1 teaspoon vanilla extract
1/3 cup sugar	1 teaspoon salt
2 eggs, room temperature	3-1/4 to 3-3/4 cups all-purpose or bread flour

In large bowl of electric mixer, dissolve yeast and 1 teaspoon sugar in water. Let stand until foamy, 5 to 10 minutes. Add 1/3 cup sugar, eggs, butter, sour cream, vanilla, salt and 1-1/2 to 2 cups flour. Beat at medium speed with electric mixer 2 minutes or, beat 200 vigorous strokes by hand. Stir in enough remaining flour to make a soft dough. Turn out dough onto a lightly floured surface. Clean and grease bowl. **Knead dough** 4 to 6 minutes or until smooth. Dough will feel soft and buttery, but not sticky. Place dough in greased bowl, turning to coat all sides. Cover with a slightly damp towel. Let rise in a warm place, free from drafts, until doubled in bulk, about 1-1/2 hours. Shape and bake as directed in specific recipes. Makes 2 loaves or 24 rolls.

Use to make: Cheddar-Pear Coffeecake, page 61; Cookie-Filled Coffeecake, below; French Mocha Ring, page 60; Grandmother's Cinnamon Rolls, page 88; Maple-Pecan Sticky Buns, page 89; Candy-Cane Bread, page 154; Raised Doughnuts, page 167; Cherry-Valentine Bread, page 142; and Fried Bread, page 40.

Variation

Overnight Sweet Dough: Shape and place in pan as recipe directs. Cover tightly with plastic wrap; refrigerate overnight. Uncover and let stand at room temperature 30 minutes before baking.

Cookie-Filled Coffeecake

Beautiful coffeecake with a delicious cookie-crumb swirl—for the kid in each of us!

1 recipe Basic Sweet Yeast Dough, above	1/3 cup sugar
1-1/2 cups finely crushed cream-filled chocolate cookies (13 to 15)	1/3 cup butter, melted
1 cup finely chopped walnuts or pecans	1 egg white blended with 1 teaspoon water for glaze

Prepare Basic Sweet Yeast Dough through first rising. Grease a large baking sheet. **Punch down dough;** knead 30 seconds. Cover and let rest 10 minutes. In a medium bowl, combine crushed cookies, nuts and sugar. Stir in butter; set aside. On a lightly floured surface, roll out dough to a 15-inch square. Sprinkle with crumb mixture to within 1/2 inch of edges. Roll up tightly, jelly-roll fashion. Pinch seam and ends to seal. Place on prepared baking sheet, seam-side down. Shape roll into a circle; pinch ends together to join. Using a sharp knife, make cuts 1 inch apart, around outside of circle, about two-thirds of way to center. Twist each cut piece in the same direction, turning so filling faces upward. Cover with a dry towel. Let rise until doubled in bulk, about 1 hour. **Preheat oven** to 350F (175C). Brush dough with egg-white glaze, being careful not to streak dark cookie-crumb filling on light dough. Bake 30 to 40 minutes or until bread sounds hollow when tapped on top. Cool on a rack at least 25 minutes before serving. Makes 1 large coffeecake.

Note: Do not use cookies that have 2 layers of cream filling.

French Mocha Ring

Meringue filling blends coffee and chocolate flavors for a special-occasion coffeecake!

1 recipe Basic Sweet Yeast Dough, page 59	**2 oz. semisweet chocolate, melted, cooled**
2 egg whites, room temperature	**1 cup chopped walnuts or pecans**
1-1/2 teaspoons instant-coffee powder	**Mocha Glaze, see below**
1/8 teaspoon salt	**Candy coffee beans, if desired**
1/2 cup sugar	

Mocha Glaze:

1 teaspoon instant-coffee powder	**1 teaspoon vanilla extract**
1 to 2 tablespoons milk	**1 cup powdered sugar**

Prepare Basic Sweet Yeast Dough through first rising. Generously grease a 10-cup fluted tube or Bundt pan. **Punch down dough;** knead 30 seconds. Cover and let rest 10 minutes. In small bowl of electric mixer, combine egg whites, coffee powder and salt. Beat until soft peaks form. Gradually beat in sugar, 2 tablespoons at a time, until meringue is firm and glossy. Fold in chocolate; set aside. On a lightly floured surface, roll out dough to a 20'' x 16'' rectangle. Spread meringue over dough to within 1 inch of edges. Sprinkle evenly with nuts. Beginning on a long side, roll up tightly, jelly-roll fashion. Pinch seam and ends to seal. Place roll in prepared pan, seam-side up. Overlap ends slightly; pinch together. Cover with a dry towel. Let rise until doubled in bulk, about 1 hour. If seam pulls apart, pinch together lightly to reseal. **Preheat oven** to 350F (175C). Bake 35 to 45 minutes or until bread sounds hollow when tapped on top. Remove from pan. Cool on a rack. Prepare Mocha Glaze. Drizzle over top of cooled coffeecake. If desired, garnish top with candy coffee beans. Makes 1 coffeecake.

Mocha Glaze:
In a small bowl, dissolve coffee powder in 1 tablespoon milk. Stir in vanilla, powdered sugar and enough additional milk to make a thick, creamy glaze of drizzling consistency.

Tip *Create instant-coffee powder out of freeze-dried-coffee granules by crushing granules in a mortar and pestle, between 2 spoons or in a food processor.*

How to Make Cheddar-Pear Coffeecake

1/Cut dough on each side of filling in 1-inch strips. Starting at ends, alternately fold at an angle over filling.

2/Loosely tie center strips; arrange attractively over filling. After baking, cool on racks before cutting.

Cheddar-Pear Coffeecake

Cheddar cheese adds golden magic to a pear, raisin and walnut filling.

Basic Sweet Yeast Dough, page 59	**1/3 cup packed brown sugar**
2 tablespoons butter, melted	**1/3 cup raisins**
1-1/2 cups finely chopped peeled pears	**1/3 cup chopped walnuts**
2 tablespoons all-purpose flour	**1 egg white blended with**
1 cup shredded Cheddar cheese (4 oz.)	**2 teaspoons water for glaze**

Prepare Basic Sweet Yeast Dough through first rising. Grease 2 baking sheets. **Punch down dough;** knead 30 seconds. Divide dough in half. Cover 1 piece; set aside. On a lightly floured surface, roll out remaining dough to a 15'' x 10'' rectangle. Brush with 1 tablespoon melted butter. In a medium bowl, toss pears and flour. Stir in cheese, brown sugar, raisins and walnuts. Spoon half of pear mixture lengthwise down center of dough. Using a sharp knife, cut dough on each side of filling into 15 (1-inch) strips. Do not cut on the diagonal. Starting at 1 end, alternately fold 7 strips from each side over filling, at an angle, creating a braided effect. Repeat, starting from opposite end with 7 pairs of strips. Bring remaining 2 center strips together. Tie loosely; arrange ends attractively over filling. Repeat with remaining dough and filling. Place shaped coffeecakes on prepared baking sheets. Cover with a dry towel. Let rise in a warm place, free from drafts, until doubled in bulk, 1 to 1-1/2 hours. **Preheat oven** to 350F (175C). Brush coffeecakes with egg-white glaze. Bake 20 to 30 minutes or until golden brown. Cool on racks 30 minutes before serving. Serve warm or at room temperature. Makes 2 coffeecakes.

Old-Fashioned Cinnamon Bread

Cinnamon-spiced bread with a rich cinnamon-sugar swirl for double-good flavor.

2 (1/4-oz.) pkgs. active dry yeast
   (2 tablespoons)
1 teaspoon sugar
1/3 cup warm water (110F, 45C)
1/3 cup sugar
1-1/4 cups milk, room temperature
2 eggs, room temperature
1 teaspoon vanilla extract
1/2 cup butter, melted
1-1/2 teaspoons salt

1/2 teaspoon ground nutmeg
1 tablespoon ground cinnamon
6 to 6-1/2 cups all-purpose or
   bread flour
Cinnamon-Nut Filling, see below
2 tablespoons butter, melted
1 egg yolk blended with
   1 teaspoon cream for glaze
2 teaspoons sugar blended with 1/4 teaspoon
   ground cinnamon, if desired

Cinnamon-Nut Filling:
3/4 cup packed brown sugar
2-1/2 teaspoons ground cinnamon

1/2 teaspoon ground nutmeg
1/2 cup finely chopped walnuts or pecans

In large bowl of electric mixer, dissolve yeast and 1 teaspoon sugar in water. Let stand until foamy, 5 to 10 minutes. Add 1/3 cup sugar, milk, eggs, vanilla, 1/2 cup butter, salt, nutmeg, 1 tablespoon cinnamon and 3-1/2 to 4 cups flour. Beat at medium speed with electric mixer 2 minutes or, beat 200 vigorous strokes by hand. Stir in enough of remaining flour to make a soft dough. Turn out dough onto a lightly floured surface. Clean and grease bowl. **Knead dough** 8 to 10 minutes or until smooth and elastic. Place dough in greased bowl, turning to coat all sides. Cover with a slightly damp towel. Let rise in a warm place, free from drafts, until doubled in bulk, about 1 hour. Grease 2 (9" x 5") loaf pans. Prepare Cinnamon-Nut Filling; set aside. **Punch down dough;** knead 30 seconds. Divide dough in half. Cover 1 piece; set aside. Roll out remaining dough to a 14" x 8" rectangle. Brush with 1 tablespoon melted butter. Sprinkle half of Cinnamon-Nut Filling evenly over dough to within 1/2 inch of edges. Lightly press cinnamon mixture into dough with back of a spoon. Beginning on a short side, roll up tightly, jelly-roll fashion. Pinch seam and ends to seal. Turn seam-side down. Tuck ends under; pinch again. Place in a prepared pan. Repeat with remaining dough. Cover with a dry towel. Let rise until doubled in bulk, about 45 minutes. **Preheat oven** to 350F (175C). Brush tops of loaves with egg-yolk glaze. If desired, sprinkle sugar-cinnamon mixture over tops. Bake 45 to 50 minutes or until bread sounds hollow when tapped on bottom. Remove from pans. Cool on racks. Makes 2 loaves.

Cinnamon-Nut Filling:
Combine all ingredients in a small bowl.

Tip *Store brown sugar in a thick plastic bag in a cool dry place. If sugar begins to harden, add a wedge of apple or a slice of bread to the bag.*

Polish Cheese Babka

Rich lemon-cheese filling hides inside this streusel-topped beauty.

1 (1/4-oz.) pkg. active dry yeast
  (1 tablespoon)
1 teaspoon granulated sugar
1/4 cup warm water (110F, 45C)
1/4 cup granulated sugar
1 egg, room temperature
2 egg yolks, room temperature
1/3 cup dairy sour cream, room temperature

6 tablespoons butter, melted
1 teaspoon vanilla extract
2 teaspoons freshly grated lemon peel
1/2 teaspoon salt
2-3/4 to 3-1/4 cups all-purpose flour
Lemon-Cheese Filling, see below
Streusel Topping, see below
Powdered sugar, if desired

Lemon-Cheese Filling:
2 (3-oz.) pkgs. cream cheese,
  room temperature
1 egg yolk
1 teaspoon freshly grated lemon peel

2 tablespoons sugar
1/2 teaspoon vanilla extract
1/2 cup golden raisins, if desired

Streusel Topping:
1/4 cup all-purpose flour
1/4 cup sugar
1/4 teaspoon ground cinnamon

1/4 cup cold butter
1/2 cup finely chopped walnuts or pecans

In large bowl of electric mixer, dissolve yeast and 1 teaspoon granulated sugar in water. Let stand until foamy, 5 to 10 minutes. Add 1/4 cup granulated sugar, egg, egg yolks, sour cream, butter, vanilla, lemon peel, salt and 1 to 1-1/2 cups flour. Beat at medium speed with electric mixer 2 minutes or, beat 200 vigorous strokes by hand. Stir in enough remaining flour to make a soft dough. Turn out dough onto a lightly floured surface. Clean and grease bowl. **Knead dough** 5 minutes or until smooth. Dough will be soft and buttery, but not sticky. Place dough in greased bowl, turning to coat all sides. Cover with a slightly damp towel. Let rise in a warm place, free from drafts, until doubled in bulk, about 1 hour. Grease a 9-inch springform or a round 9-inch cake pan. Prepare Lemon-Cheese Filling and Streusel Topping; set aside. **Punch down dough;** knead 30 seconds. Pinch off one-third of dough; cover and set aside. Press remaining two-thirds of dough into bottom and 1/2 inch up side of prepared pan. Spread Lemon-Cheese Filling evenly over dough to within 1/2 inch of edges. Roll or pat reserved dough into a 9-inch circle; place on top of filling. Pinch edges of 2 dough layers tightly together to seal. Use your finger or a wooden-spoon handle to press seam down to bottom of pan. Sprinkle Streusel Topping over top. Cover with a dry towel. Let rise until doubled in bulk, about 1 hour. **Preheat oven** to 375F (190C). Bake 35 to 40 minutes or until golden brown. Remove side of springform pan. Remove baked babka from bottom of pan. If using a round cake pan, turn out of pan onto a rack. Immediately invert onto another rack. Cool on rack at least 45 minutes before serving. Best served at room temperature. If desired, dust lightly with powdered sugar. Makes 1 coffeecake.

Lemon-Cheese Filling:
In a small bowl, blend all ingredients until smooth and creamy.

Streusel Topping:
In a small bowl, combine flour, sugar and cinnamon. Use a pastry cutter or 2 knives to cut in butter until mixture resembles coarse crumbs. Stir in nuts.

Ricotta-Orange Ring

Ricotta cheese in the dough and filling makes this coffeecake doubly good.

1 (1/4-oz.) pkg. active dry yeast
   (1 tablespoon)
1 teaspoon sugar
1/4 cup warm water (110F, 45C)
1 egg, room temperature
1/4 cup sugar
1 (8-oz.) carton ricotta cheese (1 cup),
   room temperature
3 tablespoons butter, melted

1 teaspoon salt
Grated peel of 1 medium orange
2-1/2 to 3 cups all-purpose or bread flour
Orange-Cheese Filling, see below
1 egg white blended with
   1 teaspoon water for glaze
Orange Glaze, see below
Freshly grated orange peel for garnish,
   if desired

Orange-Cheese Filling:
4 oz. ricotta cheese (1/2 cup),
   room temperature
2 (3-oz.) pkgs. cream cheese,
   room temperature
1 tablespoon all-purpose flour
1/4 cup sugar

1 egg yolk
2 teaspoons freshly grated orange peel
1/4 teaspoon ground nutmeg
1/8 teaspoon salt
1/2 cup toasted finely chopped almonds,
   if desired

Orange Glaze:
1 cup powdered sugar
1/4 teaspoon ground nutmeg

1 to 2 tablespoons orange juice

In large bowl of electric mixer, dissolve yeast and 1 teaspoon sugar in 1/4 cup water. Let stand until foamy, 5 to 10 minutes. Add egg, 1/4 cup sugar, ricotta cheese, butter, salt, orange peel from 1 orange and 1 to 1-1/2 cups flour. Beat at medium speed with electric mixer 2 minutes or, beat 200 vigorous strokes by hand. Stir in enough remaining flour to make a soft dough. Turn out dough onto a lightly floured surface. Clean and grease bowl. **Knead dough** 6 to 8 minutes or until smooth and elastic. Dough will be soft and pliable. Place dough in greased bowl, turning to coat all sides. Cover with a slightly damp towel. Let rise in a warm place, free from drafts, until doubled in bulk, about 1 hour. Grease a 9-inch springform pan with center tube or a 10-inch tube pan. Prepare Orange-Cheese Filling; set aside. **Punch down dough;** knead 30 seconds. Roll out dough to a 20'' x 8'' rectangle. Cut rectangle in half lengthwise. Spread half of filling down center of each strip, to within 1/2 inch of edges. Working with 1 rectangle at a time, bring sides up and pinch together over filling. Pinch ends together to seal. Turn seam-side down. Place filled rolls side by side. Keeping seam-sides down, twist rolls together; pinch ends together. Place twisted rolls in prepared pan, overlapping ends slightly. Cover with a dry towel. Let rise until doubled in bulk, about 1 hour. **Preheat oven** to 350F (175C). Brush top of ring with egg-white glaze. Bake 35 to 45 minutes or until a deep golden brown. Run knife around outside and inner edges to loosen bread from pan. Carefully remove from pan. Cool on a rack. Drizzle with Orange Glaze. Garnish with orange peel, if desired. Makes 1 loaf.

Orange-Cheese Filling:
In small bowl of electric mixer, combine all ingredients except almonds. Beat until creamy. Fold in almonds, if desired.

Orange Glaze:
In a small bowl, combine powdered sugar and nutmeg. Stir in enough orange juice to make a smooth, creamy glaze of drizzling consistency.

How to Make Ricotta-Orange Ring

1/Spread half of filling down center of each strip, to within 1/2 inch of edges. Bring sides up over filling; pinch to seal. Seal ends.

2/Keeping seam-sides down, twist rolls together; pinch ends together. Place twisted rolls in prepared pan, overlapping ends slightly.

Cinnamon-Nut Strips

A sweet treat the kids can make!

6 slices leftover bread, 1/2 inch thick
3/4 cup sugar
3/4 teaspoon ground cinnamon

1/2 cup minced almonds, walnuts or pecans
3/4 cup butter, melted

Lightly butter a large baking sheet; set aside. Preheat oven to 350F (175C). Cut crusts from bread, if desired. Cut each slice into 1/2-inch strips. On a large plate, combine sugar, cinnamon and chopped nuts. Dip bread strips quickly in and out of butter, then roll in sugar mixture. Arrange on prepared baking sheet, 1 inch apart. Turning once, bake 10 to 12 minutes or until golden brown. Cool on racks. Makes 24 to 30 strips.

 Tip *An oven thermometer, ruler and thermometer for reading liquid temperature should be in every baker's* batterie de cuisine.

Poppy-Swirl Loaves

These lightly sweet Polish loaves have an almond and poppy-seed filling scented with honey.

2 (1/4-oz.) pkgs. active dry yeast
   (2 tablespoons)
1 teaspoon sugar
1/3 cup warm water (110F, 45C)
1 cup milk, room temperature
1/3 cup sugar
1/4 cup butter, melted
2 eggs, room temperature
2 egg yolks, room temperature

Grated peel of 1 medium lemon
1 teaspoon vanilla extract
1 teaspoon salt
5-1/2 to 6 cups all-purpose or
   bread flour
Poppy-Seed Filling, see below
1 egg white blended with
   2 teaspoons honey for glaze
Poppy seeds and slivered almonds for garnish

Poppy-Seed Filling:
1-1/2 cups water
3/4 cup poppy seeds
1 cup slivered almonds
1/4 cup honey
1/3 cup sugar
1/4 teaspoon salt

3 tablespoons whipping cream or half and half
1 teaspoon freshly grated lemon peel
1 teaspoon vanilla extract
1/4 teaspoon almond extract
1 egg white, beaten until stiff but not dry

In large bowl of electric mixer, dissolve yeast and 1 teaspoon sugar in water. Let stand until foamy, 5 to 10 minutes. Stir in milk, 1/3 cup sugar, butter, eggs, egg yolks, lemon peel, vanilla, salt and 2-1/2 to 3 cups flour. Beat at medium speed with electric mixer 2 minutes or, beat 200 vigorous strokes by hand. Stir in enough remaining flour to make a soft dough. Turn out dough onto a lightly floured surface. Clean and grease bowl. **Knead dough** 6 to 8 minutes or until smooth and elastic. Place dough in greased bowl, turning to coat all sides. Cover with a slightly damp towel. Let rise in a warm place, free from drafts, until doubled in bulk, about 1 hour. Prepare Poppy-Seed Filling; set aside. Grease 2 (9" x 5") loaf pans. **Punch down dough;** knead 30 seconds. Divide dough in half. Cover; let rest 10 minutes. Roll out half of dough to an 18" x 10" rectangle. Spread with half of filling to within 1/2 inch of edges. Beginning on a long side, roll up tightly, jelly-roll fashion. Pinch seam and ends. With seam-side down, fold roll in half, bringing 1 end up, even with other end, in a tight U shape. Place in prepared pan with halves side by side, seam-side down. Repeat with remaining dough. Cover with a dry towel. Let rise until doubled in bulk, 45 to 60 minutes. **Preheat oven** to 350F (175C). Brush loaves with egg-white glaze, then sprinkle with poppy seeds. Bake 35 to 45 minutes or until bread sounds hollow when tapped on top. Remove from pans. Cool on racks. If desired, frost with Lemon Frosting, page 145, then sprinkle poppy seeds and slivered almonds over top. Makes 2 loaves.

Poppy-Seed Filling:
In a small saucepan, bring water and poppy seeds to a boil. Cover; set aside 30 minutes. Thoroughly drain. In a blender or food processor, combine drained poppy seeds and almonds. Process until almonds are coarsely ground. Pour into a medium bowl. Stir in honey, sugar, salt, cream or half and half, lemon peel, vanilla and almond extract. Fold in egg white.

Poppy-Swirl Loaf

Rais'n-Shine Bread

Start the day off right with this delicious raisin bread speckled with bits of orange.

1 (1/4-oz.) pkg. active dry yeast
  (1 tablespoon)
1 teaspoon granulated sugar
1/4 cup warm water (110F, 45C)
1/3 cup packed brown sugar
Freshly grated peel of 1 large orange
1-1/4 cups orange juice, room temperature
2 eggs, room temperature

1/3 cup vegetable oil
1-1/2 teaspoons salt
1/2 cup nonfat-milk powder
1/2 teaspoon ground cardamom
1 teaspoon ground allspice
5-1/2 to 6 cups all-purpose or bread flour
1 to 1-1/2 cups raisins
Sunshine Glaze, see below

Sunshine Glaze:
1 cup powdered sugar
1 tablespoon butter, melted

2 to 4 tablespoons orange juice

In large bowl of electric mixer, dissolve yeast and granulated sugar in water. Let stand until foamy, 5 to 10 minutes. Add brown sugar, orange peel, orange juice, eggs, oil, salt, milk powder, cardamom, allspice and 2-1/2 to 3 cups flour. Beat at medium speed with electric mixer 2 minutes or, beat 200 vigorous strokes by hand. Stir in raisins and enough remaining flour to make a soft dough. Turn out dough onto a lightly floured surface. Clean and grease bowl. **Knead dough** 8 to 10 minutes or until smooth and elastic. Place dough in greased bowl, turning to coat all sides. Cover with a slightly damp towel. Let rise in a warm place, free from drafts, until doubled in bulk, about 1 hour. Grease 2 (8" x 4") loaf pans or 2 (1-1/2-quart) casserole dishes. **Punch down dough;** knead 30 seconds. Divide dough in half. Shape into loaves; place in prepared pans. Cover with a dry towel. Let rise until doubled in bulk, about 45 minutes. **Preheat oven** to 375F (190C). Slash tops of loaves as desired. Bake 30 to 35 minutes or until bread sounds hollow when tapped on bottom. Remove from pans. Cool on racks over waxed paper. When bread is cool, prepare Sunshine Glaze. Drizzle glaze over tops of loaves. Let glaze set 5 minutes before slicing. Serve warm. Makes 2 loaves.

Sunshine Glaze:
In a small bowl, combine powdered sugar and butter. Stir in enough orange juice to make a smooth, creamy glaze of drizzling consistency.

Variation

Wheaty Rais'n-Shine Bread: Substitute 2 cups whole-wheat flour for 2 cups all-purpose flour. Add 1/4 cup wheat germ along with milk powder.

Tip *Sweet doughs take longer to rise than savory doughs.*

Fruited-Wheat Bread

Naturally sweetened with honey, fruit juice and dried fruit.

2 (1/4-oz.) pkgs. active dry yeast
  (2 tablespoons)
1 teaspoon honey
1/3 cup warm water (110F, 45C)
1 cup pineapple juice, orange juice or
  apricot nectar
1/4 cup honey
2 eggs, room temperature
1/3 cup butter, melted
2 teaspoons freshly grated orange peel
1/2 teaspoon ground cinnamon
1/2 teaspoon ground nutmeg

1/2 teaspoon ground allspice
1/4 teaspoon ground cloves
1-1/2 teaspoons salt
3 cups whole-wheat flour
3-1/2 to 4 cups all-purpose or bread flour
1 cup toasted chopped walnuts or pecans
1/2 cup chopped dried prunes
1/2 cup chopped dried apricots
1/2 cup dark or golden raisins
1/4 cup all-purpose or bread flour
1 egg white, slightly beaten
Sugar

In large bowl of electric mixer, dissolve yeast and 1 teaspoon honey in water. Let stand until foamy, 5 to 10 minutes. Add juice or nectar, 1/4 cup honey, eggs, butter, orange peel, cinnamon, nutmeg, allspice, cloves, salt, 1 cup whole-wheat flour and 2 to 2-1/2 cups all-purpose or bread flour. Beat at medium speed with electric mixer 2 minutes or, beat 200 vigorous strokes by hand. Stir in remaining 2 cups whole-wheat flour and enough remaining all-purpose or bread flour to make a soft dough. Turn out dough onto a lightly floured surface. Clean and grease bowl. **Knead dough** 8 to 10 minutes or until smooth and elastic. Place dough in greased bowl, turning to coat all sides. Cover with a slightly damp towel. Let rise in a warm place, free from drafts, until doubled in bulk, about 1 hour. In a medium bowl, combine nuts, prunes, apricots, raisins and 1/4 cup all-purpose or bread flour; set aside. Grease 2 large baking sheets. **Punch down dough;** knead 30 seconds. Roll out dough to a rectangle, 1/2 inch thick. Sprinkle fruit mixture over dough. Fold dough in half over fruit mixture. Knead until fruit and nuts are evenly distributed. Divide dough in half. Shape into 2 round balls about 6 inches in diameter. Place on prepared baking sheets. With pointed scissors or a sharp knife, make 8 evenly spaced 2-inch deep cuts around outside edge, to resemble a flower. Cover with a dry towel. Let rise until doubled in bulk, about 45 minutes. **Preheat oven** to 375F (190C). Brush tops of loaves with egg white. Sprinkle generously with sugar. Bake 25 to 35 minutes or until bread sounds hollow when tapped on bottom. Cool on racks. Makes 2 loaves.

Tip *Yeast doughs containing large amounts of fruit and nuts take longer to rise than regular doughs.*

How to Make Marzipan Coffee Ring

1/Holding scissors close to rope, make cuts 1 inch apart. Twist points sharply toward center of pan.

2/Cool baked loaf on a rack. Drizzle with Almond Glaze; sprinkle with chopped almonds.

Whipped Ginger Cream

A heavenly accompaniment to Twice Gingerbread, page 139.

1/2 cup whipping cream, chilled	1/3 cup packed brown sugar
1 (8-oz.) pkg. cream cheese, room temperature	1 teaspoon ground ginger
	1/4 cup minced crystallized ginger

In small bowl of electric mixer, beat cream until firm peaks form. Spoon whipped cream into a small bowl; set aside. In small bowl of electric mixer, combine cream cheese, brown sugar and ground ginger. Beat until brown sugar dissolves and mixture is smooth. Fold whipped cream and crystallized ginger into cheese mixture until evenly distributed. Spoon into a medium serving dish. Cover and refrigerate. If mixture is too firm when ready to serve, let stand at room temperature 15 minutes. Makes about 2-1/2 cups.

Tip   *Almond paste freezes well if tightly wrapped. Thaw at room temperature before using.*

Marzipan Coffee Ring

Impressive and delicious, this petal-topped bread hides a delectable marzipan swirl inside.

1 (1/4-oz.) pkg. active dry yeast
  (1 tablespoon)
1 teaspoon sugar
1/4 cup warm water (110F, 45C)
1 cup dairy sour cream, room temperature
1/4 cup sugar
2 eggs, room temperature
1/2 teaspoon almond extract

1 teaspoon salt
4-1/4 to 4-3/4 cups all-purpose or
  bread flour
Marzipan Filling, see below
3/4 cup toasted finely chopped almonds
1 egg white blended with
  2 teaspoons water for glaze
Almond Glaze, see below

Marzipan Filling:
1/2 cup packed almond paste
1/4 cup packed brown sugar
1 tablespoon butter, room temperature
1 egg white

1/4 teaspoon ground nutmeg
1/2 teaspoon almond extract
1/8 teaspoon salt

Almond Glaze:
1 cup powdered sugar
1/2 teaspoon vanilla extract

1/4 teaspoon almond extract
1 to 2 tablespoons Amaretto liqueur or milk

In large bowl of electric mixer, dissolve yeast and 1 teaspoon sugar in 1/4 cup water. Let stand until foamy, 5 to 10 minutes. Stir in sour cream, 1/4 cup sugar, eggs, almond extract, salt and 1 to 1-1/2 cups flour. Beat at medium speed with electric mixer 2 minutes or, beat 200 vigorous strokes by hand. Stir in enough remaining flour to make a soft dough. Turn out dough onto a lightly floured surface. Clean and grease bowl. **Knead dough** 6 to 8 minutes or until smooth and elastic. Place dough in greased bowl, turning to coat all sides. Cover with a slightly damp towel. Let rise in a warm place, free from drafts, until doubled in bulk, about 1 hour. Grease a 10-inch tube pan. Prepare Marzipan Filling; set aside. **Punch down dough;** knead 30 seconds. Pinch off one-fourth of dough. Cover; set aside. On a lightly floured surface, roll out remaining dough to a 20" x 12" rectangle. Spread evenly with Marzipan Filling to within 1 inch of edges. Sprinkle 1/2 cup chopped almonds over top. Beginning on a long side, roll up tightly, jelly-roll fashion. Pinch seam and ends to seal. Place seam-side down in prepared pan, overlapping ends slightly. Brush surface lightly with water. Roll reserved dough into a 24-inch rope. Lay rope around outside edge of dough in pan. Overlap and pinch ends together to seal. Holding pointed scissors almost parallel to rope, make cuts in rope, 1 inch apart, to within 1/4 inch of outside edge. Twist each pointed piece of dough sharply toward center of pan, to resemble petals. Cover with a dry towel. Let rise until doubled in bulk, about 1 hour. **Preheat oven** to 350F (175C). Brush top of dough with egg-white glaze. Bake 30 to 40 minutes or until bread sounds hollow when tapped on top. Cool on a rack. Drizzle Almond Glaze over top. Sprinkle remaining 1/4 cup chopped almonds over glaze. Makes 1 coffeecake.

Marzipan Filling:
In small bowl of electric mixer, combine all ingredients. Beat at medium speed until smooth.

Almond Glaze:
In a small bowl, combine powdered sugar, vanilla and almond extract. Stir in enough liqueur or milk to make a smooth, creamy glaze of drizzling consistency.

Viennese Striezel   Photo on page 98.

Beautiful bread from Austria—shaped into a three-tier braid.

1 (1/4-oz.) pkg. active dry yeast
  (1 tablespoon)
1 teaspoon sugar
1/4 cup warm water (110F, 45C)
3/4 cup milk, room temperature
1 egg, room temperature
2 egg yolks, room temperature
1/3 cup butter, melted

1/3 cup sugar
3/4 teaspoon salt
2 teaspoons freshly grated lemon peel
4-1/2 to 5 cups all-purpose or bread flour
1 cup golden raisins
1 egg white, slightly beaten
2 tablespoons slivered or sliced almonds
Sugar

In large bowl of electric mixer, dissolve yeast and 1 teaspoon sugar in water. Let stand until foamy, 5 to 10 minutes. Stir in milk, egg, egg yolks, butter, 1/3 cup sugar, salt, lemon peel and 2 to 2-1/2 cups flour. Beat at medium speed with electric mixer 2 minutes or, beat 200 vigorous strokes by hand. Stir in raisins and enough remaining flour to make a soft dough. Turn out dough onto a lightly floured surface. Clean and grease bowl. **Knead dough** 8 to 10 minutes or until smooth and elastic. Place dough in greased bowl, turning to coat all sides. Cover with a slightly damp towel. Let rise in a warm place, free from drafts, until doubled in bulk, about 1 hour. Grease 1 large baking sheet. **Punch down dough;** knead 30 seconds. Divide dough in half. Cover 1 piece; set aside. Divide remaining dough into 3 equal pieces. Shape each piece into a 15-inch rope. Place 3 ropes side by side; braid, starting from middle. Pinch ends together to seal; tuck under and pinch again. Place braid on prepared baking sheet. Pinch off one-third of remaining dough. Divide into 3 pieces. Shape each piece into an 8-inch rope. Braid and set aside. Shape remaining dough into 3 (12-inch) ropes. Braid and set aside. With side of your hand, make a 1/2-inch depression down center of large braid on baking sheet. Brush depression with egg white. Center next largest braid on top. Make a depression down center of second braid. Brush with egg white. Center smallest braid on top; press down lightly. Cover with a dry towel. Let rise until doubled in bulk, about 1 hour. **Preheat oven** to 350F (175C). Brush top of loaf with egg white. Sprinkle with almonds and sugar. Wipe sugar off baking sheet so it will not burn. Bake 30 to 40 minutes or until bread sounds hollow when tapped on bottom. Cool on a rack. Makes 1 large loaf.

Tip   *Braiding from the middle toward each end creates a more uniform braid. Slightly taper ends of braid for a pretty effect.*

Braiding Dough

Rope positions in a braid are numbered from left to right, beginning with 1 to however many ropes are to be braided. Numbers refer to positions, not the ropes themselves. If rope 1 is crossed over rope 2, the former rope 2 becomes rope 1 and the former rope 1 becomes rope 2.

Three-Rope Braid: Using half the dough, divide into 3 equal pieces. Roll each piece into a 12-inch rope. Lay 3 ropes, side-by-side, on a greased baking sheet. Pinch at top to seal. Braid as follows:

- 1 over 2
- 3 over 2
- 1 over 2
- 3 over 2
- Repeat until braid is completed. Pinch ends; tuck under and pinch again to seal.

Four-Rope Braid: Divide dough into 4 equal pieces. Roll each piece into a 14-inch rope. Lay 4 ropes, side-by-side, on a greased baking sheet. Pinch at top to seal. Braid as follows:

- 1 over 4 (This is the only time you will do this.)
- 3 over 1
- 4 over 3
- 2 over 4
- 1 over 2
- Repeat, beginning with 3 over 1, until braid is completed. Pinch ends; tuck under and pinch again to seal.

Five-Rope Braid: Divide dough into 5 equal pieces. Roll each piece into a 14-inch rope. Lay 5 ropes, side-by-side, on a greased baking sheet. Pinch at top to seal. Braid as follows:

- 2 over 3
- 5 over 2
- 1 over 3
- Repeat until braid is completed. Pinch ends; tuck under and pinch again to seal.

Six-Rope Braid: Divide dough into 6 equal pieces. Roll each piece into a 14-inch rope. Lay 6 ropes, side-by-side, on a greased baking sheet. Pinch at top to seal. Braid as follows:

- 5 over 1
- 6 over 4
- 2 over 6
- 1 over 3
- Repeat until braid is completed. Braid may appear to be unbraiding, but it is not. Pinch ends; tuck under and pinch again to seal.

Piggyback Braid: Pinch off one-third of dough. Divide into 3 equal pieces. Roll each piece into an 8-inch rope. Braid in a 3-rope braid. Pinch ends; tuck under and pinch again to seal. Divide remaining two-thirds dough into 3 pieces. Roll each piece into a 12-inch rope; braid in a 3-rope braid. Pinch ends; tuck under and pinch again to seal. Place large braid on a greased baking sheet. Press down center of braid with side of your hand to make a shallow indentation. Set small braid, lengthwise, on top. Lightly press top braid into surface of bottom braid.

Batter Breads

Batter breads, one of my favorites in the bread family, are magical yeast breads you don't have to knead! Extra yeast and vigorous beating with an electric mixer or, beating with a wooden spoon and a little muscle, are all it takes to create an easy and delicious loaf. Because the gluten isn't completely developed by a long kneading process, the texture is more open and coarse. The flavor is slightly more yeasty because of extra yeast. But these differences only add to its charm.

In theory, almost any yeast-bread recipe can be converted to a batter bread by simply adding less flour. Keep in mind that the batter should be stiff enough for a spoon to stand up—similar to a very soft dough. If you're in a real hurry, with company coming in a couple of hours, turn the batter right into the baking pan after beating and let it rise only once before popping it into the oven. The texture won't be as refined as with two risings, but your guests will be so delighted with fragrant homemade bread, I guarantee you won't hear any complaints!

Don't think, because of their easy beginnings, that batter breads can't be elegant. Regal Austrian Guglhupf is full of butter, eggs, rum-soaked raisins and toasted almonds. Crowned with a dusting of powdered sugar, it can compete with the best of the kneaded yeast breads. It's so popular in Europe that Austrian, Alsatian, German and Polish bakers all claim credit for its creation.

Another European legacy, rich, slightly sweet Sally Lunn, has several tales of origin. One is that Sally Lunn, an 18th-century English lass born in Bath, created the delicate cake-like bread in her tiny bakery for her prominent patrons' tea parties. The original Sally Lunns were baked as large buns, split horizontally and slathered with thick clotted cream.

Planter's Nuts sponsored a contest for the International Association of Cooking Schools that motivated me to combine heady Amaretto liqueur with toasted almonds for Amaretto-Almond Bread. The luck of the Irish held fast and I won first prize in the breads category for my efforts!

Blueberry-Yogurt Bread

Speckled with bits of blueberry and orange peel, this bread is as pretty as it is delicious!

2 (1/4-oz.) pkgs. active dry yeast
  (2 tablespoons)
1 teaspoon sugar
1/3 cup warm water (110F, 45C)
1/3 cup sugar
1 (8-oz.) carton blueberry-flavored yogurt
  (1 cup), room temperature
2 cups fresh blueberries

3 tablespoons butter, melted
2 teaspoons salt
1/2 teaspoon ground nutmeg
1-1/2 tablespoons freshly grated orange peel
3-3/4 to 4-1/4 cups all-purpose or
  bread flour
1 tablespoon butter, melted

In large bowl of electric mixer, dissolve yeast and 1 teaspoon sugar in water. Let stand until foamy, 5 to 10 minutes. Add 1/3 cup sugar, yogurt, 1 cup blueberries, 3 tablespoons melted butter, salt, nutmeg, orange peel and 1-1/2 to 2 cups flour. Beat at medium speed with electric mixer 4 minutes or, beat 400 vigorous strokes by hand. Stir in enough remaining flour to make a stiff batter. Gently fold remaining 1 cup blueberries into batter. Cover with a slightly damp towel. Let rise in a warm place, free from drafts, until doubled in bulk, about 1-1/2 hours. Grease 2 (8" x 4") loaf pans; set aside. **Stir down batter.** Turn into prepared pans. Butter your fingers and a 12-inch square of waxed paper. Smooth batter with your buttered fingers. Cover with buttered waxed paper. Let rise until doubled in bulk, about 1 hour. **Preheat oven** to 375F (190C). Bake 35 to 40 minutes or until bread sounds hollow when tapped on top. For browner bottom crusts, remove from pans. Place directly on oven rack during final 5 minutes of baking. Brush melted butter over tops. Cool on racks. Makes 2 loaves.

Hawaiian Sweet Bread

Save leftover mashed potatoes for this delicate, moist bread scented with pineapple.

2 (1/4-oz.) pkgs. active dry yeast
  (2 tablespoons)
1-1/2 cups warm pineapple juice (110F, 45C)
1/2 cup sugar
1 cup mashed cooked potatoes
2 eggs, room temperature

1/4 cup butter, melted
1 teaspoon salt
1 teaspoon vanilla extract
1/4 teaspoon ground ginger
4-1/2 to 5 cups all-purpose or bread flour
1 tablespoon butter, melted

In large bowl of electric mixer, stir yeast into pineapple juice until dissolved. Let stand until foamy, 5 to 10 minutes. Add sugar, potatoes, eggs, 1/4 cup butter, salt, vanilla, ginger and 2 to 2-1/2 cups flour. Beat at medium speed with electric mixer 4 minutes or, beat 400 vigorous strokes by hand. Stir in enough remaining flour to make a stiff batter. Cover with a slightly damp towel. Let rise in a warm place, free from drafts, until doubled in bulk, about 1 hour. Grease 2 (9" x 5") loaf pans or 2 (2-quart) casseroles; set aside. **Stir down batter.** Turn into prepared pans. Butter your fingers and 2 (12-inch) squares of waxed paper. Smooth batter with your buttered fingers. Cover with buttered waxed paper. Let rise until doubled in bulk, about 45 minutes. **Preheat oven** to 375F (190C). Bake 30 to 40 minutes or until bread sounds hollow when tapped on bottom. For browner bottom crusts, remove from pans. Place directly on oven rack during final 5 minutes of baking. Brush melted butter over tops. Cool on racks. Makes 2 loaves.

How to Make Peaches 'N Cream Coffeecake

1/Arrange peach slices decoratively on bottom over Sugar Topping and butter. Spoon batter over peaches.

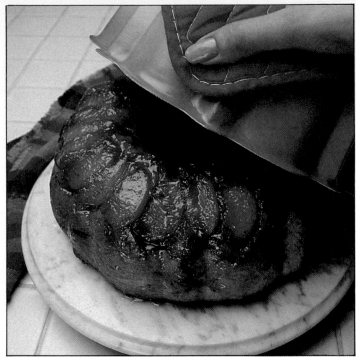

2/Invert onto a serving plate. Spoon topping from pan over coffeecake. Let stand 20 minutes before serving.

Wheaty Waldorf Bread

Inspired by the classic salad combining apples, walnuts and mayonnaise.

2 (1/4-oz.) pkgs. active dry yeast
   (2 tablespoons)
2 teaspoons granulated sugar
1/3 cup warm water (110F, 45C)
1/3 cup packed brown sugar
1 (13-oz.) can evaporated milk
1/4 cup mayonnaise or
   mayonnaise-style salad dressing
1-1/2 teaspoons salt

1/2 teaspoon ground nutmeg
1/2 teaspoon ground cinnamon
1-1/2 cups whole-wheat flour
2-1/2 to 3 cups all-purpose or bread flour
1 cup finely chopped peeled or
   unpeeled apple
3/4 cup chopped walnuts
1 teaspoon mayonnaise, melted, or
   vegetable oil

In large bowl of electric mixer, dissolve yeast and granulated sugar in water. Let stand until foamy, 5 to 10 minutes. Add brown sugar, evaporated milk, 1/4 cup mayonnaise, salt, nutmeg, cinnamon, whole-wheat flour and 1 to 1-1/2 cups all-purpose or bread flour. Beat at medium speed with electric mixer 4 minutes or, beat 400 vigorous strokes by hand. Stir in apples, nuts and enough remaining flour to make a stiff batter. Cover with a slightly damp towel. Let rise in a warm place, free from drafts, until doubled in bulk, 1-1/2 to 2 hours. Grease 2 (8" x 4") loaf pans or 2 (1-1/2-quart) casserole dishes; set aside. **Stir down batter.** Turn into prepared pans. Butter your fingers and a 12-inch square of waxed paper. Smooth batter with your buttered fingers. Cover with buttered waxed paper. Let rise until doubled in bulk, about 1 hour. **Preheat oven** to 375F (190C). Gently brush melted mayonnaise or oil over tops of loaves. Bake 30 to 40 minutes or until bread sounds hollow when tapped on bottom. Remove from pans. Cool on racks. Makes 2 loaves.

Peaches 'N Cream Coffeecake

An easy and delicious upside-down coffeecake you can start the night before.

1 (1/4-oz.) pkg. active dry yeast
  (1 tablespoon)
1 teaspoon sugar
1/4 cup warm water (110F, 45C)
1 large peach, peeled, pureed (1/2 cup)
1/2 cup half and half
1/2 cup sugar
2 eggs, room temperature
1/2 cup butter, melted
1 tablespoon vanilla extract
1-1/2 teaspoons salt

1/2 teaspoon ground nutmeg
1/2 teaspoon ground cinnamon
3-3/4 to 4-1/4 cups all-purpose flour
1/2 cup toasted chopped pecans
Sugar Topping, see below
1/4 cup butter, melted
2 ripe medium peaches, peeled,
  cut in 1/4-inch slices
2 to 3 tablespoons chopped pecans,
  if desired

Sugar Topping:
1/2 cup packed brown sugar
1/2 teaspoon ground cinnamon

1/4 teaspoon ground nutmeg

In large bowl of electric mixer, dissolve yeast and 1 teaspoon sugar in water. Let stand until foamy, 5 to 10 minutes. Add peach puree, half and half, 1/2 cup sugar, eggs, 1/2 cup butter, vanilla, salt, nutmeg, cinnamon and 2-1/2 to 3 cups flour. Beat at medium speed with electric mixer 4 minutes or, beat 400 vigorous strokes by hand. Stir in 1/2 cup pecans and enough remaining flour to make a stiff batter. Cover with a slightly damp towel. Let rise in a warm place, free from drafts, until doubled in bulk, 1 to 1-1/2 hours. Prepare Sugar Topping. Generously butter a 10-cup Bundt or tube pan. Sprinkle Sugar Topping over bottom. Drizzle with 1/4 cup melted butter. Arrange peach slices decoratively on bottom over Sugar Topping and butter. **Stir down batter.** Spoon over peaches in pan. Butter your fingers and a 12-inch square of waxed paper. Smooth batter with your buttered fingers. If desired, sprinkle additional chopped pecans over top. Cover with buttered waxed paper. Let rise until almost doubled in bulk, about 45 minutes. **Preheat oven** to 350F (175C). Bake 40 to 50 minutes or until a metal skewer inserted in center comes out clean. Carefully invert onto a serving plate. Remove pan. Spoon any topping remaining in pan over coffeecake. Let stand 20 minutes; serve warm. Makes 1 coffeecake.

Sugar Topping:
In a small bowl, combine all ingredients.

Tip *Let batter breads rise overnight in the refrigerator. Transfer to baking pan for second rise in the morning. If batter is refrigerated, second rise will take longer than indicated in recipe.*

Austrian Guglhupf

A marvelously rich bread studded with rum-soaked raisins and toasted almonds.

1 cup golden raisins
1/3 cup light rum
3/4 cup finely chopped, toasted almonds
1 (1/4-oz.) pkg. active dry yeast
  (1 tablespoon)
1 teaspoon granulated sugar
1/4 cup warm water (110F, 45C)
3/4 cup butter, room temperature

1/2 cup granulated sugar
4 eggs, room temperature
3/4 cup milk, room temperature
1 tablespoon freshly grated lemon peel
1 teaspoon salt
3-3/4 to 4-1/4 cups all-purpose flour
Powdered sugar for garnish

In a small bowl, combine raisins and rum. Cover; let stand overnight or 3 to 4 hours to soak. Generously butter a large guglhupf mold or 10-cup Bundt pan. Sprinkle bottom and sides with 1/4 cup almonds; set aside. In another small bowl, dissolve yeast and 1 teaspoon granulated sugar in water. Let stand until foamy, 5 to 10 minutes. In large bowl of electric mixer, cream butter and 1/2 cup granulated sugar until light. Add eggs, 1 at a time, beating well after each addition. Slowly beat in yeast mixture and milk. Add lemon peel, salt and 2-1/2 to 3 cups flour. Beat at medium speed with electric mixer 4 minutes or, beat 400 vigorous strokes by hand. Stir in raisin mixture, remaining 1/2 cup almonds and enough remaining flour to make a stiff batter. **Spoon batter into prepared pan.** Butter your fingers and a 12-inch square of waxed paper. Smooth batter with your buttered fingers. Cover with buttered waxed paper. Let rise in a warm place, free from drafts, until batter comes to within 1/2 inch of top of pan, about 2 hours. **Preheat oven** to 375F (190C). Bake 50 to 60 minutes or until a metal skewer inserted in center comes out clean. Remove from pan. Cool, rounded-side up, on a rack, at least 30 minutes. Dust lightly with powdered sugar. Serve warm or at room temperature. Makes 1 large loaf.

Sally Lunn

This popular English cake-like bread is rich with butter and eggs.

1 (1/4-oz.) pkg. active dry yeast
  (1 tablespoon)
1 teaspoon sugar
1/4 cup warm water (110F, 45C)
3 eggs, room temperature

3/4 cup milk, room temperature
1/3 cup sugar
1/2 cup butter, melted
1 teaspoon salt
3-1/2 to 4 cups all-purpose flour

In large bowl of electric mixer, dissolve yeast and 1 teaspoon sugar in water. Let stand until foamy, 5 to 10 minutes. Add eggs, milk, 1/3 cup sugar, butter, salt and 2 to 2-1/2 cups flour. Beat at medium speed with electric mixer 4 minutes or, beat 400 vigorous strokes by hand. Stir in enough remaining flour to make a stiff batter. Cover with a slightly damp towel. Let rise in a warm place, free from drafts, until doubled in bulk, about 1-1/2 hours. Generously butter a 9- or 10-inch tube pan; set aside. **Stir down batter.** Turn into prepared pan. Butter your fingers and a 12-inch square of waxed paper. Smooth batter with your buttered fingers. Cover with buttered waxed paper. Let rise until doubled in bulk, about 1 hour. **Preheat oven** to 375F (190C). Bake 35 to 45 minutes or until a metal skewer inserted in center comes out clean. Remove from pan. Let stand 20 minutes. Serve warm. Makes 1 loaf.

Austrian Guglhupf

Danish Prune Bread

Lavishly spread thick slices with Prune-Cheese Spread, page 94.

2 (1/4-oz.) pkgs. active dry yeast
 (2 tablespoons)
1 tablespoon brown sugar
1-1/2 cups warm water (110F, 45C)
1/2 cup packed brown sugar
2/3 cup nonfat-milk powder
1/4 cup butter, melted
2 teaspoons freshly grated lemon peel
2 teaspoons freshly grated orange peel

1-1/2 teaspoons ground cinnamon
1/2 teaspoon ground nutmeg
2 teaspoons salt
4 to 4-1/2 cups all-purpose or bread flour
1 cup chopped pitted prunes
2 tablespoons all-purpose flour
3/4 cup chopped walnuts
1 to 2 tablespoons butter, melted

In large bowl of electric mixer, dissolve yeast and 1 tablespoon brown sugar in water. Let stand until foamy, 5 to 10 minutes. Add 1/2 cup brown sugar, milk powder, 1/4 cup butter, lemon and orange peel, cinnamon, nutmeg, salt and 2-1/2 to 3 cups flour. Beat at medium speed with electric mixer 4 minutes or, beat 400 vigorous strokes by hand. Stir in enough remaining flour to make a very stiff batter. Cover with a slightly damp towel. Let rise in a warm place, free from drafts, until doubled in bulk, about 1 hour. In a medium bowl, combine prunes with 2 tablespoons flour. Toss to separate and coat prunes with flour; set aside. Grease and flour 2 (1-pound) coffee cans or 2 (1-1/2-quart) casserole dishes; set aside. **Stir down batter.** Add floured prunes and nuts; stir until evenly distributed. Turn into prepared cans or dishes. Butter your fingers and 2 (12-inch) squares waxed paper. Smooth batter with your buttered fingers; brush with melted butter. Cover with buttered waxed paper. Let rise until doubled in bulk, about 1 hour. **Preheat oven** to 375F (190C). Bake 35 to 40 minutes or until bread sounds hollow when tapped on top. Remove from pans. Brush melted butter over tops. Cool on racks. Makes 2 loaves.

Variation

Danish Apricot Bread: Substitute 1-1/2 cups warm orange juice (110F, 45C) for water. Substitute 1/2 teaspoon ground cinnamon, 1/4 teaspoon ground ginger and 1/4 teaspoon ground allspice for 1-1/2 teaspoons ground cinnamon. Substitute 1 cup chopped dried apricots for prunes.

Tip *Freshly grated orange or lemon peel gives a fuller flavor than dried peel.*

How to Make Danish Prune Bread

1/Combine prunes with 2 tablespoons flour. Toss to separate and coat prunes with flour.

2/Stir down batter. Add floured prunes and nuts; stir to distribute. Turn into prepared cans or casserole dishes.

Toasted Wheat-Germ Bread

Nutritious, delicious and wonderful for sandwiches or French toast.

2 (1/4-oz.) pkgs. active dry yeast
  (2 tablespoons)
1 teaspoon honey
1 cup warm water (110F, 45C)
1/3 cup honey
1/3 cup nonfat-milk powder
1 egg, room temperature

2 tablespoons butter, melted
1-1/2 teaspoons salt
3/4 cup toasted wheat germ
2-1/4 to 2-3/4 cups all-purpose or
  bread flour
3-1/2 tablespoons toasted wheat germ

In large bowl of electric mixer, dissolve yeast and 1 teaspoon honey in water. Let stand until foamy, 5 to 10 minutes. Add 1/3 cup honey, milk powder, egg, butter, salt, 3/4 cup wheat germ and 1 to 1-1/2 cups flour. Beat at medium speed with electric mixer 4 minutes or, beat 400 vigorous strokes by hand. Stir in enough remaining flour to make a stiff batter. Cover with a slightly damp towel. Let rise in a warm place, free from drafts, until doubled in bulk, 1 to 1-1/2 hours. Generously grease a 9'' x 5'' loaf pan or 2-quart casserole dish. Sprinkle 3 tablespoons wheat germ over bottom and sides of pan; set aside. **Stir down batter.** Turn into prepared pan. Butter your fingers and a 12-inch square of waxed paper. Smooth batter with your buttered fingers. Sprinkle with remaining wheat germ. Cover with buttered waxed paper. Let rise until doubled in bulk, about 45 minutes. **Preheat oven** to 375F (190C). Bake 35 to 40 minutes or until bread sounds hollow when tapped on bottom. Remove from pan. Cool on a rack. Makes 1 loaf.

Note: Toasted wheat germ is available in most supermarkets. Or, toast raw wheat germ in a large, ungreased skillet over medium heat, 2 to 3 minutes. Stir often to prevent scorching.

Amaretto-Almond Bread

Serve Amaretto Butter, below, with this fragrant bread, crunchy with toasted almonds.

1 cup golden raisins
1/3 cup Amaretto liqueur or
    other almond-flavored liqueur
2 (1/4-oz.) pkgs. active dry yeast
    (2 tablespoons)
1 teaspoon sugar
1/2 cup warm water (110F, 45C)
2/3 cup milk, room temperature
6 tablespoons butter, melted
1/2 cup honey

2 eggs, room temperature
1 teaspoon salt
2 teaspoons vanilla extract
Freshly grated peel of 1 large lemon
4-1/4 to 4-3/4 cups all-purpose or
    bread flour
1-1/2 cups toasted finely chopped almonds
Whole blanched almonds for decoration
1-1/2 to 2 tablespoons sugar

In a small bowl, combine raisins and liqueur. Cover; let stand overnight or 3 to 4 hours to soak. In large bowl of electric mixer, dissolve yeast and 1 teaspoon sugar in water. Let stand until foamy, 5 to 10 minutes. Add milk, butter, honey, eggs, salt, vanilla, lemon peel and 2 to 2-1/2 cups flour. Beat at medium speed with electric mixer 4 minutes or, beat 400 vigorous strokes by hand. Stir in 1 cup chopped almonds and enough remaining flour to make a stiff batter. Cover with a slightly damp towel. Let rise in a warm place, free from drafts, until doubled in bulk, about 1-1/2 hours. Generously grease 2 (8'' x 4'') loaf pans or a 10-cup Bundt pan. Sprinkle bottom and sides of pans with remaining 1/2 cup chopped almonds. If using Bundt pan, arrange whole blanched almonds in bottom of pan; set aside. **Stir down batter.** Turn into prepared pans. Butter your fingers and a 12-inch square of waxed paper. Smooth batter with your buttered fingers. Sprinkle 1 tablespoon sugar over top of batter in each loaf pan. Sprinkle 1-1/2 tablespoons sugar over batter in Bundt pan. If using loaf pans, arrange whole almonds in a decorative pattern over sugar-coated batter. Gently press almonds into batter. Cover with buttered waxed paper. Let rise until doubled in bulk, about 1 hour. **Preheat oven** to 350F (175C). Bake 40 to 45 minutes for loaf pans and 45 to 50 minutes for Bundt pan or until bread sounds hollow when tapped on top. Remove from pans. Cool on a rack. Makes 1 large or 2 medium loaves.

Amaretto Butter

Scented with Amaretto and sweetened with honey—great on anything from pancakes to dinner rolls!

1-1/4 cups butter, room temperature
3 tablespoons honey
1/4 teaspoon grated orange peel

1/4 teaspoon almond extract
1/4 cup Amaretto liqueur or
    other almond-flavored liqueur

In small bowl of electric mixer, beat butter, honey, orange peel and almond extract until blended. Beating constantly, slowly add liqueur. Beat until thoroughly blended. Spoon into a small serving bowl. Cover and refrigerate. Let stand at room temperature 20 to 30 minutes before serving. Makes about 1-1/2 cups.

Variations

Amaretto-Nut Butter: Stir in 1/4 cup toasted finely chopped almonds.
Spirited Butter: Substitute 1/4 cup orange-flavored liqueur, rum or brandy for almond-flavored liqueur. Omit almond extract.

Dill-Cheese Bread

Flecks of Cheddar cheese and dill dot this tender bread.

1 (1/4-oz.) pkg. active dry yeast
  (1 tablespoon)
Pinch of sugar
1/4 cup warm water (110F, 45C)
2 tablespoons sugar
1 cup creamed cottage cheese (8 oz.),
  room temperature
2 eggs, room temperature
2 tablespoons butter, melted
2 tablespoons minced sweet onion or
  2 teaspoons dried minced onion

1 teaspoon salt
2 teaspoons dill weed or
  1-1/2 tablespoons minced fresh dill
1-3/4 to 2-1/4 cups all-purpose or
  bread flour
1 cup shredded Cheddar cheese (4 oz.)
1 egg white blended with
  1 tablespoon water for glaze
1/2 teaspoon dill weed or
  1 teaspoon minced fresh dill for garnish

In large bowl of electric mixer, dissolve yeast and pinch of sugar in 1/4 cup water. Let stand until foamy, 5 to 10 minutes. Add 2 tablespoons sugar, cottage cheese, eggs, butter, onion, salt, 2 teaspoons dry or 1-1/2 tablespoons fresh dill and 1 to 1-1/2 cups flour. Beat at medium speed with electric mixer 4 minutes or, beat 400 vigorous strokes by hand. Stir in enough remaining flour to make a stiff batter. Cover with a slightly damp towel. Let rise in a warm place, free from drafts, until doubled in bulk, about 1-1/2 hours. Grease and flour a 2-quart casserole or a 9" x 5" loaf pan; set aside. **Stir down batter.** Stir in Cheddar cheese. Turn into prepared pan. Smooth top; brush with egg-white glaze. Sprinkle with 1/2 teaspoon dry or 1 teaspoon fresh dill. Butter a 12-inch square of waxed paper. Place over batter. Let rise until doubled in bulk, 45 to 60 minutes. **Preheat oven** to 350F (175C). Bake 30 to 40 minutes or until bread sounds hollow when tapped on top. Remove from pan. Cool on a rack. Makes 1 loaf.

Peanut-Butter & Bacon Bread

Wonderful toasted—great for bacon, lettuce and tomato sandwiches.

2 (1/4-oz.) pkgs. active dry yeast
  (2 tablespoons)
1 teaspoon granulated sugar
1/3 cup warm water (110F, 45C)
2 eggs, room temperature
1/2 cup chunky peanut butter
1/3 cup packed brown sugar

3/4 cup milk, room temperature
1 teaspoon salt
2-3/4 to 3-1/4 cups all-purpose or
  bread flour
1/2 lb. bacon, cooked crisp, crumbled
1 teaspoon butter, melted

In large bowl of electric mixer, dissolve yeast and granulated sugar in water. Let stand until foamy, 5 to 10 minutes. Add eggs, peanut butter, brown sugar, milk, salt and 1-1/2 to 2 cups flour. Beat at medium speed with electric mixer 4 minutes or, beat 400 vigorous strokes by hand. Stir in enough remaining flour to make a very stiff batter. Cover with a slightly damp towel. Let rise in a warm place, free from drafts, until doubled in bulk, about 1-1/2 hours. Generously grease a 9" x 5" loaf pan or 2-quart casserole dish; set aside. **Stir down batter.** Stir in bacon until evenly distributed. Turn into prepared pan. Butter a 12-inch square of waxed paper. Smooth batter; cover with buttered waxed paper. Let rise until doubled in bulk, about 45 minutes. **Preheat oven** to 375F (190C). Bake 35 to 40 minutes or until bread sounds hollow when tapped on bottom. Remove from pan. Brush melted butter over top. Cool on a rack. Makes 1 loaf.

Corn-Kernel Batter Bread

Golden kernels of corn dot this fragrant herb-enhanced loaf.

1 (1/4-oz.) pkg. active dry yeast
   (1 tablespoon)
1 teaspoon sugar
1/4 cup warm water (110F, 45C)
1 (7-oz.) can whole-kernel corn
Buttermilk
2 tablespoons sugar
2 tablespoons vegetable oil

2 teaspoons salt
1/2 teaspoon dried leaf basil, crushed, or
   1 teaspoon minced fresh basil
1/2 teaspoon dried leaf tarragon, crushed, or
   1 teaspoon minced fresh tarragon
1/2 cup yellow cornmeal
3-1/2 to 4 cups all-purpose or bread flour
2 tablespoons yellow cornmeal

In large bowl of electric mixer, dissolve yeast and 1 teaspoon sugar in water. Let stand until foamy, 5 to 10 minutes. Drain corn, reserving liquid; set corn aside. Add buttermilk to corn liquid to make 2 cups. Add to yeast mixture. Stir in 2 tablespoons sugar, oil, salt, basil, tarragon, 1/2 cup cornmeal and 2 to 2-1/2 cups flour. Beat at medium speed with electric mixer 4 minutes or, beat 400 vigorous strokes by hand. Stir in reserved corn and enough remaining flour to make a stiff batter. Cover with a slightly damp towel. Let rise in a warm place, free from drafts, until doubled in bulk, 1 to 1-1/2 hours. Grease 2 (8" x 4") loaf pans or 2 (1-1/2-quart) casserole dishes. Sprinkle 1 tablespoon cornmeal over bottom and sides of each pan; set aside. **Stir down batter.** Turn into prepared pans. Butter your fingers and a 12-inch square of waxed paper. Smooth tops with your buttered fingers. Cover with buttered waxed paper. Let rise until doubled in bulk, about 45 minutes. **Preheat oven** to 375F (190C). Bake 35 to 40 minutes or until bread sounds hollow when tapped on bottom. Remove from pans. Cool on racks. Makes 2 loaves.

Italian-Sausage Bread

Makes a hearty breakfast bread, a meal with soups and a perfect picnic mainstay.

1 lb. mild Italian sausage
2 (1/4-oz.) pkgs. active dry yeast
   (2 tablespoons)
1 teaspoon sugar
1/2 cup warm water (110F, 45C)
1-1/2 cups milk, room temperature
2-1/2 tablespoons sugar

1 egg, room temperature
1 teaspoon salt
1/2 teaspoon freshly ground black pepper
1/2 teaspoon dried leaf basil, crumbled, or
   1 teaspoon minced fresh basil
4-3/4 to 5-1/4 cups all-purpose or
   bread flour

Remove sausage from casings. In a large skillet, cook sausage over medium heat until no longer pink. As sausage cooks, crumble into small pieces. Remove from skillet with a slotted spoon; drain on paper towels. Set aside. Reserve 2 tablespoons sausage drippings. In large bowl of electric mixer, dissolve yeast and 1 teaspoon sugar in water. Let stand until foamy, 5 to 10 minutes. Add milk, 2-1/2 tablespoons sugar, egg, salt, pepper, basil, reserved sausage drippings and 3 to 3-1/2 cups flour. Beat at medium speed with electric mixer 4 minutes or, beat 400 vigorous strokes by hand. Stir in crumbled sausage and enough remaining flour to make a stiff batter. Cover with a slightly damp towel. Let rise in a warm place, free from drafts, until doubled in bulk, about 1 hour. Grease 2 (9" x 5") loaf pans or 2 (2-quart) casserole dishes; set aside. **Stir down batter.** Turn into prepared pans. Butter your fingers and 2 (12-inch) squares of waxed paper. Smooth batter with your buttered fingers. Cover with buttered waxed paper. Let rise until doubled in bulk, 30 to 45 minutes. **Preheat oven** to 400F (205C). Bake 35 to 40 minutes or until bread sounds hollow when tapped on bottom. Remove from pans. Cool on racks. Refrigerate leftovers. Makes 2 loaves.

Green-Chili & Cheese Bread

Cheese soup makes quick work of this easy batter bread—delicious with chili con carne!

1 (1/4-oz.) pkg. active dry yeast
  (1 tablespoon)
1 teaspoon sugar
1/4 cup warm water (110F, 45C)
1 (11-oz.) can condensed Cheddar-cheese soup
1/4 cup vegetable oil
2 eggs, room temperature

1 teaspoon salt
1/4 teaspoon baking powder
1/2 cup yellow cornmeal
2-1/2 to 3 cups all-purpose or bread flour
1 (4-oz.) can diced green chilies
2 tablespoons yellow cornmeal
1 tablespoon butter, melted

In large bowl of electric mixer, dissolve yeast and sugar in water. Let stand until foamy, 5 to 10 minutes. Add soup, oil, eggs, salt, baking powder, 1/2 cup cornmeal and 1 to 1-1/2 cups flour. Beat at medium speed with electric mixer 4 minutes or, beat 400 vigorous strokes by hand. Stir in chilies and enough remaining flour to make a stiff batter. Cover with a slightly damp towel. Let rise in a warm place, free from drafts, until doubled in bulk, about 1-1/2 hours. Grease 2 (8" x 4") loaf pans or 2 (1-1/2-quart) casserole dishes. Sprinkle 1 tablespoon cornmeal over bottom and sides of each pan; set aside. **Stir down batter.** Turn into prepared pans. Butter your fingers and 2 (12-inch) squares of waxed paper. Smooth batter with your buttered fingers. Cover with buttered waxed paper. Let rise until doubled in bulk, about 1 hour. **Preheat oven** to 375F (190C). Bake 30 to 35 minutes or until bread sounds hollow when tapped on bottom. For browner bottom crusts, remove from pans. Place directly on oven rack during final 5 minutes of baking. Brush melted butter over tops. Cool on racks. Makes 2 loaves.

Cheddar Butter

Wonderful with savory breads—delicious on baked potatoes.

1/2 cup butter, room temperature
3/4 cup shredded Cheddar cheese (3 oz.),
  room temperature

3 drops hot pepper sauce
Salt to taste

In a blender or food processor fitted with a metal blade, combine all ingredients. Scraping container often, process until almost smooth. Cheese will retain some texture. Spoon into a small serving dish. Cover and refrigerate. Let stand at room temperature 20 to 30 minutes before serving. Makes about 3/4 cup.

Variation

Substitute 3/4 cup (3 ounces) shredded Swiss cheese or 1/4 cup (1 ounce) crumbled Roquefort or Bleu cheese for Cheddar cheese. Add 1 teaspoon crumbled dried herbs, if desired.

Little Yeast Breads

Little yeast breads are the perfect answer for hurried, on-the-run breakfasts, sack-lunch fillers, quick and delicious snacks and lunch or dinner accompaniments. They're perfect for almost any occasion! Don't get in a rut by thinking of little breads as only muffins and biscuits. There are dozens of yeast creations so easy to make you'll soon be including them as a regular part of your baking. Little yeast breads are easy to make, easy to eat and easy to freeze. What more can you ask of your bread?

What is a bagel? According to an old Yiddish recipe, "First you take a hole, then you put some dough around it." Wonderfully chewy Water Bagels are delicious and the whole family can have fun making them. They are first simmered in water, then baked in an oven. The water-bath reduces their starch and creates satisfyingly chewy crusts.

In contrast are elegant Danish Pastries and Classic Croissants—bursting with butter. These flaky creations are the perfect way to begin your day. I'll never forget my first true French croissant—unbelievably big and flaky, undeniably tender. It was accompanied by a creamy cup of *café au lait* and served on a sunny hotel terrace in Cannes.

If you haven't the time for Croissants and Danish, by all means try Quick Cheese Pastries. Taking only 1-1/2 hours from start to finish, these crisp yeast twists with a citrus and cream-cheese filling are definitely worth getting up for!

I'd get up at any hour for a taste of Grandmother's Cinnamon Rolls! They are fully three inches in diameter and boast a cinnamon-raisin swirl and cinnamon frosting. Grandmother never did anything in a small way!

Buttermilk Yeast Biscuits

Serve these old-fashioned, yeast-raised biscuits for breakfast, lunch or dinner.

1 (1/4-oz.) pkg. active dry yeast
   (1 tablespoon)
2 teaspoons sugar
1/4 cup warm water (110F, 45C)
2-1/2 cups all-purpose flour
1 teaspoon salt

1 teaspoon baking powder
1/2 teaspoon baking soda
1/3 cup cold lard or butter
3/4 cup buttermilk, room temperature
1 egg white blended with
   2 teaspoons water for glaze

Grease 2 large baking sheets; set aside. In a small bowl, dissolve yeast and sugar in 1/4 cup water. Let stand until foamy, 5 to 10 minutes. In a large bowl, combine flour, salt, baking powder and baking soda. Use a pastry blender or 2 knives to cut in lard or butter until mixture resembles coarse crumbs. Stir in yeast mixture and buttermilk. Turn out dough onto a lightly floured surface. **Knead dough** 2 to 3 minutes or until mixture holds together. Roll out dough until 1/2 inch thick. Cut with a round 2- or 2-1/2-inch cutter. Arrange biscuits 2 inches apart on prepared baking sheets. Gather leftover dough together; knead, roll and cut as before. Butter an 18-inch piece of waxed paper. Place over biscuits. Let rise in a warm place, free from drafts, until doubled in bulk, about 1 hour. **Preheat oven** to 425F (220C). Brush biscuits with egg-white glaze. Bake 12 to 15 minutes or until golden brown. Serve warm or, cool on racks. Makes about 22 biscuits.

Variations

Double-Butter Biscuits: Melt 1/3 cup butter; set aside. Roll out dough until 1/4 inch thick. Cut as directed above. Dip each round in melted butter, then top with another butter-dipped round. Place 2 inches apart on ungreased baking sheets.

Sugar 'N Spice Biscuits: In a small bowl, combine 1 cup sugar, 1/2 teaspoon ground cinnamon, 1/4 teaspoon ground nutmeg and 1/4 teaspoon ground allspice. Proceed as for Double-Butter Biscuits, dipping each biscuit in butter, then in sugar mixture.

Chili-Cheese Biscuits: Reduce buttermilk to 2/3 cup. Add 1 (2-ounce) can diced green chilies, drained on paper towels. Add 1 cup (4 ounces) shredded Cheddar cheese. If necessary, knead in additional flour only until dough is no longer sticky.

Sesame-Yeast Biscuits: Place about 1/2 cup sesame seeds in a small bowl. Proceed as for Double-Butter Biscuits, dipping first in butter, then in sesame seeds.

Tip *Twisting a biscuit cutter compresses the dough. Cut out biscuits with a clean, sharp downward motion for high-rising end results.*

Grandmother's Cinnamon Rolls Photo on page 98.

Shape and refrigerate the dough tonight—bake and serve hot rolls in the morning.

Basic Sweet Yeast Dough, page 59
3/4 cup packed brown sugar
2 teaspoons ground cinnamon

3 tablespoons butter, room temperature
3/4 to 1 cup raisins, if desired
Cinnamon Glaze, see below

Cinnamon Glaze:
1 cup powdered sugar
1/4 teaspoon ground cinnamon

1/2 teaspoon vanilla extract
1 to 2 tablespoons cream or milk

Prepare Basic Sweet Yeast Dough as directed through first rising. **Punch down dough;** knead 30 seconds. Cover dough; let stand 10 minutes. Generously grease a 13" x 9" baking pan; set aside. In a small bowl, combine brown sugar and cinnamon; set aside. On a lightly floured surface, roll out dough to a 24" x 12" rectangle. Spread with butter, leaving 1/2 inch not buttered on 1 narrow end. Sprinkle evenly with brown-sugar mixture. Sprinkle with raisins, if desired. Lightly press raisins and brown-sugar mixture into surface of dough with your fingers or back of a spoon. Beginning on buttered short side, roll up tightly, jelly-roll fashion. Pinch seam to seal. Cut roll into 12 equal slices. Arrange cut-side down about 1/2 inch apart in prepared pan. Cover tightly with plastic wrap. Let rise in a warm place, free from drafts, until doubled in bulk, about 1-1/2 hours. **Preheat oven** to 375F (190C). Bake 30 to 35 minutes or until deep golden brown. Prepare Cinnamon Glaze. Place a rack over waxed paper. Turn out rolls onto rack; turn rolls top-side up. Drizzle with glaze. Makes 12 large rolls.

Cinnamon Glaze:

In a small bowl, combine powdered sugar and cinnamon. Stir in vanilla and enough cream or milk to make a smooth, creamy glaze of drizzling consistency.

Variation

Cinnamon-Nut Rolls: Substitute 1 cup chopped walnuts or pecans for raisins. Or, reduce raisins to 1/2 cup and add 1/2 cup chopped walnuts.

Tip *To cut rolled dough or delicate breads into slices, wrap a long piece of thread around area to be cut; pull thread-ends together slowly. Thread will slice cleanly through dough or bread.*

Maple-Pecan Sticky Buns

Gooey-good and sticky-sweet, these rolls boast a rich spiral of cinnamon and nuts!

Basic Sweet Yeast Dough, page 59
Maple Topping, see below
1 cup toasted finely chopped pecans

Cinnamon-Nut Filling, see below
3 tablespoons butter, room temperature

Maple Topping:
1/2 cup pure maple syrup
1/4 cup packed brown sugar

1/3 cup butter
1/4 teaspoon salt

Cinnamon-Nut Filling:
2/3 cup packed brown sugar
1 teaspoon ground cinnamon

1/2 cup toasted finely chopped pecans

Prepare Basic Sweet Yeast Dough as directed through first rising. **Punch down dough;** knead 30 seconds. Cover and let stand 10 minutes. Butter an 18-inch length of waxed paper; set aside. Generously grease a 13" x 9" baking pan. Prepare Maple Topping; pour into prepared pan. Sprinkle evenly with 1 cup chopped pecans; set aside. Prepare Cinnamon-Nut Filling; set aside. On a lightly floured surface, roll out dough to a 24" x 12" rectangle. Spread with butter, leaving 1/2 inch not buttered on 1 long side. Sprinkle evenly with Cinnamon-Nut Filling. Beginning on buttered long side, roll up tightly, jelly-roll fashion. Pinch seam to seal. Cut roll into 24 equal slices. Arrange rolls cut-side down in prepared baking pan. Cover with buttered waxed paper. Let rise in a warm place, free from drafts, until doubled in bulk, about 1 hour. **Preheat oven** to 350F (175C). Bake 30 to 35 minutes or until golden brown. Let stand in pan 1 minute; invert baked rolls onto a platter or a wire rack set over waxed paper. Spoon any topping remaining in pan over rolls. Let stand 5 minutes. Serve warm. Separate rolls by gently pulling apart with 2 forks. Makes 24 rolls.

Maple Topping:
Combine all ingredients in a small saucepan. Cook over medium heat, stirring occasionally, until mixture begins to simmer.

Cinnamon-Nut Filling:
Combine all ingredients in a small bowl.

Variation
Raisin-Nut Sticky Buns: Add 1 cup raisins to Cinnamon-Nut Filling.

 If breads are browning too fast, cover them with a tent of foil.

Rolls & Buns   Photo on page 98.

Make plain rolls interesting by trying the shapes and toppings listed below.

1 recipe Basic White Bread, page 19,
   or other bread dough
1 egg white blended with
   2 teaspoons water for glaze

Topping as indicated

Prepare Basic White-Bread dough or other bread dough through first rising. Punch down dough and shape as desired. Arrange on prepared baking sheets. Cover and let rise until doubled in bulk, 30 to 45 minutes. Brush with egg-white glaze or top as directed below. Preheat oven to 375F (190C). Bake 15 minutes or until golden brown. Yields are for Basic White-Bread dough; other doughs may yield more or less.

Parker-House Rolls: Grease 2 large baking sheets; set aside. Roll out dough until 1/2 inch thick. Cut dough with a floured 3- to 3-1/2-inch biscuit cutter or inverted drinking glass. Make a crease barely off-center with back edge of a knife. Fold at crease, pressing down slightly. Place 2 inches apart on prepared baking sheets. Let rise; brush with melted butter. Sprinkle with sesame seeds, if desired. Bake as directed above. Makes 20 to 25 rolls.

Cloverleaf Rolls: Grease 24 muffin cups; set aside. Divide dough into 24 portions. Divide each portion into 3 pieces. Roll each into a smooth ball. Place 3 balls in each prepared muffin cup. Let rise; brush with melted butter or milk. Bake as directed above. Makes 24 rolls.

Spiral Rolls: Grease 2 large baking sheets; set aside. Shape dough into 24 (12-inch) ropes. Shape each rope into a tight spiral. Tuck ends under slightly; pinch to seal. Place 2 inches apart on greased baking sheets. Flatten slightly with your hand. Let rise; brush with egg-white glaze. Sprinkle with sesame or poppy seeds, if desired. Bake as directed above. Makes 24 rolls.

Knot-Shape Rolls: Grease 2 large baking sheets; set aside. Shape dough into 24 (12-inch) ropes. Tie each rope into a loose knot. Place 2 inches apart on prepared baking sheets. Let rise; brush with melted butter. Bake as directed above. Makes 24 rolls.

How to Shape Rolls

1/Parker House Rolls: Make a crease barely off-center with back edge of a knife. Fold at crease. Place 2 inches apart on prepared baking sheets.

2/Cloverleaf Rolls: Roll each small piece of dough into a smooth ball. Place 3 balls in each prepared muffin cup.

Oval Rolls: Grease 2 large baking sheets; set aside. Divide dough into 24 pieces. Shape each piece into a football-shape, slightly tapering ends. Place 2 inches apart on prepared baking sheets. Let rise. Using a razor blade, cut a 1/4-inch-deep lengthwise slash down center top of each roll. Brush with egg-white glaze. Bake as directed above. Makes 24 rolls.

Round Rolls: Grease 2 large baking sheets; set aside. Shape dough into 24 smooth balls, pinching undersides to seal. Place 2 inches apart on prepared baking sheets. Let rise. Using a razor blade, cut a cross in top of each roll. Brush with egg-white glaze. Bake as directed above. Makes 24 rolls.

Pan Rolls: Grease a 13'' x 9'' baking pan; set aside. Shape dough into 24 smooth balls. Place balls in prepared pan in 6 rows of 4 each. Let rise; brush with melted butter or milk. Bake as directed above. Makes 24 rolls.

Hand-Print Rolls: Grease 2 large baking sheets; set aside. Roll out dough 1/2 inch thick. Place your hand or a child's hand, palm down, fingers spread, on surface of dough. Using a sharp knife, cut around hand. Place cut dough 2 inches apart on prepared baking sheet, curving fingers as desired. Let rise; brush with egg-white glaze. Bake as directed above. Makes 8 to 12 rolls.

Hamburger Buns: Grease 2 large baking sheets; set aside. Divide dough into 18 pieces. Shape each piece into a smooth ball; flatten into a 5-inch circle. Place 2 inches apart on prepared baking sheets. Let rise; brush with butter. Sprinkle sesame seeds over top, if desired. Bake 20 to 25 minutes or until golden brown. Makes 18 buns.

Hot-Dog Buns: Grease 2 large baking sheets; set aside. Divide dough into 18 pieces. Shape each piece into a 6-inch rope. Place 2 inches apart on prepared baking sheets. Let rise; brush with butter. Bake 20 to 25 minutes or until golden brown. Makes 18 buns.

Onion Buns: In a large skillet, sauté 1-1/4 cups finely chopped onion in 1/4 cup butter called for in Basic White-Bread recipe. Sauté over medium heat until soft. Set aside to cool. Reserve 1/4 cup sautéed onion for topping. Stir remaining sautéed onion into flour mixture. Complete bread through first rising. Grease 2 large baking sheets; set aside. Divide dough into 18 pieces; shape as for Hamburger Buns. Place 2 inches apart on prepared baking sheets. Press some of reserved sautéed onion into surface of each bun. Cover with buttered waxed paper. Let rise; bake 20 to 25 minutes or until golden brown. Makes 18 buns.

3/Spiral Rolls: Roll each piece into a 12-inch rope. Shape each rope into a tight spiral. Tuck end under; pinch to seal.

4/Knot-Shape Rolls: Roll each piece into a 12-inch rope. Tie each rope into a loose knot. Place 2 inches apart on prepared baking sheets.

Water Bagels

Water bagels are chewier than egg bagels because they contain no fat.

1 (1/4-oz.) pkg. active dry yeast
  (1 tablespoon)
1 teaspoon sugar
1-1/2 cups warm water from cooking potatoes
  or other water (110F, 45C)
1/4 cup sugar
2 teaspoons salt

4 to 4-1/2 cups all-purpose or bread flour
3 quarts water
1 egg yolk blended with
  1 tablespoon water for glaze
Coarse salt, onion flakes, sesame seeds,
  poppy seeds or caraway seeds for
  topping, if desired

In large bowl of electric mixer, dissolve yeast and 1 teaspoon sugar in 1-1/2 cups water. Let stand until foamy, 5 to 10 minutes. Add 2 tablespoons sugar, salt and 2 to 2-1/2 cups flour. Beat at medium speed with electric mixer 2 minutes or, beat 200 vigorous strokes by hand. Stir in enough remaining flour to make a soft dough. Turn out dough onto a lightly floured surface. Clean and grease bowl; set aside. **Knead dough** 8 to 10 minutes or until smooth and elastic. Place dough in greased bowl, turning to coat all sides. Cover with a slightly damp towel. Let rise in a warm place, free from drafts, until doubled in bulk, about 1 hour. **Punch down dough;** knead 30 seconds. Divide dough into 14 pieces. Roll each piece into a cigar shape about 8 inches long. Hold 1 end of dough with thumb and index finger. Wrap dough around hand to make a doughnut shape. Moisten ends slightly with water; pinch firmly to seal. Or, shape each piece of dough into a ball. Flatten slightly. Press your thumb through center of each ball of dough. Gently enlarge hole; smooth edges. Place bagels on a lightly floured surface. Cover with a dry towel. Set in a warm place, free from drafts, 10 minutes. Grease 2 large baking sheets; set aside. **Preheat oven** to 375F (190C). In a large pot or kettle, combine remaining 2 tablespoons sugar and 3 quarts water. Bring to a boil. Reduce heat so water boils gently. Carefully lower bagels into water, 1 at a time. Cook 3 to 4 bagels at a time. Bagels will sink, then rise to surface almost immediately. Boil 30 seconds on each side, turning with a slotted spoon. Remove from water with slotted spoon; drain on paper towels. Place boiled bagels on prepared baking sheets. Brush with egg-yolk glaze. Sprinkle with topping, if desired. Bake 25 to 30 minutes or until golden brown. Cool on racks. Eat whole or, split and toast. Makes 14 bagels.

Variations

Egg Bagels: Reduce water to 1 cup; add 2 eggs.
Beer-Rye Bagels: Substitute a 12-ounce can or bottle of warm beer (110F, 45C) for 1-1/2 cups water. Substitute 1-1/2 cups rye flour for 1-1/2 cups all-purpose or bread flour. Add 1 tablespoon each additional caraway seeds and freshly grated orange peel. Sprinkle additional caraway seeds over tops of boiled, glazed bagels.
Cheddar-Cheese Bagels: Reduce salt to 1-1/2 teaspoons; add 1 cup (4 ounces) shredded Cheddar cheese. Sprinkle additional shredded Cheddar cheese over tops of boiled, glazed bagels.
Almond-Raisin Bagels: Add 1/2 cup toasted chopped almonds, 1 cup raisins, 1 teaspoon vanilla extract, 1 teaspoon grated lemon peel and 1/2 teaspoon each ground cinnamon and ground nutmeg. Sprinkle a cinnamon-sugar mixture over tops of boiled, glazed bagels.
Onion Bagels: Sauté 1/2 cup finely chopped onions in 1 tablespoon butter until soft. Add with second addition of flour or, add 2 tablespoons dried minced onion. Sprinkle poppy seeds and minced fresh onion over tops of boiled, glazed bagels.
Seeded Bagels: Add 1 tablespoon poppy seeds, 1 tablespoon caraway seeds or 2 tablespoons toasted sesame seeds with first addition of flour. Sprinkle same seeds over tops of boiled, glazed bagels.

Cocktail Bagels

Fill or spread these miniature bagels with your favorite spread for an hors d'oeuvre.

Water Bagels, opposite
2 tablespoons sugar
3 qts. water
1 egg yolk blended with
   1 tablespoon water for glaze

Lox & Cream-Cheese Spread,
   Nutty Mushroom Spread, below, or
   other spread

Prepare Water Bagels through first rising. Divide dough in half. Divide each half into 25 equal pieces. Cover dough not being shaped. Roll each piece into a cigar shape, about 4 inches long. Shape as directed for Water Bagels. Cover and set aside 10 minutes. Grease 2 large baking sheets; set aside. **Preheat oven** to 375F (190C). In a large pot or kettle, combine 2 tablespoons sugar and 3 quarts water. Bring to a boil. Reduce heat so water boils gently. Carefully lower bagels into water, 1 at a time. Cook 8 to 10 cocktail bagels at a time. Bagels will sink, then rise to surface almost immediately. Boil 30 seconds on each side, turning with a slotted spoon. Remove from water with slotted spoon; drain on paper towels. Place boiled bagels on prepared baking sheets. Brush with egg-yolk glaze. Bake 15 to 20 minutes or until golden brown. Cool on racks. Split, toast, if desired, and top with spread of your choice. Makes 50 miniature bagels.

Cocktail-Bagel Spreads

Nutty Mushroom Spread:
1/3 cup butter
1 lb. fresh mushrooms, finely chopped
1/4 cup finely chopped green onions
   with tops
1 large garlic clove, minced
1/4 cup finely chopped fresh parsley
2 tablespoons Madeira

1/2 teaspoon salt
1/8 teaspoon pepper
1/8 teaspoon ground nutmeg
1/2 cup dairy sour cream
1/2 cup toasted finely chopped walnuts
   or pecans
Chopped fresh parsley for garnish

Melt butter in a large skillet over medium heat. Add mushrooms, green onions, garlic and parsley; sauté 3 minutes. Add Madeira. Stirring occasionally, cook until liquid evaporates, 6 to 8 minutes. Cool to room temperature. Stir in salt, pepper, nutmeg, sour cream and nuts. Spread on cocktail bagels. Serve hot or cold, garnished with parsley. To serve hot, preheat oven to 350F (175C). Bake 5 to 8 minutes or until mixture sizzles. Makes about 2 cups.

Lox & Cream-Cheese Spread:
1 (8-oz.) pkg. cream cheese,
   room temperature
1/2 cup dairy sour cream
1 teaspoon minced fresh dill or
   1/4 teaspoon dried dill weed

4 to 6 oz. smoked salmon, diced
1 tablespoon finely chopped onion or
   1/2 teaspoon dried minced onion
Salt and pepper to taste

In small bowl of electric mixer, beat cream cheese, sour cream and dill until creamy. Stir in salmon and onion. Cover; refrigerate 6 to 8 hours or overnight for flavors to blend. Season with salt and pepper. Makes about 2 cups.

Wheat-Bran Buns

Cottage cheese and bran give these delicious, light rolls a nutritional bonus!

2 (1/4-oz.) pkgs. active dry yeast
   (2 tablespoons
1 teaspoon brown sugar
1/2 cup warm water (110F, 45C)
1/3 cup packed brown sugar
1 cup small-curd cottage cheese (8 oz.),
   room temperature
2 eggs, room temperature

2 teaspoons salt
1/2 cup unprocessed bran flakes
1 cup whole-wheat flour
3-1/4 to 3-3/4 cups all-purpose or
   bread flour
1/4 cup butter, melted
2/3 cup unprocessed bran flakes

In large bowl of electric mixer, dissolve yeast and 1 teaspoon brown sugar in water. Let stand until foamy, 5 to 10 minutes. Add 1/3 cup brown sugar, cottage cheese, eggs, salt, 1/2 cup bran flakes, whole-wheat flour and 1/2 to 1 cup all-purpose or bread flour. Beat at medium speed with electric mixer 2 minutes or, beat 200 vigorous strokes by hand. Stir in enough remaining all-purpose or bread flour to make a soft dough. Turn out dough onto a lightly floured surface. Clean and grease bowl; set aside. **Knead dough** 8 to 10 minutes or until smooth and elastic. Place dough in greased bowl, turning to coat all sides. Cover with a slightly damp towel. Let rise in a warm place, free from drafts, until doubled in bulk, about 1 hour. Grease a 13" x 9" baking pan; set aside. **Punch down dough;** knead 30 seconds. Divide dough into 24 pieces. Roll each piece into a smooth ball. Dip each ball in melted butter, then roll in 2/3 cup bran flakes. Arrange coated balls in prepared pan. Cover with a dry towel. Let rise until doubled in bulk, about 45 minutes. **Preheat oven** to 375F (190C). Bake 20 to 25 minutes or until golden brown. Remove from pan. Cool on a rack 5 minutes. Makes 24 rolls.

Orange & Cream-Cheese Spread

This spread makes you think of sunshine and is especially good on whole-grain breads!

2 (3-oz.) pkgs. cream cheese,
   room temperature
1/4 cup orange juice

2 tablespoons powdered sugar
2 teaspoons grated orange peel

In small bowl of electric mixer or food processor fitted with a metal blade, process all ingredients until smooth and light. Spoon into a small serving dish. Cover and refrigerate. Let stand at room temperature 20 to 30 minutes before serving. Makes about 1 cup.

Variations

Ginger-Orange Spread: Add 1 tablespoon minced crystallized ginger.
Prune-Cheese Spread: Add 1/2 cup finely chopped prunes.

Wheat-Bran Buns with Orange & Cream-Cheese Spread

Oatmeal Honor Rolls

Go to the top of your class with these orange-scented, raisin-studded winners!

3/4 cup raisins
2 tablespoons orange-flavored liqueur
1 (1/4-oz.) pkg. active dry yeast
   (1 tablespoon)
1 teaspoon honey
1/4 cup warm water (110F, 45C)
1/4 cup honey
2 eggs, room temperature
1 cup milk, room temperature

1/4 cup butter, melted
1-1/2 teaspoons salt
1/4 teaspoon ground cinnamon
2 teaspoons freshly grated orange peel
1-1/4 cups regular or quick-cooking
   rolled oats
3-1/2 to 4 cups all-purpose or bread flour
3 tablespoons butter, melted
Rolled oats for garnish

In a small bowl, combine raisins and orange-flavored liqueur. Cover; let stand overnight or 3 to 4 hours to soak. In large bowl of electric mixer, dissolve yeast and 1 teaspoon honey in water. Let stand until foamy, 5 to 10 minutes. Add 1/4 cup honey, eggs, milk, 1/4 cup butter, salt, cinnamon, orange peel, 1-1/4 cups oats and 1 to 1-1/2 cups flour. Beat at medium speed with electric mixer 2 minutes or, beat 200 vigorous strokes by hand. Stir in enough remaining flour to make a soft dough. Turn out dough onto a lightly floured surface. Clean and grease bowl; set aside. **Knead dough** 5 minutes or until smooth. Place dough in greased bowl, turning to coat all sides. Cover with a slightly damp towel. Let rise in a warm place, free from drafts, until doubled in bulk, about 1-1/2 hours. **Punch down dough;** knead 30 seconds. Cover and let stand 10 minutes. Grease 2 large baking sheets; set aside. Roll out dough to a 15" x 9" rectangle. Cut into 15 (3-inch) squares. Brush with melted butter. With back of a knife, score each square horizontally across center. Fold squares at crease. Place rolls 2 inches apart on prepared baking sheets. Butter 2 (18-inch) pieces of waxed paper. Place over rolls. Let rise until almost doubled in bulk, 30 to 45 minutes. **Preheat oven** to 400F (205C). Brush rolls with melted butter; sprinkle with oats. Bake 15 to 20 minutes or until evenly browned. Cool on racks 5 minutes. Makes 15 large rolls.

Potato-Chive Rolls   Photos on pages 44-45 and 98.

No kneading for these fluffy sour-cream and chive rolls—perfect for company dinners!

2 (1/4-oz.) pkgs. active dry yeast
   (2 tablespoons)
1-1/2 tablespoons sugar
3/4 cup warm water (110F, 45C)
1 cup dairy sour cream, room temperature
1 cup mashed cooked potatoes

3 eggs, room temperature
1 tablespoon salt
4-1/2 to 5 cups all-purpose or bread flour
1 to 1-1/2 tablespoons finely
   chopped chives

In large bowl of electric mixer, dissolve yeast and sugar in water. Let stand until foamy, 5 to 10 minutes. Add sour cream, potatoes, eggs, salt and 2 to 2-1/2 cups flour. Beat at medium speed with electric mixer 4 minutes or, beat 400 vigorous strokes by hand. Stir in chives and enough remaining flour to make a stiff dough. Cover with a slightly damp towel. Let rise in a warm place, free from drafts, until doubled in bulk, about 1-1/2 hours. Grease a 13" x 9" pan; set aside. Butter a 14-inch length of waxed paper; set aside. **Punch down dough.** On a generously floured surface, toss dough until no longer sticky. Divide dough into 24 equal pieces. Shape each piece into a ball; place smooth-side up in prepared pan. Cover with buttered waxed paper. Let rise until doubled in bulk, about 45 minutes. **Preheat oven** to 375F (190C). Bake 30 to 35 minutes or until deep golden brown. Remove from pan. Place rolls on a rack; dust lightly with flour. Let cool 5 minutes. Makes 24 rolls.

Quick Cheese Pastries

Buttery pastries with a citrus and cream-cheese filling—quick and delicious!

1 (1/4-oz.) pkg. active dry yeast
  (1 tablespoon)
1 teaspoon sugar
1/4 cup warm water (110F, 45C)
2 tablespoons sugar
2-1/4 cups all-purpose flour
1/4 teaspoon salt
1 cup cold butter, cut in 16 pieces

1 egg, slightly beaten
1 teaspoon vanilla extract
Cream-Cheese Filling, see below
1 cup finely chopped walnuts or pecans
1 egg yolk blended with
  1 tablespoon cream for glaze
Powdered sugar

Cream-Cheese Filling:
2 (3-oz.) pkgs. cream cheese,
  room temperature
3/4 cup sugar
1/2 teaspoon ground cinnamon

1-1/2 teaspoons freshly grated
  lemon peel
1-1/2 teaspoons freshly grated
  orange peel

In a small bowl, dissolve yeast and 1 teaspoon sugar in water. Let stand until foamy, 5 to 10 minutes. In a large bowl, combine 2 tablespoons sugar, flour and salt. Use a pastry cutter or 2 knives to cut butter into flour mixture until mixture resembles coarse crumbs; set aside. Stir egg and vanilla into yeast mixture. Stir into flour mixture until combined but still crumbly. Turn out onto a well-floured surface. **Knead 12 to 15 strokes** or until dough holds together. Dough will be very moist and sticky. Use a pastry scraper or metal spatula to scrape dough off work surface. Divide dough in half. Wrap each half in plastic wrap; refrigerate. Lightly grease 2 large baking sheets; set aside. Prepare Cream-Cheese Filling; set aside. **Preheat oven** to 375F (190C). Remove half of dough from refrigerator. On a well-floured surface, roll out dough to a 20" x 10" rectangle. Spread with half of Cream-Cheese Filling. Sprinkle with 1/2 cup chopped nuts. Loosen pastry from work surface with a pastry scraper or metal spatula, if necessary. Fold dough in half lengthwise. Cut into 20 (1-inch) strips. Holding each strip at both ends, twist in opposite directions, twice, making spirals. Place 1-1/2 inches apart on prepared baking sheets, pressing ends down lightly to secure. Repeat with remaining dough. Pastries may be covered and refrigerated overnight. If refrigerated, let stand 30 minutes at room temperature before baking. Brush pastries with egg-yolk glaze. Bake 15 to 25 minutes or until golden brown. Remove to racks; dust lightly with powdered sugar. Serve slightly warm or at room temperature. Makes about 40 pastries.

Cream-Cheese Filling:
In small bowl of electric mixer, beat cream cheese, sugar and cinnamon until light and creamy. Stir in lemon peel and orange peel.

Tip   *Reduce heat by 25F (15C) when substituting glass baking containers for metal containers.*

Beer Sticks

Choose your favorite topping for these thin, crunchy breadsticks flavored with beer!

1 (1/4-oz.) pkg. active dry yeast (1 tablespoon)	**1 egg blended with** 1 tablespoon water for glaze
1 (12-oz.) can warm, flat beer (110F, 45C)	**Poppy, caraway, sesame or dill seeds,** dill weed, coarse salt or
3/4 cup olive oil or vegetable oil	cracked pepper for topping
1-1/2 teaspoons salt	
4-3/4 to 5-1/4 cups all-purpose or bread flour	

In large bowl of electric mixer, dissolve yeast in beer. Let stand until foamy, 5 to 10 minutes. Add oil, salt and 2-1/2 to 3 cups flour. Beat at medium speed with electric mixer 2 minutes or, beat 200 vigorous strokes by hand. Stir in enough remaining flour to make a soft dough. Turn out dough onto a lightly floured surface. Clean and grease bowl; set aside. **Knead dough** 6 to 8 minutes or until smooth and elastic. Place dough in greased bowl, turning to coat all sides. Cover with a slightly damp towel. Let rise in a warm place, free from drafts, until doubled in bulk, about 1 hour. Grease 2 to 4 large baking sheets; set aside. **Punch down dough;** knead 30 seconds. Divide dough in half. Cover and set 1 piece aside. Roll or pat remaining dough to a 20" x 6" rectangle. Cut crosswise in 40 (1/2-inch) strips. Arrange on prepared baking sheets, stretching strips to 8 inches. Make sure strips are of a uniform thickness. Brush with egg glaze; sprinkle with poppy, caraway, sesame or dill seeds, dill weed, coarse salt or cracked pepper. Repeat with remaining dough. Let rise, uncovered, 20 minutes. **Preheat oven** to 350F (175C). Bake 20 to 30 minutes or until golden brown. Cool on racks. Makes about 80 breadsticks.

Variations

Pepper Sticks: With first addition of flour, add 1-1/2 teaspoons ground pepper. Brush tops of strips with egg glaze. Sprinkle with cracked pepper and coarse salt.

Fennel Sticks: With first addition of flour, add 1/2 teaspoon ground pepper, 1 teaspoon crushed fennel seeds and 1/2 teaspoon crushed anise seeds. Brush tops of strips with egg glaze. Sprinkle with crushed fennel seeds and coarse salt.

Breadsticks Italiano: With first addition of flour, add 1 crushed garlic clove, 1 teaspoon dried leaf basil, 1 teaspoon dried leaf oregano, 1/2 teaspoon freshly ground black pepper and 1/2 cup (1-1/2 ounces) grated Parmesan cheese. Complete mixing dough as directed; let rise. Brush with egg glaze; sprinkle with coarse salt or sesame seeds.

Shaping Variation

Divide dough into fourths. Cover 3 pieces; set aside. Divide remaining fourth into 12 equal pieces. Shape each piece into an 8- to 12-inch rope. Thin ropes will be crisper. Place ropes 1 inch apart on prepared baking sheets. Repeat with remaining dough. Let rise, uncovered, 20 minutes. Bake in a preheated 350F (175C) oven, 35 to 40 minutes. Makes about 48 breadsticks.

Clockwise from top left: Spiral and Knot-Shape Rolls, pages 90-91; Potato-Chive Rolls, page 96; Basic White Bread, page 19; Butterflake Bread, page 26; Molasses-Bran Bread, page 49; Whole-Earth Date Bread, page 44-46; Grandmother's Cinnamon Rolls, page 88; Hot Dog Onion Rolls and Cloverleaf Rolls with seed toppings, pages 90-91; Viennese Striezel, page 72; Beer Sticks with salt and fennel seeds, above.

Classic Croissants   Photo on pages 44 and 45.

These tender, butter-layered classics will earn you raves!

1 (1/4-oz.) pkg. active dry yeast
   (1 tablespoon)
Pinch of sugar
1/4 cup warm water (110F, 45C)
3/4 cup milk, room temperature
1 tablespoon sugar
1/2 teaspoon salt

2 tablespoons unsalted butter, melted
2-1/2 to 3 cups all-purpose flour
2 tablespoons all-purpose flour
1 cup cold unsalted butter
2 egg yolks blended with
   2 teaspoons cream or milk for glaze

In a large bowl, dissolve yeast and pinch of sugar in water. Let stand until foamy, 5 to 10 minutes. Add milk, 1 tablespoon sugar, salt, 2 tablespoons butter and about 2-1/2 cups flour. Stir until dough forms a ball. Add more flour, if necessary. Turn out dough onto a lightly floured surface. Cover; let stand 5 minutes. Clean and butter bowl; set aside. **Knead dough** about 1 minute or until smooth but not elastic. Use a pastry scraper, if necessary; dough will be very soft. Handle dough gently to prevent over-developing gluten. Place dough in buttered bowl, turning to coat all sides. Cover with plastic wrap. Let rise in a warm place, free from drafts, until *tripled* in bulk, about 1-1/2 hours. Gently punch down dough. Cover; let rise again until *doubled* in bulk, about 2 hours. Punch down dough again; cover and refrigerate 30 minutes or overnight. **To prepare butter:** Sprinkle 2 tablespoons flour over work surface. Place 1 cup cold butter on floured surface. Lightly pound butter with a floured rolling pin until softened. With heel of your hand or a pastry scraper, knead butter into flour on work surface until of spreading consistency yet still cold. If butter begins to melt, refrigerate immediately until firm. Butter should be as close as possible to consistency of croissant dough. Set butter mixture aside; do not refrigerate. **To combine butter and dough:** On a lightly floured surface, roll out dough to a 16" x 12" rectangle; brush excess flour from dough. Using a rubber spatula, spread butter mixture over center and another third of dough, leaving a 1/2-inch margin around outside edges. Fold unbuttered third over center third. Fold remaining third over top. Press edges together to seal. This is called *turn one.* Lightly flour work area and surface of dough. Keeping dough 12 inches wide, work rapidly and use firm, even pressure, to roll out dough again to a 16" x 12" rectangle. Roll from center of dough to within 1 inch of sides to avoid pushing butter through seams. Fold again in thirds for *turn two.* Dust surface of dough lightly with flour; wrap in plastic wrap. Refrigerate 1 hour. Lightly flour work surface and top of refrigerated dough. Roll and fold again for *turn three.* Repeat for *turn four.* Dust surface of dough lightly with flour. Wrap in plastic wrap. Refrigerate 1-1/2 hours or overnight. If refrigerated overnight, place a small board or baking sheet and a 5-pound weight on top of dough to prevent rising. **To shape dough:** On a lightly floured surface, roll out dough to a 24" x 16" rectangle, about 1/8 inch thick. Cut rectangle in half lengthwise, making 2 (24" x 8") strips. Lightly dust 1 strip with flour, fold in thirds and wrap in plastic wrap; refrigerate. Score remaining strip, on 1 long side, at 6-inch intervals. On other long side, starting 3 inches from 1 end, score at 6-inch intervals. Cut strip, from 3-inch mark to opposite 6-inch mark. Continue cutting in triangles. Each triangle will have a 6-inch base and 8-1/2-inch sides. Press edges of end pieces together, making a triangle. Brush excess flour from triangles. Beginning at 6-inch base, roll up triangle toward point. If necessary, dampen triangle point with a drop of water so it will stick to roll. Curve ends slightly into a crescent shape. Lightly spray cold water on 2 large baking sheets or, wipe with a wet cloth. Arrange crescents, 1-1/2 to 2 inches apart on damp baking sheets. Point of crescent should rest on baking sheet. Do not tuck under roll. Repeat with remaining dough. Butter as much waxed paper as needed to cover croissants; place over croissants. Let rise in a warm place (not over 80F, 25C), free from drafts, until doubled in bulk, about 1-1/2 hours. **Preheat oven** to 400F (205C). Brush croissants with egg-yolk glaze. Bake 15 to 20 minutes or until lightly browned. Cool on racks 10 to 15 minutes. Serve warm. Makes about 16 croissants.

How to Make Classic Croissants

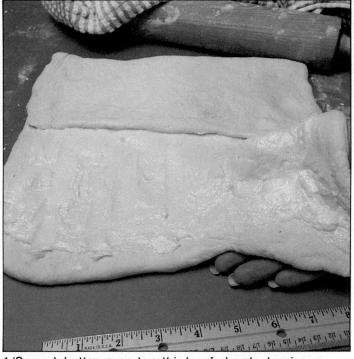

1/Spread butter over two-thirds of dough, leaving a 1/2-inch margin. Fold unbuttered third over center and remaining third over top. Press edges to seal in butter.

2/Pinch edges to seal. Roll from center of dough to within 1 inch of ends to avoid pushing butter through seams.

3/On a long side, score at 6-inch intervals. Starting 3 inches from end, score other long side at 6-inch intervals. Cut from 3-inch mark to opposite 6-inch mark. Continue cutting in triangles.

4/Beginning at 6-inch base of triangles, roll up toward point. Curve ends slightly to make crescents. Let point of crescents rest on baking sheet; do not tuck under.

Quick Croissants

A little easier, a lot quicker—these buttery taste-alikes will fool most croissant lovers!

5 cups all-purpose flour
2 cups cold unsalted butter
2 (1/4-oz.) pkgs. active dry yeast
  (2 tablespoons)
3 tablespoons sugar
1-3/4 cups warm milk (110F, 45C)

2 teaspoons salt
1/4 cup butter, melted
Additional butter, if desired,
  room temperature
2 egg yolks blended with
  2 teaspoons cream or milk for glaze

In large bowl of electric mixer or a food processor fitted with metal blade, combine 3 cups flour and 2 cups butter. Mix at low speed or use on and off pulses of food processor until butter particles are similar in size to small lima beans. Cover and refrigerate. In a large bowl, dissolve yeast and sugar in milk. Stir in 2 cups flour; beat until batter is smooth. Cover tightly with plastic wrap. Let rise in a warm place, free from drafts, until doubled in bulk, 20 to 30 minutes. **Stir down batter.** Stir in salt and 1/4 cup melted butter until blended. Add refrigerated butter mixture. Fold in only until flour is moistened and mixture is crumbly. Butter will remain in large pieces. Turn out crumbly dough onto a lightly floured surface. Handle dough as little as possible with your hands. Gently roll out dough to a large rectangle 1/2 inch thick. Brush excess flour from surface. Dough will be sticky. Using a pastry scraper or metal spatula, fold top third of dough down over middle third; fold opposite end over top, as if folding a letter. This is called *turn one*. Repeat rolling and folding dough 3 more times. If butter becomes soft and breaks through dough, place dough in a plastic bag. Refrigerate or freeze 10 to 20 minutes to refirm. Sprinkle flour over work surface and top of dough between each *turn*. Wrap folded dough airtight in plastic wrap. **Refrigerate** 1-1/2 to 2 hours or up to 24 hours, if desired. Lightly butter 2 large baking sheets; set aside. Place chilled dough on a lightly floured surface. **Deflate dough** by rapping firmly with a rolling pin. Divide dough into 4 equal pieces. Cover and refrigerate 3 pieces of dough. Roll remaining dough into a 14-inch circle. If a more buttery flavor is desired, spread a thin layer of softened butter over dough to within 1/4 inch of edges. Cut circle into 8 triangles. Beginning at outer edge of each triangle and stretching ends slightly, roll up dough toward point. If necessary, dampen tip of triangle with a drop of water so it will stick to roll. Curve ends slightly. Arrange 1-1/2 inches apart on prepared baking sheets. Point of crescent should rest on baking sheet. Do not tuck under roll. Repeat with remaining dough, removing 1 piece at a time from refrigerator. Cover loosely with plastic wrap. Let rise in a warm place (not over 80F, 25C), free from drafts, until almost doubled in bulk, about 1 hour. **Preheat oven** to 400F (205C). Brush croissants with egg-yolk glaze. Bake 12 to 18 minutes or until puffy and evenly browned. Cool on racks 10 to 15 minutes before serving. Makes 32 croissants.

Croissant Variations

Petits Pains au Chocolat: *(Croissant pastry wrapped around chocolate.)* To use a full Classic Croissant recipe, use 8 ounces semisweet chocolate pieces or minced semisweet chocolate. Lightly butter 2 large baking sheets; set aside. Roll out dough until 1/8 inch thick. Cut into 4-inch squares. Place about 1 tablespoon chocolate in a row, 1/2 inch from 1 edge of square. Roll up, jelly-roll fashion. Arrange 1-1/2 inches apart on prepared baking sheets. Cover; let rise. Bake as directed above. Cool at least 30 minutes before serving.

Whole-Wheat Croissants: Substitute 1-1/2 cups whole-wheat pastry flour for 1-1/2 cups all-purpose flour. Substitute 2 tablespoons honey or brown sugar for 1 tablespoon granulated sugar. If honey is used, additional flour may be needed. Add 1/4 cup toasted wheat germ. Before baking, brush with egg-yolk glaze; sprinkle with toasted wheat germ.

Croissant Fillings

Prepare filling mixture as directed below. Spread 1 heaping teaspoonful at base of each dough triangle. Roll from base to point. Arrange on damp baking sheets. Cover and let rise until doubled in bulk, about 1 hour. Brush croissants with egg-yolk glaze. Bake at 400F (205C), 12 to 18 minutes or until evenly browned and puffy.

Sweet Cheese Filling:
1 (8-oz.) pkg. cream cheese,
   room temperature
1 tablespoon rum or brandy
3 tablespoons sugar

1 teaspoon vanilla extract
1 teaspoon grated lemon peel
2 tablespoons currants, if desired

Combine all ingredients in a small bowl.

Herb-Cheese Filling:
1 (8-oz.) pkg. cream cheese,
   room temperature
Salt and pepper to taste

1-1/2 to 2 tablespoons minced
   fresh herbs or
   1 to 2 teaspoons dried leaf herbs

Combine all ingredients in a small bowl.

Cherry-Cheese Filling:
2 (3-oz.) pkgs. cream cheese,
   room temperature
2 tablespoons sugar

1/2 teaspoon almond extract
2/3 cup cherry preserves

In small bowl of electric mixer, beat cream cheese, sugar and almond extract until smooth. Stir in cherry preserves until combined.

Spiced-Apple Filling:
1 cup finely chopped peeled apple
1 tablespoon brown sugar
1/4 teaspoon ground cinnamon

1/8 teaspoon ground allspice
1/8 teaspoon ground nutmeg
1/4 cup currants or dark raisins, if desired

In a medium bowl, combine all ingredients.

Almond Filling:
1/2 cup almond paste, room temperature
1/4 cup butter, room temperature
1 egg white

1/2 teaspoon vanilla extract
Finely chopped sliced almonds, if desired

In small bowl of electric mixer or a food processor fitted with metal blade, beat almond paste and butter until smooth. Beat in egg white and vanilla until blended. Sprinkle almonds over glazed croissants before baking.

 Tip *Unsalted butter allows you to control the amount of salt added to your bread. It is a must for delicate pastries like croissants and Danish pastry.*

Danish Pastries

Buttery-rich pastries with a variety of shapes and fillings—a special breakfast treat.

2 (1/4-oz.) pkgs. active dry yeast (2 tablespoons)	3 tablespoons unsalted butter, room temperature
1 teaspoon sugar	4 to 5 cups all-purpose flour
1/2 cup warm water (110F, 45C)	3 tablespoons all-purpose flour
1/2 cup milk	2 cups cold unsalted butter
2 eggs	Choice of Danish Pastry Fillings, opposite
1/2 cup sugar	1 egg blended with
1 teaspoon salt	2 tablespoons cream or milk for glaze
1 teaspoon vanilla extract	Sugar, if desired
1/4 teaspoon ground cardamom	

In a large bowl, dissolve yeast and 1 teaspoon sugar in water. Let stand until foamy, 5 to 10 minutes. Add milk, eggs, 1/2 cup sugar, salt, vanilla, cardamom, 3 tablespoons butter and 4 cups flour. Stir until dry ingredients have absorbed liquid. Turn out dough onto a lightly floured surface. **Knead dough** 2 to 3 minutes or until smooth. Dust surface of dough lightly with flour. Place in a plastic bag. Refrigerate 1 to 1-1/2 hours. **To prepare butter:** Sprinkle 3 tablespoons flour over work surface. Place 2 cups cold butter on floured surface. Lightly pound butter with a floured rolling pin until softened. With heel of your hand or a pastry scraper, knead butter into flour on work surface until of spreading consistency, yet still cold. If butter begins to melt, refrigerate immediately until firm. Butter should be as close as possible to consistency of pastry dough. Set butter mixture aside; do not refrigerate. **To combine butter and dough:** On a lightly floured surface, roll out dough to an 18" x 12" rectangle. Brush excess flour from dough. Using a rubber spatula, spread butter mixture over center and another third of dough, leaving a 1/2-inch margin around outside edges. Fold unbuttered third over center third. Fold remaining third over top. Press edges together to seal in butter. Keeping dough 12 inches wide, work rapidly and use firm even pressure to roll out dough again to an 18" x 12" rectangle. Roll from center of dough to within 1 inch of ends to avoid pushing butter through seams. Fold as before. Repeat rolling and folding of dough a third time. Work rapidly, using firm, even pressure. If butter breaks through dough, lightly sprinkle flour over break. Cover dough and place in freezer 5 minutes. After third rolling of dough, dust surface lightly with flour. Place dough in a plastic bag. Refrigerate 45 minutes. Brush excess flour from dough. On a lightly floured surface, repeat rolling and folding 3 more times. If butter begins to soften, refrigerate dough 15 minutes between rollings. After final folding, chill dough at least 2 hours or overnight. Lightly butter several large baking sheets; set aside. **To shape pastries:** Choose desired filling; then shape, page 106. For variety, use 2 or 3 different shapes and fillings. Deflate dough by rapping firmly with a rolling pin. Shape half of dough at a time; keep remaining dough refrigerated. After shaping, place pastries 2 inches apart on prepared baking sheets. Cover with plastic wrap; refrigerate at least 30 minutes. **Preheat oven** to 400F (205C). Brush pastries with egg glaze. If desired, sprinkle lightly with sugar. Bake 5 minutes. Reduce heat to 350F (175C). Bake 10 minutes longer or until golden brown. Cool on racks at least 5 minutes. Makes about 48 pastries.

Variation

Quick Danish Pastry: Prepare Quick Croissant dough, page 102, reducing salt to 1 teaspoon and adding 1/3 cup sugar, 1/4 teaspoon ground cardamom and 1 teaspoon vanilla extract. Roll and fold as directed above, to first refrigeration. Refrigerate 45 minutes only. Roll and fold 2 more times. Refrigerate 1-1/2 to 2 hours. Shape and fill as desired.

Danish-Pastry Fillings

Currant-Cheese Filling:

2 tablespoons currants
1 tablespoon rum
1 (8-oz.) pkg. cream cheese,
   room temperature
1/4 cup sugar

1 tablespoon all-purpose flour
Pinch of salt
1 egg yolk
1/2 teaspoon grated lemon peel
1/2 teaspoon vanilla extract

In a small bowl, combine currants and rum. Cover; set aside overnight or 3 to 4 hours to soak. In small bowl of electric mixer, beat cream cheese and sugar until light. Beat in flour, salt, egg yolk, lemon peel and vanilla until blended. Stir in currant mixture. Makes about 1 cup.

Crunchy-Almond Filling:

1 egg white
1/2 cup packed almond paste,
   room temperature

1/4 cup butter, room temperature
Pinch of salt
1/2 cup toasted finely chopped almonds

In small bowl of electric mixer, beat egg white until foamy. With mixer on low speed, add almond paste in small pieces. Increase speed to medium; beat until smooth. Beat in butter and salt. Fold in almonds. Makes about 1 cup.

Rum-Cream Filling:

3 tablespoons sugar
2 tablespoons cornstarch
1/4 teaspoon salt
3/4 cup half and half

1/4 cup light rum
2 egg yolks, slightly beaten
1 teaspoon vanilla extract

In top of a double boiler, combine sugar, cornstarch and salt. Slowly stir in half and half, rum and egg yolks. Stirring constantly, cook over simmering water until mixture thickens, about 10 minutes. Cook 5 minutes longer. Pour into a small bowl; stir in vanilla. Cool to room temperature. Makes about 1 cup.

Apricot or Prune Filling:

1 cup dried apricots or pitted prunes
1/2 cup apricot nectar or prune juice
1/2 cup orange- or almond-
   flavored liqueur

1/2 cup sugar
Pinch of salt
2 tablespoons butter, room temperature

In a medium saucepan, combine dried fruit, nectar or juice and liqueur. Cover; simmer over medium heat 20 to 25 minutes or until fruit is tender. Stir in sugar; cook 2 to 3 minutes longer or until sugar is dissolved. Stir in salt and butter. Let cool slightly. In a blender or food processor fitted with metal blade, process until mixture is smooth. Cool to room temperature. Makes about 1 cup.

Ground-Nut Filling:

1 egg
1/2 cup packed brown sugar
3/4 cup ground walnuts or pecans

1/2 teaspoon ground cinnamon
Pinch of salt

In a small bowl, lightly beat egg. Stir in brown sugar, ground nuts, cinnamon and salt until blended. Makes about 1 cup.

Danish-Pastry Shapes

Cockscombs:
Dust work surface with granulated sugar. Roll dough into a strip 9 inches wide and 1/8 inch thick. Spread a thin layer of filling over half of dough, lengthwise, to within 1/4 inch of edges. Fold dough lengthwise over top of filling, making a 4-1/2-inch strip. Gently pinch edges to seal. Cut crosswise into 2-1/2-inch strips. Make 4 cuts along 1 long side of each strip to within 1/2 inch of opposite edge. Place pastry strips 2 inches apart on buttered baking sheets, curving slightly to separate fingers of dough. *Suggested fillings:* Currant-Cheese, Ground-Nut or Apricot.

Danish Twists:
Dust work surface with granulated sugar. Roll out dough 10 inches wide and 1/8 inch thick. Cut dough in half crosswise. Spread a thin layer of filling over 1 piece of dough, to within 1/4 inch of edges. Place second piece of dough over filling; press together lightly. Cut filled dough in half lengthwise, making 2 (5-inch-wide) strips. Cut strips crosswise into 1/2-inch pieces. Lift pieces and carefully twist 3 or 4 times. Place 2 inches apart on buttered baking sheets. Brush pastries with egg glaze. Sprinkle finely chopped almonds or nuts used in Ground-Nut Filling over top. *Suggested fillings:* Crunchy-Almond or Ground-Nut.

Cream-Filled Rum Buns:
Dust work surface with granulated sugar. Roll out dough to an 18" x 12" rectangle, about 1/8 inch thick. Cut into 24 (3-inch) squares. Place 1 teaspoonful Rum-Cream Filling in center of each square. Bring all 4 corners to center; pinch slightly to seal. Corners will open during baking.

Fans, Baskets & Spectacles:
Dust work surface with granulated sugar. Roll out dough 10 inches wide and 1/8 inch thick. Spread a thin layer of Apricot Filling, Prune Filling or raspberry jam to within 1/4 inch of edges. Beginning on 1 long side, roll tightly, jelly-roll fashion. Cover; refrigerate 20 to 30 minutes to make slicing easier. **To make Fans:** Cut dough crosswise in 1-1/2-inch slices. Cutting from top of slice, use a sharp knife or scissors to make 2 cuts, 1/2 inch apart to within 1/4 inch of bottom. Lay flat on buttered baking sheet. Spread slices apart in fan shapes. **To make Baskets:** Cut as for fans. On a buttered baking sheet, lay 2 outside slices flat; leave center slice upright for handle. **To make Spectacles:** With a sharp knife, cut roll almost through, 1/2 inch from end. Move knife over 1/2 inch and cut roll all the way through. Repeat cutting until all dough is cut. On a buttered baking sheet, pull joined sections apart so they lay flat, like spectacles with strip of dough forming a bridge between 2 "eye glasses."

Freezing Croissants & Danish Pastries

• To freeze *unbaked* croissants and Danish pastries, place shaped dough on a large baking sheet. Freeze until firm. Wrap frozen dough airtight; store in freezer 2 to 3 weeks.
• To bake frozen unbaked croissants, place on unbuttered baking sheets. Let rise at room temperature until doubled in bulk, 2 to 2-1/2 hours. Bake in a preheated 400F (205C) oven, 15 to 20 minutes or until lightly browned.
• To bake frozen unbaked Danish pastries, place on lightly buttered baking sheets. Place frozen pastries in a preheated 425F (220C) oven. Bake 10 minutes or until golden brown.
• To freeze *baked* croissants and Danish pastries, cool, then wrap airtight. Store in freezer up to 4 months.
• To reheat, place frozen baked croissants or pastries on unbuttered baking sheets. Heat croissants in a preheated 400F (205C) oven, 5 to 8 minutes. Heat pastries in a preheated 350F (175C) oven, 5 to 10 minutes.

Little Quick Breads

"You've heard about the muffin man,
the muffin man, the muffin man,
You've heard about the muffin man
who lives in Drury Lane?
Well, here you see that muffin man,
that celebrated muffin man,
And if you try his muffins,
You're sure to buy again!"

So sang the English muffin man as he strolled the streets of London, balancing a basket of savory crumpets and buns on his head, and ringing a handbell to announce his coming.

Today's quick muffins are different than those sold on the streets of old England, but every bit as tender and fragrantly delicious. The basic rules for making little quick breads are the same as with big quick breads—work fast and with a light touch. Overmixing muffin batter will create coarse-textured muffins with pointed tops. Over-handling biscuit dough produces tough, dense biscuits. Turn baked muffins on their sides in the muffin pans for a couple of minutes to release steam before serving. Muffins and biscuits should be eaten hot with plenty of butter and jam. Any leftovers can be split and toasted the next day for a tasty encore.

When I was eight years old, my Grandfather Buck taught me how to make Easy Cream Biscuits. Now, if an eight-year-old and grandpa can make them, you *know* they're easy! No cutting together of butter and flour is necessary. Instead, whipping cream is stirred into the dry ingredients. The heavier the cream, the richer the biscuit. In lieu of the traditional round shape, we used to cut the dough into squares—big, for grandpa-size appetites—and dip them in melted butter before baking.

Any muffin can be made lighter by separating the eggs, beating the whites, and folding them in after the rest of the ingredients are combined. Open Sesames use this method, creating a light, fine-textured muffin, special enough to serve with your best entree.

Blueberry-Streusel Muffins

Blueberry-flavored yogurt enhances these tender muffins crowned with a yummy streusel topping.

Streusel Topping, see below
2 cups all-purpose flour
2 teaspoons baking powder
1/2 teaspoon baking soda
3/4 teaspoon salt
1/3 cup sugar
1/2 teaspoon ground cinnamon
1/4 teaspoon ground nutmeg

2 teaspoons freshly grated lemon peel
2 eggs, room temperature
1 (8-oz.) carton blueberry-flavored yogurt,
   room temperature
1/4 cup butter, melted
1/2 teaspoon vanilla extract
1-1/4 cups fresh or frozen blueberries,
   not thawed

Streusel Topping:
1/4 cup cold butter, cut in 4 pieces
1/4 cup sugar
3/4 cup all-purpose flour

1 teaspoon freshly grated lemon peel
1/2 teaspoon ground cinnamon

Prepare Streusel Topping; set aside. Grease 18 muffin cups or line with paper liners. Preheat oven to 400F (205C). In a large bowl, combine flour, baking powder, baking soda, salt, sugar, cinnamon, nutmeg and lemon peel; set aside. In a medium bowl, lightly beat eggs. Stir in yogurt, butter and vanilla. Stir into flour mixture only until dry ingredients are moistened. Fold in blueberries until evenly distributed. Spoon batter into prepared muffin cups until 1/2 full. Sprinkle top of each muffin with about 2 rounded teaspoons Streusel Topping. Bake 15 to 20 minutes or until a wooden pick inserted in center comes out clean. Serve hot. Makes 16 to 18 muffins.

Streusel Topping:
Combine all ingredients in a medium bowl. Use a pastry blender or 2 knives to cut in butter until mixture resembles coarse crumbs.

Variation
Lemon-Blueberry Muffins: Substitute lemon-flavored yogurt for blueberry-flavored yogurt. Increase lemon peel to 4 teaspoons.

Candied-Apple Muffins

Colorful muffins that invoke childhood memories of shiny red, candy-coated apples.

2 cups all-purpose flour
1 tablespoon baking powder
3/4 teaspoon salt
1/2 teaspoon ground cinnamon
1/3 cup sugar

2 eggs, room temperature
1 cup unsweetened applesauce
1/4 cup butter, melted
1/4 cup miniature cinnamon candies
   (red hots)

Grease 12 muffin cups or line with paper liners. Preheat oven to 400F (205C). In a large bowl, combine flour, baking powder, salt, cinnamon and sugar; set aside. In a medium bowl, lightly beat eggs. Stir in applesauce and butter. Stir into flour mixture only until dry ingredients are moistened. Add cinnamon candies; stir in quickly to prevent color from running. Spoon batter into prepared muffin cups until 2/3 to 3/4 full. Bake 25 to 30 minutes or until a wooden pick inserted in center comes out clean. Serve hot. Makes 10 to 12 muffins.

Lemon-Ambrosia Muffins

Lemon yogurt and shredded coconut combine to give these tender muffins a heavenly flavor.

Ambrosia Topping, see below
2 cups all-purpose flour
2 teaspoons baking powder
1/2 teaspoon baking soda
3/4 teaspoon salt
1/4 cup sugar
1/2 cup shredded coconut

1 tablespoon freshly grated lemon peel
2 eggs, room temperature
1 (8-oz.) carton lemon-flavored yogurt, room temperature
1 teaspoon vanilla extract
1/4 cup butter, melted

Ambrosia Topping:
1/4 cup shredded coconut
2 tablespoons finely chopped pecans or walnuts

2 tablespoons brown sugar
1/8 teaspoon ground nutmeg

Prepare Ambrosia Topping; set aside. Grease 12 muffin cups or line with paper liners. Preheat oven to 400F (205C). In a large bowl, combine flour, baking powder, baking soda, salt, sugar, coconut and lemon peel; set aside. In a medium bowl, lightly beat eggs. Stir in yogurt, vanilla and butter. Stir into flour mixture only until dry ingredients are moistened. Spoon batter into prepared muffin cups until 2/3 to 3/4 full. Sprinkle top of each muffin with a heaping teaspoon of Ambrosia Topping. Bake 25 to 30 minutes or until a wooden pick inserted in center comes out clean. Serve hot. Makes 10 to 12 muffins.

Ambrosia Topping:
Combine all ingredients in a small bowl.

Maple-Banana & Bran Muffins

This childhood favorite is wonderful with Maple Butter, page 48.

1-1/4 cups all-purpose flour
1 cup unprocessed bran flakes
2-1/2 teaspoons baking powder
1/2 teaspoon baking soda
3/4 teaspoon ground cinnamon
1/2 teaspoon salt

2 eggs, room temperature
1/3 cup pure maple syrup
1 cup pureed ripe banana
3 tablespoons butter, melted
3/4 cup chopped walnuts or pecans

Grease 12 muffin cups or line with paper liners. Preheat oven to 400F (205C). In a large bowl, combine flour, bran flakes, baking powder, baking soda, cinnamon and salt; set aside. In a medium bowl, lightly beat eggs. Stir in maple syrup, banana and butter. Stir into flour mixture only until dry ingredients are moistened. Stir in nuts. Spoon into prepared muffin cups until 2/3 to 3/4 full. Bake 12 to 18 minutes or until a wooden pick inserted in center comes out clean. Serve hot. Makes 10 to 12 muffins.

Open Sesames

No magic words necessary to create these light muffins—elegant enough for special dinners!

1/4 cup toasted sesame seeds	2 eggs, separated, room temperature
2 cups all-purpose flour	1/4 cup vegetable oil or
2 teaspoons baking powder	1 tablespoon sesame oil and
1/2 teaspoon baking soda	3 tablespoons vegetable oil
3/4 teaspoon salt	1 cup buttermilk, room temperature
2 tablespoons sugar	2 tablespoons sesame seeds for garnish
1/3 cup toasted sesame seeds	Honey Butter, page 46, or other spread

Generously grease 12 muffin cups. Do not use paper liners. Sprinkle 1 teaspoon toasted sesame seeds over bottom and side of each cup. Preheat oven to 400F (205C). In a large bowl, combine flour, baking powder, baking soda, salt, sugar and 1/3 cup sesame seeds; set aside. In a medium bowl, lightly beat egg yolks. Stir in oil and buttermilk. Stir into flour mixture only until dry ingredients are moistened; set aside. In small bowl of electric mixer, beat egg whites until stiff but not dry. Stir 2 to 3 tablespoons beaten egg whites into batter, then fold in remaining beaten egg whites. Spoon batter into prepared muffin cups until 2/3 to 3/4 full. Sprinkle remaining 2 tablespoons sesame seeds over tops of unbaked muffins. Bake 25 to 30 minutes or until a wooden pick inserted in center comes out clean. Serve hot with Honey Butter or another spread. Makes 10 to 12 muffins.

Hominy Honeys   Photo on page 114.

Old-fashioned corn muffins, fragrant with honey.

2 cups all-purpose flour	2 eggs, room temperature
1 tablespoon baking powder	1/4 cup butter, melted
1 teaspoon salt	1/4 cup honey
1 (15-oz.) can golden hominy	Honey Dip, see below
Milk, if needed	

Honey Dip:
1/2 cup honey
2 tablespoons butter

Grease 12 muffin cups or line with paper liners. Preheat oven to 400F (205C). In a large bowl, combine flour, baking powder and salt; set aside. Drain hominy, reserving 1/2 cup liquid. If necessary, add milk to make 1/2 cup. Reserve 12 hominy kernels for garnish. In a blender or food processor fitted with a metal blade, process 1 cup hominy until finely ground but not pureed. In a medium bowl, lightly beat eggs. Stir in reserved hominy liquid, ground hominy, butter and honey. Stir into flour mixture only until dry ingredients are moistened. Spoon batter into prepared muffin cups until 2/3 to 3/4 full. Lightly press 1 reserved hominy kernel in center of each unbaked muffin. Bake 25 to 30 minutes or until a wooden pick inserted in center comes out clean. Prepare Honey Dip. Remove baked muffins from muffin cups; dip tops in Honey Dip. Let stand 3 to 4 minutes before serving. Serve remaining Honey Dip with muffins. Makes 10 to 12 muffins.

Honey Dip:
In a small saucepan, stir honey and butter over medium heat only until butter is melted and mixture is blended. Pour into a small bowl.

How to Make Praline-Rum Rolls

1/Stand 2 slices, side by side on edge, in each muffin cup. Gently spread slices apart.

2/Spoon 1 teaspoon reserved brown-sugar mixture in center of each roll. Top each with a pecan half.

Praline-Rum Rolls

Elegant rum-glazed treats flavored by a rich praline spiral.

Easy Cream Biscuit dough, page 113,
**   made with 1/2 teaspoon salt**
1/4 cup butter, room temperature
2/3 cup packed brown sugar

1/3 cup finely chopped pecans
1 teaspoon ground cinnamon
12 pecan halves
Rum Glaze, see below

Rum Glaze:
1 cup powdered sugar
2 teaspoons rum or
**   1/4 teaspoon rum extract plus**
**   1-3/4 teaspoons milk**

2 to 4 teaspoons milk

Grease 12 muffin cups. Do not use paper liners. Preheat oven to 425F (220C). Prepare Easy Cream Biscuit dough. Turn out dough onto a lightly floured surface. Gently knead 10 to 12 strokes. Roll out dough to an 18" x 12" rectangle. Spread with butter. In a small bowl, combine brown sugar, chopped pecans and cinnamon; reserve 1/4 cup for topping. Sprinkle remaining mixture evenly over buttered dough. Beginning on a long side, roll up tightly, jelly-roll fashion. Pinch seam to seal. Cut roll into 24 slices, 3/4 inch wide. Stand 2 slices, side by side and on edge, in each muffin cup. Gently spread slices apart. Spoon 1 teaspoon reserved brown-sugar mixture in center of each roll. Top each with a pecan half, pressing down lightly. Bake 15 to 20 minutes or until golden brown. Prepare Rum Glaze. Remove rolls from muffin cups; place on a rack over waxed paper. Drizzle with Rum Glaze. Let stand 5 minutes before serving. Makes 12 rolls.

Rum Glaze:
In a small bowl, combine powdered sugar, rum or rum extract and enough milk to make a smooth, creamy glaze of drizzling consistency.

Popovers

Eggs and steam make popovers "pop." Serve hot with plenty of butter and jam!

1 cup all-purpose flour	**1 cup milk, room temperature**
1/4 teaspoon salt	**2 eggs, room temperature**
2 teaspoons sugar	**1 tablespoon vegetable oil**

Generously butter 8 (5- to 6-ounce) custard cups, 10 muffin cups or 12 popover cups. Place custard cups on a heavy baking sheet. Place muffin cups, popover cups or baking sheet with custard cups on center rack of oven. Preheat oven to 450F (230C). Combine all ingredients in a blender, food processor or small bowl of electric mixer. Blend until batter is smooth, scraping sides of container as necessary. Remove hot baking cups from oven; spoon in batter until 2/3 full. Immediately return filled cups to oven. Bake 20 minutes. Reduce heat to 350F (175C). Bake 20 to 25 minutes longer or until browned. Run a knife around edge of baking cups to loosen popovers. Remove from cups. Serve hot. Makes 8 to 12 popovers.

Note: After batter is prepared, it can be stored at room temperature 2 to 3 hours before baking. Keep oven door closed during first 30 minutes of baking. A draft will collapse popovers. Popovers have a moist interior. For a drier popover, remove baked popovers from oven. Prick in several places with tip of a knife. Return to turned-off oven. With door ajar, let stand 5 to 10 minutes.

Variations

Parmesan Popovers: Add 1/2 cup (1-1/2 ounces) grated Parmesan cheese or 3/4 cup (3 ounces) shredded Cheddar cheese. Add 1/4 teaspoon pepper.
Wheaty Popovers: Substitute 1/2 cup whole-wheat flour for 1/2 cup all-purpose flour. Substitute 1 tablespoon brown sugar for 2 teaspoons granulated sugar. Add 2 tablespoons wheat germ.
Maple-Pecan Popovers: Substitute 1/4 cup pure maple syrup for 1/4 cup milk. Add 1/4 teaspoon ground cinnamon and 3 tablespoons minced pecans.
Sunshine Popovers: Substitute 1/2 cup orange juice for 1/2 cup milk. Add 1/4 teaspoon ground nutmeg and 1 tablespoon freshly grated orange peel.

Ham & Cheese Drop Biscuits

Using a prepared spread makes these savory bites quick and delicious!

1-3/4 cups all-purpose flour	**1/4 cup cold bacon grease or butter**
1 tablespoon baking powder	**1/2 cup shredded Cheddar cheese (2 oz.)**
1/2 teaspoon salt	**1 (4-1/2-oz.) can deviled-ham spread**
2 teaspoons sugar	**Milk**

Grease 2 large baking sheets. Preheat oven to 450F (230C). In a large bowl, combine flour, baking powder, salt and sugar. Use a pastry blender or 2 knives to cut in bacon grease or butter until mixture resembles coarse crumbs. Add cheese, tossing until coated with flour mixture; set aside. Spoon deviled ham into a 1-cup liquid measure. Gradually stir in milk to make 1 cup; blend well. Stir into flour mixture only until dry ingredients are moistened. Drop by heaping tablespoons, 2 inches apart on prepared baking sheets. Bake 12 to 15 minutes or until golden brown. Makes about 18 biscuits.

Easy Cream Biscuits

Whipping cream takes the place of butter and milk in these quick and delicious biscuits.

2 cups all-purpose flour
4 teaspoons baking powder
2 teaspoons sugar

1 teaspoon salt
3/4 to 1 cup whipping cream,
    room temperature

Preheat oven to 425F (220C). In a large bowl, combine flour, baking powder, sugar and salt. Stir in enough cream to make a soft dough. Turn out onto a lightly floured surface. Gently knead 12 to 15 strokes until dough holds together. Pat or roll out dough until 1/2 inch thick. Cut dough with a round 2-inch cutter or, cut in 2-inch squares. Arrange biscuits 2 inches apart on 1 or 2 ungreased large baking sheets. Bake 15 to 18 minutes or until golden brown. Serve hot. Makes about 12 biscuits.

Variations

Butter Biscuits: Melt 1/4 to 1/3 cup butter. Dip each biscuit in melted butter before baking.
Whole-Wheat Biscuits: Substitute 1 cup whole-wheat flour for 1 cup all-purpose flour. Add 2 tablespoons wheat germ to dry ingredients.
Herbed Cheese Biscuits: Add 1/2 teaspoon each of crumbled dried leaf oregano and basil and 3/4 cup (3 ounces) shredded Cheddar cheese to dry ingredients.
Seeded Biscuits: Add 1 tablespoon poppy seeds or toasted sesame seeds or, 1-1/2 to 2 teaspoons caraway seeds to dry ingredients.
Onion Biscuits: Add 3 tablespoons finely chopped onion to dry ingredients.
Raisin-Nut Biscuits: Increase sugar to 2 tablespoons. Add 1/2 teaspoon ground cinnamon, 1/3 cup raisins and 1/3 cup chopped walnuts to dry ingredients.
Rye Biscuits: Substitute 2/3 cup rye flour for 2/3 cup all-purpose flour. Add 2 teaspoons caraway seeds to dry ingredients.
Sunflower-Seed Biscuits: Add 1/3 cup toasted raw hulled sunflower seeds to dry ingredients.

Crunchy Onion Sticks

Serve these crisp breadsticks as an appetizer or with soup.

Easy Cream Biscuit dough, above
2 eggs, room temperature
2 tablespoons butter, melted

1 tablespoon all-purpose flour
2 (3-oz.) cans French-fried onions, crushed

Grease 2 large baking sheets. Preheat oven to 375F (190C). Prepare Easy Cream Biscuit dough; set aside. In a medium bowl, beat eggs, butter and flour until combined; set aside. Place crushed onions on a large plate; set aside. On a lightly floured surface, roll out biscuit dough to a 15" x 6" rectangle. Cut crosswise into 30 (1/2-inch) strips. Dip strips into egg mixture; roll in crushed onions. Holding each strip at both ends, twist in opposite directions, twice, making a spiral. Arrange spirals 1-1/2 inches apart on prepared baking sheets. Press ends onto baking sheets to secure. Bake 20 to 25 minutes or until golden brown and crisp. Serve warm or at room temperature. Makes 30 breadsticks.

Sherried Tea Biscuits

Buttery little biscuits scented with sherry—perfect with tea or coffee!

1-1/2 cups all-purpose flour
1 tablespoon baking powder
1/2 teaspoon salt
1 tablespoon sugar
1/2 cup cold butter, cut in 8 pieces

1/3 cup plus 1 to 2 tablespoons dry sherry
1/3 cup currants
1 tablespoon melted butter blended with
   1 teaspoon sherry and
   1 teaspoon sugar for glaze

Preheat oven to 400F (205C). In a large bowl, combine flour, baking powder, salt and 1 tablespoon sugar. Use a pastry blender or 2 knives to cut in 1/2 cup butter until mixture resembles coarse crumbs. Add 1/3 cup sherry and currants. Stir only until dough holds together. If necessary, stir in remaining 1 to 2 tablespoons sherry, 1 teaspoon at a time, until dough holds together. Turn out onto a lightly floured surface. Gently knead 12 to 15 strokes. Pat or roll out dough until 1/2 inch thick. Cut dough with a round 1-1/2- or 2-inch cutter. Place cut dough 1-1/2 inches apart on ungreased baking sheets. Brush with sherry glaze. Bake 6 to 8 minutes or until lightly browned. Makes about 26 biscuits.

Italian Cheese Crescents

Ricotta cheese and toasted almonds give these tiny treats a melt-in-your-mouth flavor.

2-1/2 cups all-purpose flour
2 teaspoons baking powder
1/2 teaspoon salt
1/3 cup granulated sugar
1 (8-oz.) carton ricotta cheese (1 cup),
   room temperature
1 cup butter, room temperature
1 teaspoon freshly grated lemon peel

1/2 teaspoon almond extract
3/4 cup packed brown sugar
3/4 cup toasted finely chopped almonds
1/2 teaspoon ground cinnamon
1/4 cup butter, melted
1 egg blended with
   1 tablespoon granulated sugar for glaze

Grease 2 or 3 large baking sheets. In a medium bowl, combine flour, baking powder, salt and 1/3 cup granulated sugar; set aside. In large bowl of electric mixer, beat ricotta cheese, 1 cup butter, lemon peel and almond extract until smooth and creamy. Fold in flour mixture in 3 parts, blending only until dry ingredients are moistened. Turn out onto a lightly floured surface. Using a pastry scraper or metal spatula, gently knead dough 10 to 12 strokes. Dough will be moist. Divide dough into 3 pieces. Place on a large plate; cover and refrigerate 20 minutes. Preheat oven to 400F (205C). In a small bowl, combine brown sugar, almonds and cinnamon; set aside. Remove 1 piece of dough from refrigerator. On a lightly floured surface, roll or pat into a 13-inch circle, about 1/8 inch thick. Brush with about one-third of melted butter. Sprinkle one-third of cinnamon-nut mixture over top. Press lightly into surface. Cut circle into 16 pie-shaped pieces. Roll each piece from outer edge to point. Place on prepared baking sheets with points down. Curve ends slightly to make crescents. Brush with egg glaze. Repeat with remaining refrigerated dough. Bake 15 to 20 minutes or until golden brown. Serve hot. Makes 48 rolls.

Clockwise from top left: Sherried Tea Biscuits, above; Italian Cheese Crescents, above; Hominy Honeys, page 110; and Orange-Pecan Spirals, page 117.

How to Make Orange-Pecan Spirals

1/Spread rolled-out dough with marmalade; sprinkle with 1/3 cup pecans. Fold dough in half lengthwise.

2/Cut crosswise into 15 (1-inch) strips. Holding each strip at both ends, twist in opposite directions twice.

Scandinavian Brittlebread

Break off pieces of this crunchy, beer-flavored cracker to serve with your favorite spread.

1-1/2 cups all-purpose flour	**3 tablespoons brown sugar**
1 cup medium rye flour	**2 teaspoons caraway seeds**
1 teaspoon baking powder	**1/4 cup cold butter, cut in 4 pieces**
1 teaspoon salt	**1/2 cup warm, flat dark beer (110F, 45C)**

Grease 3 baking sheets. Preheat oven to 325F (165C). In a large bowl, combine all-purpose flour, rye flour, baking powder, salt, brown sugar and caraway seeds. Use a pastry blender or 2 knives to cut in butter until mixture resembles coarse crumbs. Stir in beer only until dough holds together. Turn out onto a lightly floured surface. Gently knead 10 to 12 strokes. Divide dough into 6 pieces; shape each piece into a ball. Roll out each ball to an 8-inch circle. Use your index finger to make a 1-inch hole in center of each circle. Roll again with a rolling pin to flatten edges of hole. Place 2 rounds on each baking sheet. Prick entire surface of each round with a fork. Bake 15 minutes. Turn breads over; bake 7 to 9 minutes longer or until lightly browned. Cool on racks. Bread will become crisp as it cools. Makes 6 large crackers.

Orange-Pecan Spirals   Photo on page 114.

Easy pastries filled with orange marmalade and pecans—great hot or at room temperature!

2 cups all-purpose flour	1/2 cup whipping cream, room temperature
1 tablespoon baking powder	1/3 cup orange marmalade, room temperature
1/2 teaspoon salt	1/3 cup finely chopped pecans
1/4 cup sugar	Cinnamon-Orange Glaze, see below
1/2 cup cold butter, cut in 8 pieces	1/4 cup minced pecans for garnish,
1 egg, room temperature	if desired

Cinnamon-Orange Glaze:

1 cup powdered sugar	2 to 4 tablespoons orange juice
1/2 teaspoon ground cinnamon	

Lightly grease 2 baking sheets. Preheat oven to 450F (230C). In a large bowl, combine flour, baking powder, salt and sugar. Use a pastry blender or 2 knives to cut in butter until mixture resembles coarse crumbs; set aside. In a medium bowl, lightly beat egg and cream until blended. Stir into flour mixture only until dough holds together. Turn out onto a lightly floured surface. Gently knead 10 to 12 strokes. Roll out dough to a 15" x 8" rectangle. Spread with marmalade; sprinkle with 1/3 cup pecans. Fold dough in half lengthwise, making a 15" x 4" rectangle. Cut crosswise into 15 (1-inch) strips. Holding each strip at both ends, twist in opposite directions, twice, making a spiral. Arrange spirals 2 inches apart on prepared baking sheets. Press ends onto baking sheets to secure. Bake 10 to 12 minutes or until golden brown. Place twists on racks over waxed paper. Drizzle with Cinnamon-Orange Glaze. If desired, sprinkle with minced pecans. Let stand 3 to 4 minutes before serving. Spirals become crisp as they cool. Makes 15 spirals.

Cinnamon-Orange Glaze:
In a small bowl, combine powdered sugar and cinnamon. Stir in enough orange juice to make a smooth, creamy glaze of drizzling consistency.

Toasted-Oat Crisps

Crispy, rich bites that are perfect with salads and soups or as hors d'oeuvres!

1-1/2 cups regular or quick-cooking rolled oats	1 tablespoon sugar
1/2 cup all-purpose flour	5 tablespoons cold butter, cut in 5 pieces
1/2 teaspoon baking powder	2 to 3 tablespoons cold water
1 teaspoon salt	2 tablespoons butter, melted

Preheat oven to 375F (190C). In a blender or food processor fitted with a metal blade, process oats until finely ground. In a large bowl, combine ground oats, flour, baking powder, salt and sugar. Use a pastry blender or 2 knives to cut in 5 tablespoons butter until mixture resembles coarse crumbs. Stir in enough water so mixture holds together. Turn out onto a lightly floured surface. Knead 15 to 20 strokes or until dough is no longer sticky. Roll out dough until 1/8 inch thick. Cut dough with a round 2-inch cutter. Use a metal spatula to lift and place cut dough 1-1/2 inches apart on ungreased baking sheets. Flatten slightly with a rolling pin or palm of your hand. Prick all surfaces with a fork or, imprint with a patterned meat mallet to create surface indentations. Brush lightly with melted butter. Bake 10 to 15 minutes or until golden brown. Cool on racks. Makes about 48 crackers.

Savory Quick Breads

Of all the bread classes I teach, the quick-breads series is one of the most popular with my beginning students. Discovering that they can actually create delicious homemade bread in about an hour from start to finish, amazes and delights them. It also bolsters confidence to move on to higher-rising aspirations.

Quick breads blossom to mouth-watering tenderness without the aid of yeast. They're referred to as *quick* because you don't have to knead them or wait for them to rise. Baking powder and baking soda are the magic ingredients; the magic words are *easy* and *delicious!*

The key to success with quick breads is gentle but speedy handling. When combined with a liquid, baking soda and baking powder release carbon dioxide, giving an almost "instant-rise" power. Oven heat gives double-acting baking powder a second burst of energy. Because of this quick-rising action, make sure your pans are greased and the oven preheated before you begin mixing. Have ingredients at room temperature to get a good gas expansion, ensuring light and tender breads. Stir *only* until the dry ingredients are moistened. Vigorous beating or stirring will stretch the gluten and dissipate the carbon dioxide, producing a tough, heavy loaf.

Few quick breads flood my taste-memories with warmth more than Irish Soda Bread. On the coldest of school days, my Irish grandmother would have this wonderful bread-cake ready when I came through her back door, stomping the snow off my boots. With a leprechaun twinkle in her eye, she would warm my little hands between hers and then seat me at the huge kitchen table. The bread, rustic and brown with a rough-hewn cross cut in the top—to scare away the devil—was placed on an old wooden bread plate. Then we would tear chunks off the still-warm loaf. Sitting there together in that great warm kitchen, we'd eat and talk, my legs swinging happily under the chair to the rhythm of the moment.

Honey-Bran Bread

Moist and flavorful—lightly scented with honey.

2 tablespoons whole-bran cold cereal
1-3/4 cups all-purpose flour
1-1/2 cups whole-bran cold cereal
2 teaspoons baking powder
1/2 teaspoon baking soda
1/2 teaspoon salt

2 eggs, room temperature
1/3 cup butter, melted
2 tablespoons honey
1 cup buttermilk, room temperature
1 tablespoon whole-bran cold cereal

Generously grease an 8" x 4" loaf pan. Sprinkle 2 tablespoons whole-bran cereal over bottom and sides; set aside. Preheat oven to 350F (175C). In a large bowl, combine flour, 1-1/2 cups whole-bran cereal, baking powder, baking soda and salt; set aside. In a medium bowl, lightly beat eggs. Stir in butter, honey and buttermilk. Stir into flour mixture only until dry ingredients are moistened. Turn into prepared pan. Smooth top; sprinkle with 1 tablespoon whole-bran cereal. Bake 45 to 50 minutes or until a wooden pick inserted in center comes out clean. Let stand in pan 10 minutes. Turn out onto a rack to cool. Makes 1 loaf.

Bran Brown Bread

A wonderfully wholesome bread for snacks or breakfast.

1 cup all-purpose flour
1/2 cup whole-wheat flour
1/2 cup medium rye flour
1 cup unprocessed bran flakes
2 teaspoons baking powder
1 teaspoon baking soda
1 teaspoon salt

1/2 teaspoon ground nutmeg
1 teaspoon grated orange peel
3 tablespoons butter, melted
1/3 cup molasses
1 cup orange juice
1 cup raisins, if desired

Grease an 8" x 4" loaf pan; set aside. Preheat oven to 350F (175C). In a large bowl, combine all-purpose flour, whole-wheat flour, rye flour, bran flakes, baking powder, baking soda, salt, nutmeg and orange peel; set aside. In a medium bowl, combine butter, molasses, orange juice and raisins, if desired. Stir into flour mixture only until dry ingredients are moistened. Turn into prepared pan; smooth top. Bake 55 to 65 minutes or until a wooden pick inserted in center comes out clean. Let stand in pan 10 minutes. Turn out onto a rack to cool. Makes 1 loaf.

Tip *Breads made with honey and molasses brown more quickly than breads made with other sugars.*

How to Make Zucchini-Cheese Bread

1/Combine cheese and shredded zucchini with dry ingredients.

2/Quick bread is done when a wooden pick inserted in center comes out clean.

Zucchini-Cheese Bread

Moist and delicious—serve with a Mexican or Italian dinner.

2 cups all-purpose flour	1 tablespoon sugar
2 teaspoons baking powder	3/4 cup shredded Cheddar cheese (3 oz.)
1/2 teaspoon baking soda	3/4 cup shredded unpeeled zucchini
3/4 teaspoon salt	2 eggs
1/8 teaspoon red (cayenne) pepper	1/2 cup pureed unpeeled zucchini
1/4 teaspoon dried leaf oregano, crushed	1/4 cup vegetable oil
1/4 teaspoon dried leaf basil, crushed	1 tablespoon lemon juice
1/2 teaspoon dried minced onion	

Grease and flour an 8" x 4" loaf pan; set aside. Preheat oven to 350F (175C). In a large bowl, combine flour, baking powder, baking soda, salt, red pepper, oregano, basil, onion, sugar, cheese and 3/4 cup shredded zucchini; set aside. In a medium bowl, lightly beat eggs. Stir in 1/2 cup pureed zucchini, oil and lemon juice. Stir into flour mixture only until dry ingredients are moistened. Turn into prepared pan; smooth top. Bake 45 to 50 minutes or until a wooden pick inserted in center comes out clean. Let stand in pan 10 minutes. Turn out onto a rack to cool. Makes 1 loaf.

Poppy-Parmesan Bread

Great with soups and salads—wonderful for grilled cheese sandwiches!

2 teaspoons poppy seeds
2 cups all-purpose flour
2 teaspoons baking powder
1/2 teaspoon baking soda
3/4 teaspoon salt
1 cup grated Parmesan cheese (3 oz.)

1-1/2 tablespoons poppy seeds
1 egg, room temperature
1 tablespoon vegetable oil
1 cup buttermilk, room temperature
1 teaspoon poppy seeds

Grease and flour an 8'' x 4'' loaf pan or 1-1/2-quart casserole dish. Sprinkle 2 teaspoons poppy seeds over bottom and sides of pan; set aside. Preheat oven to 350F (175C). In a large bowl, combine flour, baking powder, baking soda, salt, cheese and 1-1/2 tablespoons poppy seeds; set aside. In a medium bowl, lightly beat egg. Stir in oil and buttermilk. Stir into flour mixture only until dry ingredients are moistened. Turn into prepared pan. Smooth top; sprinkle with 1 teaspoon poppy seeds. Bake 45 to 50 minutes or until a wooden pick inserted in center comes out clean. Let stand in pan 10 minutes. Turn out onto a rack to cool. Makes 1 loaf.

Variation
Poppy-Cheddar Bread: Substitute 1 cup (4 ounces) shredded Cheddar cheese for Parmesan cheese.

Pepperoni-Pizza Bread

Pizza-flavored snack bread to serve with soup for a hearty winter meal.

1 tablespoon yellow cornmeal
2 cups all-purpose flour
2 teaspoons baking powder
1/2 teaspoon baking soda
1/4 teaspoon dried leaf basil, crushed
1/4 teaspoon dried leaf oregano, crushed
1 cup shredded provolone cheese (4 oz.)
3/4 cup grated Parmesan cheese (2-1/4 oz.)

1 cup finely chopped pepperoni or
   Italian salami (about 4 oz.)
2 eggs, room temperature
1 (8-oz.) can tomato sauce
2 tablespoons olive oil or vegetable oil
1 medium garlic clove, minced, or
   1/8 teaspoon garlic powder
9 slices pepperoni, 1/8 inch thick

Generously grease an 8- or 9-inch square baking pan. Sprinkle 1 tablespoon cornmeal over bottom of pan; set aside. Preheat oven to 375F (190C). In a large bowl, combine flour, baking powder, baking soda, basil and oregano; set aside. In a small bowl, combine provolone and Parmesan cheeses. Reserve 1 cup for topping. Toss remaining cheese mixture and 1 cup pepperoni or salami with dry ingredients; set aside. In a medium bowl, lightly beat eggs. Stir in tomato sauce, oil and garlic. Stir into flour mixture only until dry ingredients are moistened. Turn into prepared pan. Smooth top; sprinkle with reserved cheese mixture. Arrange pepperoni slices in 3 rows over top of batter. Lightly press into surface of batter. Bake 35 to 40 minutes or until a wooden pick inserted in center comes out clean. Let stand in pan 15 minutes. Cut and serve hot. Or, turn out onto a rack to cool. Refrigerate leftovers. Makes 9 to 16 servings.

Nutty Double-Cheese Bread

Makes wonderful oven toast to serve with soup.

2 cups all-purpose flour
1 tablespoon baking powder
1 teaspoon salt
2 tablespoons sugar
1 cup shredded Cheddar cheese (4 oz.)
3 eggs, room temperature
1/3 cup milk, room temperature

3/4 cup cottage cheese (6 oz.),
  room temperature
2 tablespoons walnut oil or vegetable oil
1 tablespoon finely chopped onion or
  1 teaspoon dried minced onion
3/4 cup finely chopped walnuts

Grease and flour a 9" x 5" loaf pan or a 2-quart casserole dish; set aside. Preheat oven to 350F (175C). In a large bowl, combine flour, baking powder, salt, sugar and Cheddar cheese; set aside. In a medium bowl, lightly beat eggs. Stir in milk, cottage cheese, oil and onion. Stir into flour mixture only until dry ingredients are moistened. Stir in nuts. Turn into prepared pan; smooth top. Bake 55 to 65 minutes or until a wooden pick inserted in the center comes out clean. Let stand in pan 10 minutes. Turn out onto a rack to cool. Makes 1 loaf.

Pull-Apart Cheese Ring

Guests can pull off their own helpings of this fragrant wine-and-cheese bread.

2 tablespoons cheese-cracker crumbs or
  dry breadcrumbs
2 cups all-purpose flour
1 tablespoon baking powder
1 teaspoon salt
1/2 teaspoon dry mustard
Dash of red (cayenne) pepper

1 cup shredded Cheddar cheese (4 oz.)
1/3 cup dry white wine, room temperature
1/3 cup vegetable oil
1/3 cup milk, room temperature
6 tablespoons butter, melted
1 cup grated Parmesan cheese (3 oz.)

Generously grease an 8-inch tube pan or ring mold. Sprinkle crumbs over bottom and side of pan; set aside. Preheat oven to 400F (205C). In a large bowl, combine flour, baking powder, salt, mustard, red pepper and Cheddar cheese; set aside. In a 1-cup measure, combine wine, oil and milk. Stir into dry ingredients only until mixture no longer sticks to bowl. Shape dough into 26 (1-inch) balls. Dip balls in melted butter; roll in Parmesan cheese. Arrange in 2 layers in prepared pan. Drizzle with remaining butter; sprinkle with remaining Parmesan cheese. Bake 25 to 30 minutes or until a wooden pick inserted in center comes out clean. Let stand in pan 10 minutes. Turn out onto a serving dish. Serve warm. Makes 1 loaf.

Tip *Your bread will only be as good as the ingredients that go into it. Be sure to use full-flavored wines and beers when called for. Never substitute so-called cooking wines or light beers.*

How to Make Olive-Cheese Bread

1/Spoon half of batter into prepared pan. Arrange 28 olives, on their sides, on top of batter. Cover with remaining batter.

2/Place 6 olives, pimiento-end up, down center of batter. When baked loaf is cut, olives are exposed.

Olive-Cheese Bread

A surprise layer of pimiento-stuffed olives hides inside this cheese-flecked loaf!

2 cups all-purpose flour
2 teaspoons baking powder
1/2 teaspoon baking soda
1/4 teaspoon salt
1 tablespoon sugar
1 cup shredded Cheddar cheese (4 oz.)
1 egg, room temperature

1/4 cup vegetable oil
3/4 cup buttermilk
1 tablespoon finely chopped onion or
   3/4 teaspoon dried minced onion
34 pimiento-stuffed green olives
1-1/2 teaspoons olive oil

Grease an 8'' x 4'' loaf pan; set aside. Preheat oven to 350F (175C). In a large bowl, combine flour, baking powder, baking soda, salt, sugar and cheese; set aside. In a medium bowl, lightly beat egg. Stir in oil, buttermilk and onion. Stir into flour mixture only until dry ingredients are moistened. Spoon half of batter into prepared pan. Arrange 28 olives on their sides on top of batter, making 4 rows of 7 olives each. Cover with remaining batter; smooth top. Place 6 olives, pimiento-end up, evenly spaced down center of batter. Brush top with olive oil. Bake 35 to 45 minutes or until a wooden pick inserted in center comes out clean. Let stand in pan 10 minutes. Turn out onto a rack to cool. Makes 1 loaf.

Mexican-Cornbread Ring

Serve this moist, spicy and colorful bread with a crock of Cheddar Butter, page 85. Olé!

1-1/4 cups all-purpose flour
1-1/4 cups yellow cornmeal
1 tablespoon baking powder
1 teaspoon salt
1 tablespoon sugar
1/2 teaspoon dried leaf oregano, crushed, or
   1 teaspoon minced fresh oregano
2 cups shredded Cheddar cheese (8 oz.)
1 (1-lb.) can whole-kernel corn

Milk
3 eggs, room temperature
1/3 cup vegetable oil
1/3 cup finely chopped green onions with tops
1 (4-oz.) can diced green chilies or
   2 to 3 tablespoons jalapeño chilies
1 (4-oz.) jar diced pimientos, well drained
1/3 cup shredded Cheddar cheese
   (about 1-1/2 oz.)

Grease a 9-inch springform pan with center tube, an 8- to 10-cup ring mold or a 13'' x 9'' baking pan; set aside. Preheat oven to 400F (205C). In a large bowl, combine flour, cornmeal, baking powder, salt, sugar, oregano and 2 cups Cheddar cheese; set aside. Drain liquid from corn into a 1-cup liquid measure. If necessary, add milk to make 1 cup liquid; set corn and liquid aside. In a medium bowl, lightly beat eggs. Stir in reserved corn liquid, oil, onions, chilies and pimientos. Stir into flour mixture only until dry ingredients are moistened. Turn into prepared pan. Smooth top; sprinkle with 1/3 cup Cheddar cheese. Bake 35 to 45 minutes or until a wooden pick inserted in center comes out clean. Baked bread will be moist, but no particles will cling to pick. Let stand in pan 15 minutes. Carefully turn out onto a rack, then immediately turn top-side up on a serving plate to cool. Handle gently to avoid breaking. Makes 1 loaf.

Nutty Pumpkin Cornbread

Spicy but not sweet, this cornbread is wonderful with hearty soups.

1 tablespoon yellow cornmeal
1 cup all-purpose flour
1/2 cup yellow cornmeal
1 teaspoon baking powder
1/2 teaspoon baking soda
3/4 teaspoon salt
1/4 teaspoon ground cinnamon
1/4 teaspoon ground nutmeg
1/4 teaspoon ground allspice

2 eggs, room temperature
1 cup mashed cooked pumpkin or
   canned pumpkin
1/4 cup butter, melted
3 tablespoons molasses
1/2 cup buttermilk
1/2 cup chopped walnuts
1 tablespoon finely chopped walnuts

Grease an 8-inch square baking pan. Sprinkle 1 tablespoon cornmeal over bottom and sides of pan; set aside. Preheat oven to 375F (190C). In a large bowl, combine flour, 1/2 cup cornmeal, baking powder, baking soda, salt, cinnamon, nutmeg and allspice; set aside. In a medium bowl, lightly beat eggs. Stir in pumpkin, butter, molasses and buttermilk. Stir into flour mixture only until dry ingredients are moistened. Stir in nuts until evenly distributed. Turn into prepared pan. Smooth top; sprinkle with 1 tablespoon nuts. Bake 30 to 35 minutes or until a wooden pick inserted in center comes out clean. Let stand in pan 10 minutes. Cut into squares; remove from pan. Makes 16 servings.

Traditional Cornbread

Preheating the baking pan gives this tender buttermilk cornbread a crisper crust!

1 tablespoon vegetable oil or
  bacon or meat drippings
1/2 cup all-purpose flour
1-1/2 cups yellow cornmeal
2 teaspoons baking powder
1/2 teaspoon baking soda

1 teaspoon salt
2 tablespoons sugar
2 eggs, room temperature
1 cup buttermilk, room temperature
1/4 cup vegetable oil or bacon grease or
  meat drippings

Grease an 8- or 9-inch square baking pan. Pour in 1 tablespoon oil or drippings. Spread over bottom and sides of pan. Place pan in oven; preheat oven to 400F (205C). In a large bowl, combine flour, cornmeal, baking powder, baking soda, salt and sugar; set aside. In a medium bowl, lightly beat eggs. Stir in buttermilk and 1/4 cup oil or drippings. Stir into flour mixture only until dry ingredients are moistened. Remove baking pan from oven. Turn batter into preheated pan. Bake 20 to 30 minutes or until a wooden pick inserted in center comes out clean. Let stand in pan 10 minutes. Cut in squares; serve warm. Makes 9 to 12 servings.

Variations

Sweet Cornbread: Add 2 tablespoons sugar and 1/4 teaspoon ground nutmeg to dry ingredients.
Peanut-Butter & Sausage Cornbread: In a small saucepan, melt 3 tablespoons peanut butter over medium heat. Stir into liquid mixture. After stirring liquid mixture into dry ingredients, add 1/2 pound cooked, crumbled sausage or bacon.
Cheesy Sunflower Cornbread: Add 1 cup (4 ounces) shredded sharp Cheddar cheese and 3/4 cup toasted hulled raw sunflower seeds to dry ingredients. Sprinkle 1/3 cup (about 1-1/2 ounces) shredded Cheddar cheese and 2 tablespoons hulled sunflower seeds over top before baking.
Herbed Cornbread: To dry ingredients, add 1/2 teaspoon rubbed sage, 1/2 teaspoon dried leaf tarragon, 1/2 teaspoon dried leaf basil, 1/4 teaspoon crushed dried rosemary and 1/4 teaspoon ground black pepper.

Sunflower-Wheat Loaf

Raw hulled sunflower seeds are available at health-food stores and many supermarkets.

1 cup all-purpose flour
1 cup whole-wheat flour
1/2 cup wheat germ
1 tablespoon baking powder
1 teaspoon salt
1-1/2 tablespoons poppy seeds
1 egg, room temperature

2 tablespoons vegetable oil
2 tablespoons honey
1 cup milk, room temperature
1 cup toasted raw hulled sunflower seeds
2 teaspoons raw hulled sunflower seeds for
  topping

Grease an 8" x 4" loaf pan; set aside. Preheat oven to 350F (175C). In a large bowl, combine all-purpose flour, whole-wheat flour, wheat germ, baking powder, salt and poppy seeds; set aside. In a medium bowl, lightly beat egg. Stir in oil, honey and milk. Stir into flour mixture only until dry ingredients are moistened. Stir in 1 cup sunflower seeds until evenly distributed. Turn into prepared pan. Smooth top; sprinkle with 2 teaspoons sunflower seeds. Bake 60 to 70 minutes or until a wooden pick inserted in center comes out clean. Let stand in pan 10 minutes. Turn out onto a rack to cool. Makes 1 loaf.

Irish Soda Bread

My Irish grandmother added whiskey, honey and orange peel for a true leprechaun's delight!

4 cups all-purpose flour	1 cup currants
1 tablespoon baking powder	1/4 cup honey
1 teaspoon baking soda	1-1/2 cups buttermilk, room temperature
1 teaspoon salt	1/4 cup Irish whiskey or buttermilk
2 teaspoons grated orange peel	1/2 tablespoon milk blended with
2 teaspoons caraway seeds, if desired	1/2 tablespoon Irish whiskey for glaze
1/4 cup butter, room temperature	

Generously grease 2 round 8-inch cake or pie pans; set aside. Preheat oven to 350F (175C). In a large bowl, combine flour, baking powder, baking soda, salt, orange peel and caraway seeds, if desired. Use a pastry cutter or your fingers to blend butter into flour mixture. Stir in currants; set aside. In a medium bowl, combine honey, 1-1/2 cups buttermilk and 1/4 cup whiskey or buttermilk. Stir into flour mixture only until dry ingredients are moistened. Turn out dough onto a generously floured surface. Dough will be sticky. Knead 1 minute. Cut dough in half. Shape each piece into a round loaf. Place in prepared pans. Dip a sharp knife or razor blade into flour. Cut a cross, 1/2 inch deep, in top of each loaf. Brush loaves with milk glaze. Let loaves stand 10 minutes. Bake 35 to 40 minutes or until bread sounds hollow when tapped on bottom. Remove from pans. Cool on racks. Slice thinly or cut in wedges. Makes 2 loaves.

Variations

For a lighter texture, the Irish invert deep, round cake pans over loaves as they bake. To brown crusts, remove upper pans during final 15 minutes of baking.

Add 3/4 cup finely chopped dried apricots. Omit currants, if desired.

Whole-Wheat Irish Soda Bread: Substitute 2 cups whole-wheat flour for 2 cups all-purpose flour. After brushing loaves with milk glaze, sprinkle 2 to 3 teaspoons wheat germ over top of each.

Creamy Lemon Loaf

Spread sweet butter over this non-sweet loaf laced with lemon zest—then serve with tea!

2 cups all-purpose flour	1/4 cup sugar
2 teaspoons baking powder	1 cup whipping cream
1 teaspoon baking soda	1/2 cup finely chopped walnuts or pecans
1 teaspoon salt	2 teaspoons finely chopped walnuts or
Freshly grated peel from 1-1/2 large lemons	pecans
4 eggs, room temperature	

Grease and flour a 1-1/2-quart casserole dish or an 8" x 4" loaf pan; set aside. Preheat oven to 325F (165C). In a large bowl, combine flour, baking powder, baking soda, salt and lemon peel; set aside. In small bowl of electric mixer, beat eggs and sugar until light and creamy. Add whipping cream; beat 2 minutes longer. Stir into flour mixture only until dry ingredients are moistened. Stir in 1/2 cup nuts until evenly distributed. Turn into prepared pan. Smooth top; sprinkle with 2 teaspoons nuts. Bake 55 to 65 minutes or until a wooden pick inserted in center comes out clean. Let stand in pan 10 minutes. Turn out onto a rack to cool. Makes 1 loaf.

Sweet Quick Breads & Coffeecakes

The discovery of baking powder in 1855 was a boon to home bakers everywhere. Previously, the most widely used source of carbon dioxide was *saleratus* or baking soda. Because saleratus was alkaline and needed an acid ingredient to neutralize its bitter flavor, delicious sweet quick breads were not always possible. But when it was discovered that three ingredients—baking soda, an acid agent such as cream of tartar and an atmospheric moisture-absorber—such as cornstarch—could be combined in one powder, bakers everywhere rejoiced! Soon, there was a renaissance in cake and quick-bread making, the like of which hasn't been seen in the baking world since.

Fruits and nuts are natural enrichments for sweet quick breads. When working with fruits in breads, be sure they're ripe but firm. Cut away any bruised portions from the larger fruits; discard bruised or overly soft berries. Several breads in this chapter have been created to take advantage of summer's sun-ripened fruit harvest.

Dutch Apple-Streusel Bread was inspired by a delicious apple bread my husband Ron and I were served by a young Dutch couple who helped us repair a flat tire in front of their house. They insisted we refresh ourselves with wedges of a wonderful bread the wife had just baked. We didn't speak Dutch and they spoke little English, so getting the recipe was impossible. My rendition of that fragrant loaf includes sour cream, fresh apples, toasted walnuts and a cinnamon-spiced streusel topping. It's rather like a tea bread but is also marvelous for snacks or even a light dessert!

Gingerbread has long been a traditional English tea bread. The English bake it in the customary loaf and serve it thinly sliced with butter. I've given new character to this classic by adding minced crystallized ginger—therefore the name Twice Gingerbread. Even the diehard gingerhater will be seduced into trying a slice of this appealing loaf, still warm from the oven, spread with Whipped Ginger Cream!

Caramel-Apple Twist

A quick and beautiful coffeecake—fit for the finest occasion.

Caramel-Apple Filling, see below
2 cups all-purpose flour
2 teaspoons baking powder
3/4 teaspoon salt
1/4 cup sugar

1/4 cup butter
1 egg, room temperature
1/2 cup milk, room temperature
1 teaspoon vanilla extract
Apple Glaze, see below

Caramel-Apple Filling:
1/2 cup packed brown sugar
1/2 teaspoon ground cinnamon
Pinch of salt

1 cup finely chopped peeled apple
1/2 cup finely chopped walnuts or pecans
1/3 cup raisins or currants, if desired

Apple Glaze:
2 tablespoons butter
2 tablespoons apple juice

1/4 cup sugar

Grease a large baking sheet; set aside. Preheat oven to 350F (175C). Prepare Caramel-Apple Filling; set aside. In a large bowl, combine flour, baking powder, salt and sugar. Use a pastry cutter or 2 knives to cut in butter until mixture resembles coarse crumbs; set aside. In a medium bowl, lightly beat egg. Stir in milk and vanilla. Stir into flour mixture only until dry ingredients are moistened. Turn out dough onto a generously floured surface. Knead gently until dough holds together, 12 to 15 strokes. Roll out dough to a 13-inch square. Spread Caramel-Apple Filling over dough, to within 1 inch of edges. Roll up tightly, jelly-roll fashion. Pinch seam and ends to seal. Place seam-side down on prepared baking sheet. Using a sharp knife, cut 1-inch slices leaving 1/2 inch uncut and still attached to roll. Gently lift every other piece of dough to opposite side of roll. Turn each piece cut-side up. Bake 20 to 30 minutes or until golden brown. Using 2 large metal spatulas, carefully remove baked roll from baking sheet to a platter. Prepare Apple Glaze. Brush or spoon hot Apple Glaze over top of coffeecake. Let glaze set 5 minutes before serving warm. Makes 1 coffeecake.

Caramel-Apple Filling:
In a medium bowl, combine all ingredients.

Apple Glaze:
In a small saucepan, combine all ingredients. Stirring constantly, bring to a boil over medium-high heat. Boil 3 minutes without stirring.

 Fresh fruit used in breads should be fully ripe, yet firm. Cut away any bruised spots before using.

Old-Fashioned Banana Bread

Cinnamon and sour cream make this moist classic a favorite.

2 cups all-purpose flour
1/2 teaspoon baking powder
1 teaspoon baking soda
1/2 teaspoon salt
1/2 teaspoon ground cinnamon
1/2 cup butter, room temperature
1/2 cup packed brown sugar
1/2 cup granulated sugar

2 eggs, room temperature
1/2 cup dairy sour cream or plain yogurt,
   room temperature
1 cup pureed ripe bananas
   (1-1/2 to 2 medium)
1 teaspoon vanilla extract
1/2 cup toasted chopped almonds, walnuts or
   pecans, if desired

Generously grease a 9" x 5" loaf pan; set aside. Preheat oven to 350F (175C). In a large bowl, combine flour, baking powder, baking soda, salt and cinnamon; set aside. In small bowl of electric mixer, cream butter. Gradually beat in both sugars; continue beating 1 minute or until light and airy. Beat in eggs one at a time. Beat in sour cream, bananas and vanilla until blended. Stir into flour mixture only until dry ingredients are moistened. Stir in nuts, if desired. Turn into prepared pan; smooth top. Bake 55 to 60 minutes or until a wooden pick inserted in center comes out clean. Let stand in pan 10 minutes. Turn out onto a rack to cool. Makes 1 loaf.

Variations

Raisin-Banana Bread: Fold in 1/2 cup raisins with nuts.
Blueberry-Banana Bread: Toss 3/4 cup fresh or frozen blueberries with dry ingredients. Do not thaw berries.
Banana-Apricot Bread: Toss 1/2 cup finely chopped dried apricots and 1 teaspoon freshly grated orange peel with dry ingredients.
Whole-Wheat Banana Bread: Substitute 1 cup whole-wheat flour for 1 cup all-purpose flour; add 1/4 cup toasted wheat germ.

Banana-Daiquiri Bread

Rum and lime juice add a tropical flavor to this winsome loaf.

2 cups all-purpose flour
1 teaspoon baking powder
1/4 teaspoon baking soda
1/2 teaspoon salt
1/2 cup butter, room temperature
3/4 cup sugar

1/2 cup pureed ripe banana (about 1 medium)
2 eggs, room temperature
1/3 cup dark rum
2 tablespoons lime juice
1/2 teaspoon rum extract
1/2 cup toasted chopped almonds

Grease an 8" x 4" or 9" x 5" loaf pan; set aside. Preheat oven to 350F (175C). In a large bowl, combine flour, baking powder, baking soda and salt; set aside. In small bowl of electric mixer, cream butter. Gradually beat in sugar. Beat 1 minute or until light and airy. Add banana, eggs, rum, lime juice and rum extract; beat until blended. Stir into flour mixture only until dry ingredients are moistened. Stir in nuts. Turn into prepared pan; smooth top. Bake 55 to 60 minutes or until a wooden pick inserted in center comes out clean. Let stand in pan 10 minutes. Turn out onto a rack to cool. Makes 1 loaf.

Piña-Colada Bread

Like the popular Caribbean drink, this bread is heady with pineapple, rum and coconut.

1-1/2 cups shredded coconut
2-3/4 cups all-purpose flour
2 teaspoons baking powder
1/2 teaspoon baking soda
1 teaspoon salt
3/4 cup sugar
1 egg, room temperature

1 cup unsweetened pineapple juice,
  room temperature
1/2 cup light rum
1 teaspoon vanilla extract
2 tablespoons vegetable oil
Pineapple-Rum Glaze, see below

Pineapple-Rum Glaze:
3 tablespoons butter
2 tablespoons pineapple juice

1/2 cup sugar
1/4 cup light rum

Generously grease a 9" x 5" loaf pan; set aside. Preheat oven to 350F (175C). Spread coconut in a single layer in an ungreased jelly-roll pan. Stirring often, toast in oven, 4 to 6 minutes or until golden brown. Set aside to cool. In a large bowl, combine flour, baking powder, baking soda, salt, sugar and 1-1/4 cups toasted coconut; set aside. Reserve remaining toasted coconut for topping. In a medium bowl, lightly beat egg. Stir in pineapple juice, rum, vanilla and oil. Stir into flour mixture only until dry ingredients are moistened. Turn into prepared pan; smooth top. Bake 55 to 60 minutes or until a wooden pick inserted in center comes out clean. Let stand in pan 10 minutes. Prepare Pineapple-Rum Glaze. Place a rack over waxed paper. Turn out baked loaf onto rack. Drizzle Pineapple-Rum Glaze over warm bread. Sprinkle with reserved 1/4 cup toasted coconut. Cool to room temperature. Makes 1 loaf.

Pineapple-Rum Glaze:
In a small saucepan, combine butter, pineapple juice and sugar. Bring to a boil over medium heat. Cook 5 minutes, stirring constantly. Stir in rum; set aside to cool.

California Avocado-Orange Bread

Three California crops—avocados, oranges and walnuts—give this bread its sunshine flavor.

2-1/2 cups all-purpose flour
1-1/2 teaspoons baking powder
1/2 teaspoon baking soda
1/2 teaspoon salt
3/4 cup sugar
2 teaspoons freshly grated orange peel
1/2 teaspoon ground cardamom

1/2 teaspoon ground cinnamon
1/4 teaspoon ground nutmeg
1 egg, room temperature
1/2 cup mashed avocado (about 1 medium)
2 tablespoons walnut oil or vegetable oil
3/4 cup orange juice, room temperature
1 cup toasted finely chopped walnuts

Generously grease a 9" x 5" loaf pan or 2-quart casserole dish; set aside. Preheat oven to 350F (175C). In a large bowl, combine flour, baking powder, baking soda, salt, sugar, orange peel, cardamom, cinnamon and nutmeg; set aside. In a medium bowl, lightly beat egg. Stir in avocado, oil and orange juice. Stir into flour mixture only until dry ingredients are moistened. Stir in nuts. Turn into prepared pan; smooth top. Bake 50 to 55 minutes or until a wooden pick inserted in center comes out clean. Let stand in pan 10 minutes. Turn out onto a rack to cool. Makes 1 loaf.

Raspberry-Ripple Coffeecake

A swirl of red-raspberry preserves flavors this yogurt-enriched coffee bread.

2 cups all-purpose flour
1/2 teaspoon baking powder
1 teaspoon baking soda
1/2 teaspoon salt
1 cup sugar
1 egg, room temperature
1/2 cup butter, melted
1 teaspoon vanilla extract

1 (8-oz.) carton raspberry-flavored yogurt,
   room temperature
1/2 cup chopped almonds, if desired
1/3 cup seedless red-raspberry preserves
2 tablespoons seedless red-raspberry
   preserves
About 25 whole blanched almonds
Fresh raspberries for decoration, if desired

Grease a 9-inch springform pan; set aside. Preheat oven to 350F (175C). In a large bowl, combine flour, baking powder, baking soda, salt and sugar; set aside. In a medium bowl, lightly beat egg. Stir in butter, vanilla and yogurt. Stir into flour mixture only until dry ingredients are moistened. Stir in nuts, if desired. Turn into prepared pan; smooth top. Drop 1/3 cup preserves, by teaspoonfuls, over top of batter. To give a marbled effect, use a knife to cut preserves through batter several times. Bake 40 to 45 minutes or until a wooden pick inserted in center comes out clean. Let stand in pan 10 minutes. Remove side of pan. Use 2 large spatulas to remove baked coffeecake from pan bottom. Place top-side up on a plate. In a small saucepan, over low heat, melt 2 tablespoons preserves. Brush over coffeecake. Let stand 10 minutes. Arrange whole almonds around coffeecake. Decorate with fresh raspberries, if desired. Makes 1 coffeecake.

Apricot-Nectar Bread

Even better the second day, this tart-sweet bread combines dried apricots with apricot nectar.

2-1/2 cups all-purpose flour
2 teaspoons baking powder
1 teaspoon baking soda
1-1/4 teaspoons salt
1/2 cup sugar
3/4 cup finely chopped dried apricots

1 egg, room temperature
2 tablespoons butter, melted
1 (12-oz.) can apricot nectar (1-1/2 cups)
1/2 teaspoon vanilla extract
1/2 cup toasted chopped walnuts, if desired

Grease an 8" x 4" or 9" x 5" loaf pan; set aside. Preheat oven to 350F (175C). In a large bowl, combine flour, baking powder, baking soda, salt, sugar and apricots; set aside. In a medium bowl, lightly beat egg. Stir in butter, apricot nectar and vanilla. Stir into flour mixture only until dry ingredients are moistened. Stir in nuts, if desired. Turn into prepared pan; smooth top. Bake 60 to 65 minutes or until a wooden pick inserted in center comes out clean. Let stand in pan 10 minutes. Turn out onto a rack to cool. Makes 1 loaf.

Variations

Apricot-Orange Bread: Add 2 teaspoons grated orange peel. Substitute 1-1/2 cups orange juice for 12 ounces apricot nectar.

Apricot-Raisin Bread: Add 1/2 teaspoon ground cinnamon. Substitute 1/2 cup raisins for 1/2 cup chopped nuts.

Apricot & Chocolate-Chip Bread: Substitute 3/4 cup semisweet chocolate pieces for 1/2 cup chopped nuts.

Chocolate-Streusel Coffeecake

Layers of spicy chocolate streusel make this morning treat a chocoholic's delight.

Chocolate Streusel, see below
2 cups all-purpose flour
2 teaspoons baking powder
1/2 teaspoon baking soda
1/2 teaspoon salt
1/4 teaspoon ground cinnamon

1/2 cup butter, room temperature
3/4 cup sugar
3 eggs, room temperature
1 cup dairy sour cream, room temperature
2 teaspoons vanilla extract

Chocolate Streusel:
3/4 cup packed brown sugar
1/4 cup all-purpose flour
1-1/2 tablespoons unsweetened cocoa powder
1/4 teaspoon ground cinnamon

1/4 teaspoon ground nutmeg
1/4 cup cold butter
6 oz. semisweet chocolate pieces (1 cup)
1 cup finely chopped walnuts or pecans

Generously grease and flour a 10-cup tube or Bundt pan; set aside. Preheat oven to 350F (175C). Prepare Chocolate Streusel. Sprinkle 1 cup streusel mixture over bottom of prepared pan; set aside. In a large bowl, combine flour, baking powder, baking soda, salt and cinnamon; set aside. In small bowl of electric mixer, cream butter and sugar until light and airy. Add eggs one at a time, beating after each addition. Beat in sour cream and vanilla until blended. Stir into flour mixture only until dry ingredients are moistened. Spoon one-third of batter over streusel in pan. Carefully smooth surface. Sprinkle with half of remaining streusel mixture. Top with half of remaining batter. Again, carefully smooth surface. Repeat layers with remaining streusel and batter, ending with batter. Bake 45 to 50 minutes or until a wooden pick inserted in center comes out clean. Turn out immediately onto a rack to cool. Spoon topping from pan onto coffeecake. Makes 1 coffeecake.

Chocolate Streusel:
In a small bowl, combine brown sugar, flour, cocoa powder, cinnamon and nutmeg. Use a pastry cutter or 2 knives to cut in butter until mixture resembles coarse crumbs. Stir in chocolate pieces and nuts.

Tip *Measure flour and other dry ingredients by stirring, then spooning into measuring cup. Level off with flat edge of a knife.*

Dutch Apple-Streusel Bread

Crisp streusel tops this tender bread made with fresh apples, sour cream and walnuts.

Streusel Topping, see below
2 cups all-purpose flour
2 teaspoons baking powder
1 teaspoon baking soda
1 teaspoon salt
1/2 teaspoon ground cinnamon
1/2 cup butter, room temperature
1/2 cup packed brown sugar

1/2 cup granulated sugar
1/3 cup dairy sour cream, room temperature
2 eggs, room temperature
1 teaspoon vanilla extract
1 cup finely chopped unpeeled or
    peeled tart apple
1 cup toasted finely chopped walnuts

Streusel Topping:
2 tablespoons cold butter
1/4 cup granulated sugar

3 tablespoons all-purpose flour
1/4 teaspoon ground cinnamon

Generously grease an 8" x 4" or 9" x 5" loaf pan; set aside. Preheat oven to 350F (175C). Prepare Streusel Topping; set aside. In a large bowl, combine flour, baking powder, baking soda, salt and cinnamon; set aside. In small bowl of electric mixer, cream butter and both sugars until light. Beat in sour cream, eggs and vanilla until blended. Fold creamed mixture, apples and nuts into flour mixture only until dry ingredients are moistened. Turn into prepared pan; smooth top. Sprinkle Streusel Topping evenly over batter. Bake 50 to 60 minutes or until a wooden pick inserted in center comes out clean. Let stand in pan 10 minutes. Turn out onto a rack to cool. Makes 1 loaf.

Streusel Topping:
In a small bowl, combine all ingredients. Use a pastry cutter or 2 knives to cut in butter until mixture resembles coarse crumbs. Or, place all ingredients in a food processor fitted with a metal blade. Turn on and off until mixture resembles coarse crumbs.

Strawberries 'N Cream Bread

Moist bits of strawberries and rich sour cream flavor this tender loaf.

1-3/4 cups all-purpose flour
1/2 teaspoon baking powder
1/4 teaspoon baking soda
1/2 teaspoon salt
1/4 teaspoon ground cinnamon
1/2 cup butter, room temperature

3/4 cup sugar
2 eggs, room temperature
1/2 cup dairy sour cream, room temperature
1 teaspoon vanilla extract
1 cup coarsely chopped fresh strawberries
3/4 cup toasted chopped walnuts, if desired

Grease an 8" x 4" loaf pan; set aside. Preheat oven to 350F (175C). In a large bowl, combine flour, baking powder, baking soda, salt and cinnamon; set aside. In small bowl of electric mixer, cream butter. Gradually add sugar; beat 1 minute or until light and airy. Beat in eggs one at a time. Beat in sour cream and vanilla. Stir into flour mixture only until dry ingredients are moistened. Fold in strawberries and nuts, if desired. Turn into prepared pan; smooth top. Bake 60 to 65 minutes or until a wooden pick inserted in center comes out clean. Let stand in pan 10 minutes. Turn out onto a rack to cool. Makes 1 loaf.

Ginger-Peachy Blueberry Bread

Fragrant with ginger and peaches and topped with blueberry streusel. Springtime's here!

Blueberry Streusel, see below
2 cups all-purpose flour
2 teaspoons baking powder
3/4 teaspoon salt
3/4 cup sugar
1/4 teaspoon ground cinnamon
2 eggs, room temperature

1/4 cup butter, melted
1 teaspoon vanilla extract
1-1/2 to 2 teaspoons minced gingerroot
2 small peaches, peeled, finely chopped
3/4 cup fresh or frozen blueberries,
   not thawed

Blueberry Streusel:
1/4 cup fresh or frozen blueberries,
   not thawed
1/4 cup all-purpose flour
1/4 cup sugar

1 tablespoon cold butter
1/8 teaspoon ground cinnamon
1 tablespoon all-purpose flour, if needed

Grease an 8" x 4" loaf pan or 1-1/2-quart casserole dish; set aside. Preheat oven to 350F (175C). Prepare Blueberry Streusel; set aside. In a large bowl, combine flour, baking powder, salt, sugar and cinnamon; set aside. In a medium bowl, lightly beat eggs. Stir in butter, vanilla, gingerroot and peaches. Stir into flour mixture only until dry ingredients are moistened. Fold in blueberries. Do not thaw frozen berries. Turn into prepared pan; smooth top. Sprinkle with Blueberry Streusel. Bake 70 to 80 minutes or until a wooden pick inserted in center comes out clean. Let stand in pan 10 minutes. Turn out onto a rack to cool. Makes 1 loaf.

Blueberry Streusel:
In a blender or food processor fitted with a metal blade, combine blueberries, 1/4 cup flour, sugar, butter and cinnamon. Process until blueberries are minced. If using frozen blueberries, increase flour by 1 tablespoon.

Ginger-Peachy Butter

A summery spread for summery breads—try it on Ginger-Peachy Blueberry Bread, above.

1/2 cup butter, room temperature
1/4 cup powdered sugar
1/2 to 1 teaspoon minced gingerroot
   or crystallized ginger

Pinch of salt
1/2 medium peach, peeled, minced

In small bowl of electric mixer, beat butter and sugar until creamy. Fold in gingerroot or crystallized ginger, salt and peaches until evenly distributed. Spoon into a small serving dish. Cover and refrigerate. Let stand at room temperature 20 to 30 minutes before serving. Makes about 1 cup.

Variation

Substitute 1/2 cup minced fresh nectarines or apricots for peaches.

Blueberries 'N Cheese Coffeecake

A sour-cream-enriched bread studded with blueberries and chunks of cream cheese.

Cinnamon-Nut Topping, see below
3 cups all-purpose flour
4 teaspoons baking powder
1 teaspoon salt
1 cup sugar
1 teaspoon freshly grated lemon peel
1 (8-oz.) pkg. cold cream cheese,
  cut in 1/2-inch cubes

1-1/2 cups fresh or frozen blueberries,
  not thawed
3 eggs, room temperature
1/2 cup dairy sour cream, room temperature
1/2 cup butter, melted
2/3 cup milk, room temperature

Cinnamon-Nut Topping:
1/4 cup all-purpose flour
1/3 cup packed brown sugar
1 teaspoon ground cinnamon

1/4 cup cold butter
1/2 cup chopped walnuts or pecans

Grease a 13" x 9" baking pan; set aside. Preheat oven to 350F (175C). Prepare Cinnamon-Nut Topping; set aside. In a large bowl, combine flour, baking powder, salt, sugar and lemon peel. Add cream cheese and blueberries, tossing to coat with flour mixture; set aside. In a medium bowl, lightly beat eggs and sour cream. Stir in butter and milk. Stir into flour mixture only until dry ingredients are moistened. Turn into prepared pan; smooth top. Sprinkle with Cinnamon-Nut Topping. Bake 55 to 60 minutes or until a wooden pick inserted in center comes out clean. Let stand in pan 15 minutes. Cut and arrange on a platter. Serve warm or at room temperature. Makes 12 to 18 servings.

Cinnamon-Nut Topping:
In a medium bowl, combine flour, brown sugar and cinnamon. Cut in butter until mixture resembles coarse crumbs. Stir in nuts.

Rice-Pudding Bread

Moist and chewy—reminiscent of Mom's old-fashioned rice pudding.

1/3 cup raisins
1 tablespoon orange-flavored liqueur
1-3/4 cups all-purpose flour
1 cup cooked brown rice, unsalted
1 tablespoon baking powder
1 teaspoon salt
1/4 teaspoon ground cinnamon
1/4 teaspoon ground allspice

1/4 teaspoon ground nutmeg
1 teaspoon freshly grated orange peel
3 eggs, room temperature
1/3 cup packed brown sugar
1/2 cup milk, room temperature
3 tablespoons butter, melted
2 teaspoons vanilla extract

In a small bowl, combine raisins and orange liqueur. Cover; set aside overnight or 3 to 4 hours to soak. Generously grease an 8" x 4" loaf pan; set aside. Preheat oven to 350F (175C). In a large bowl, toss flour and rice together until rice is well coated and separated. Stir in baking powder, salt, cinnamon, allspice, nutmeg and orange peel; set aside. In a medium bowl, lightly beat eggs. Stir in brown sugar, milk, butter, vanilla and raisin mixture. Stir into flour mixture only until dry ingredients are moistened. Turn into prepared pan; smooth top. Bake 55 to 60 minutes or until a wooden pick inserted in center comes out clean. Let stand in pan 10 minutes. Turn out onto a rack to cool. Makes 1 loaf.

How to Make Boston Brown Bread

1/Fill cans evenly with batter. Cover cans tightly with 2 layers of foil; tie with string.

2/Place cans on a rack in a large kettle. Add boiling water until halfway up cans. Cover kettle.

Boston Brown Bread

More American than apple pie, this steamed bread boasts a trio of wholesome grains.

1 cup whole-wheat flour	1 teaspoon salt
1 cup medium rye flour	1 cup raisins, if desired
1 cup yellow cornmeal	2 cups buttermilk, room temperature
1-1/2 teaspoons baking soda	3/4 cup molasses

Generously grease 2 (1-pound) coffee cans or 3 (1-pound) vegetable or fruit cans; set aside. In a large bowl, combine whole-wheat flour, rye flour, cornmeal, baking soda and salt. Add raisins, if desired. Toss to separate and coat with flour mixture. In a medium bowl, combine buttermilk and molasses. Stir into flour mixture only until dry indredients are moistened. Turn into prepared cans, filling evenly. Cover cans tightly with 2 layers of foil; tie with string. Place a rack in a large kettle. Place cans on rack. Place kettle over low heat. Add boiling water until halfway up cans. Cover; bring water to a gentle boil. Steam bread 2-1/2 to 3 hours or until a wooden pick inserted in center comes out clean. Add more boiling water during steaming, if necessary. Carefully remove bread from cans. Cool on racks at least 30 minutes before slicing. Makes 2 or 3 small loaves.

Variations

Apricot Boston-Brown Bread: Substitute 1 cup finely chopped apricots or 1/2 cup chopped apricots plus 1/2 cup raisins for 1 cup raisins.

Baked Brown Bread: Generously grease a 2-quart casserole dish or 9" x 5" loaf pan. Preheat oven to 325F (165C). Turn batter into prepared pan. Bake 1 hour or until a wooden pick inserted in center comes out clean.

Twice Gingerbread

Candied ginger adds new magic to this old favorite.

3 cups all-purpose flour
1-1/2 teaspoons baking powder
1 teaspoon baking soda
1 teaspoon salt
1-1/2 teaspoons ground ginger
1/2 teaspoon ground allspice
1/2 teaspoon ground cinnamon
1/4 to 1/3 cup minced crystallized ginger

2 eggs, room temperature
1/2 cup butter, melted
3/4 cup dark molasses
1/2 cup packed brown sugar
1 (5.33-oz.) can evaporated milk
1 cup chopped walnuts, if desired
Butter
Whipped Ginger Cream, page 70

Grease a 9" x 5" loaf pan or an 8- or 9-inch square baking pan; set aside. Preheat oven to 350F (175C). In a large bowl, combine flour, baking powder, baking soda, salt, ground ginger, allspice, cinnamon and crystallized ginger; set aside. In a medium bowl, lightly beat eggs. Stir in 1/2 cup butter, molasses, brown sugar and milk until blended. Stir into flour mixture only until dry ingredients are moistened. Stir in nuts, if desired. Turn into prepared pan; smooth top. Bake 60 to 70 minutes for loaf pan, 50 to 60 minutes for square pan or until a wooden pick inserted in center comes out clean. If bread begins to brown too fast, cover with a foil tent. Let stand in pan 10 minutes. Turn out onto a rack to cool. Serve warm or cool with sweet butter or Whipped Ginger Cream. Makes 1 loaf.

Variations

Banana Gingerbread: Reduce ground ginger to 1 teaspoon. Substitute 1 cup pureed ripe banana for evaporated milk.
Ginger-Date Bread: Reduce crystallized ginger to 1 tablespoon. Add 1-3/4 cups coarsely chopped dates and 1 tablespoon freshly grated orange peel. Omit nuts.

Honey-Graham Loaf

Spread with Honey Butter, page 46, and serve with a fruit salad.

1-1/2 tablespoons graham-cracker crumbs
1-1/4 cups all-purpose flour
2 teaspoons baking powder
1/2 teaspoon baking soda
1/2 teaspoon salt
1-1/4 cups graham-cracker crumbs
1/4 cup toasted wheat germ
1/4 teaspoon ground cinnamon

1 egg, room temperature
1/3 cup honey
3 tablespoons butter, melted
1 cup milk, room temperature
1 teaspoon vanilla extract
3/4 cup chopped walnuts or pecans,
   if desired
1-1/2 tablespoons graham-cracker crumbs

Generously grease an 8" x 4" loaf pan or 1-1/2-quart casserole dish. Sprinkle 1-1/2 tablespoons graham-cracker crumbs over bottom and sides of pan; set aside. Preheat oven to 350F (175C). In a large bowl, combine flour, baking powder, baking soda, salt, 1-1/4 cups graham-cracker crumbs, wheat germ and cinnamon; set aside. In a medium bowl, lightly beat egg. Stir in honey, butter, milk and vanilla. Stir into flour mixture only until dry ingredients are moistened. Add nuts, if desired. Turn into prepared pan; smooth top. Sprinkle with remaining 1-1/2 tablespoons graham-cracker crumbs. Bake 35 to 40 minutes or until a wooden pick inserted in center comes out clean. Let stand in pan 10 minutes. Turn out onto a rack to cool. Makes 1 loaf.

Festive & Holiday Breads

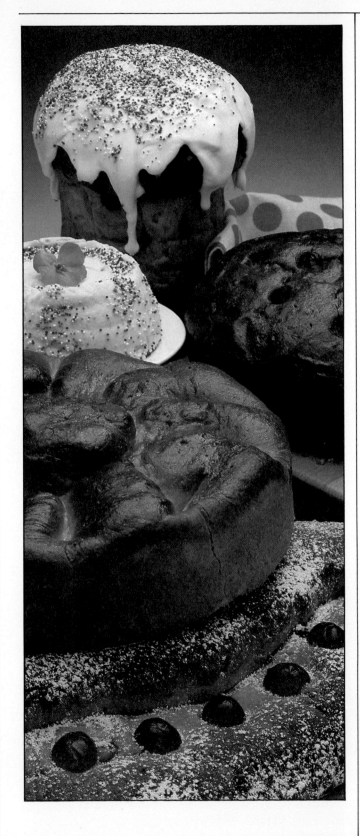

For centuries bread has played an important role in festive celebrations and religious holidays. When I was a little girl, I remember the anticipation as we toasted the nuts, gathered the candied fruits, and prepared the pans for our annual holiday bake-fest. To this day, I still feel that same excitement every year!

Many festive breads have European roots dating back hundreds of years. Said to have originated in early Britain, Hot Cross Buns were traditionally baked on Good Friday. Today these fat, fruit-filled buns, decorated with an icing cross, are more often served on Easter Sunday. If you have time, make the Easter Basket Bread and fill it with Hot Cross Buns for a show-stopping Easter brunch centerpiece!

An Easter gift from Russia is the majestically tall Kulich, crowned with a snow-white icing. Some say this white-capped loaf represents the snow-frosted domes of Russian Orthodox churches. Traditionally, a small rose or rosebud is placed on top of the loaf, perhaps to symbolize new life. The Russians serve a wonderful sweet cheese mold called Pashka with this regal Easter bread.

A traditional European Christmas bread is Germany's Dresden Stollen. It somewhat resembles a giant Parkerhouse roll, rum-spiked and laden with fruit. It's been said that the shape of the bread represents the Christ child wrapped in swaddling clothes. When Stollen begins to dry, brush it lightly all over with rum; wrap well and let stand for a day.

Don't think of festive breads only for Christmas and Easter holidays. Any celebration can be made special with the addition of personalized, homemade breads depicting a special event. Bake Cherry Valentine Bread, heart-shaped with a swirl of cherries inside, as an edible valentine for that special someone. Or, how about the colorful raisin-filled, pumpkin-flavored Jack-O-Lantern Bread for a Halloween party? Let your imagination soar!

Savory Stuffing Bread

Reminiscent of holiday stuffing — wonderful for cold turkey sandwiches!

1/4 cup butter	1-1/2 teaspoons poultry seasoning or
1/2 cup finely chopped onions	1/2 teaspoon each of ground thyme,
2 (1/4-oz.) pkgs. active dry yeast	sage and rosemary
(2 tablespoons)	1/2 teaspoon celery seeds
1 teaspoon sugar	1/2 teaspoon pepper
1 (10-3/4-oz.) can condensed chicken broth,	1-1/2 teaspoons salt
warmed to 110F, 45C	5 to 5-1/5 cups all-purpose or bread flour
2 tablespoons sugar	1 egg white blended with
2 eggs, room temperature	1 tablespoon water for glaze

Melt butter in a medium skillet over medium heat. Add onions; sauté until soft. Set aside to cool. In large bowl of electric mixer, dissolve yeast and 1 teaspoon sugar in chicken broth. Let stand until foamy, 5 to 10 minutes. Add 2 tablespoons sugar; eggs; poultry seasoning or thyme, sage and rosemary; celery seeds; pepper; salt; cooled butter-onion mixture and 2 to 2-1/2 cups flour. Beat at medium speed with electric mixer 2 minutes or, beat 200 vigorous strokes by hand. Stir in enough remaining flour to make a soft dough. Turn out dough onto a lightly floured surface. Clean and grease bowl; set aside. **Knead dough** 6 to 8 minutes or until smooth and elastic. Place dough in greased bowl, turning to coat all sides. Cover with a slightly damp towel. Let rise in a warm place, free from drafts, until doubled in bulk, 45 to 60 minutes. Grease 2 (9" x 5") loaf pans or 2 (2-quart) casserole dishes; set aside. **Punch down dough;** knead 30 seconds. Divide dough in half. Shape into loaves and place in prepared pans. Cover with a dry towel. Let rise until doubled in bulk, 30 to 45 minutes. **Preheat oven** to 375F (190C). Slash tops of loaves as desired; brush with egg-white glaze. Bake 30 to 35 minutes or until bread sounds hollow when tapped on bottom. Remove from pans. Cool on racks. Makes 2 loaves.

Variation

Braided Stuffing Bread: After first rising, divide dough in half. Divide each half into 3 equal pieces. Roll each piece into a 15-inch rope. Braid into 2 (3-rope) braids; pinch ends to seal. Place in prepared loaf pans; proceed as directed above.

Special-Occasion Breads

Let your imagination lead the way in creating personalized breads for special occasions! Hand-Print Rolls, page 91, are perfect for children's birthday parties. Let the children cut out their own handprints in dough. Then watch it bake into edible party favors! Use your favorite yeast-bread dough to create unique holiday breads. After the first rising, simply roll the dough into long ropes. Then write your message with the bread ropes. For example, for Mother's Day, divide dough into 3 pieces, roll into ropes and shape the letters **MOM**; use the letters **DAD** for Father's Day; a big shamrock is perfect for St. Patrick's Day; a big **4** for the Fourth of July; and a person's name for a special birthday. There are dozens of ways to create special-occasion breads. Surprise and delight your family and friends with your creativity!

Cherry Valentine Bread

Show your love on Valentine's Day with this cherry-filled heart!

1 recipe Basic Sweet Yeast Dough, page 59
1 (21-oz.) can cherry-pie filling
1/4 teaspoon almond extract
1/3 cup all-purpose flour
1/2 cup packed brown sugar

1/2 teaspoon ground nutmeg
3/4 cup toasted chopped almonds
1 egg white blended with
  1 teaspoon water for glaze
Cherry Glaze, see below

Cherry Glaze:
1-1/2 cups sifted powdered sugar
1/4 teaspoon almond extract
1 teaspoon vanilla extract

1 to 3 tablespoons reserved
  cherry-pie sauce

Prepare Basic Sweet Yeast Dough through first rising. Grease a large baking sheet; set aside. Using a coarse sieve or colander, strain sauce from cherries, being careful not to crush cherries; set sauce aside. Cherries will have some sauce clinging to them. In a medium bowl, stir 1/4 teaspoon almond extract into drained cherries; set aside. In another medium bowl, combine flour, brown sugar, nutmeg and almonds; set aside. **Punch down dough;** knead 30 seconds. Divide dough in half. Cover one half; set aside. Roll out remaining dough to a 14" x 8" rectangle. Top with 1 tablespoon cherry-pie sauce, spreading to within 1 inch of edges. Spoon half of cherries evenly over dough. Sprinkle with half of brown-sugar mixture. Beginning on a long side, roll up, jelly-roll fashion. When almost to opposite edge, stop rolling. Bring dough up to meet roll. Tightly pinch seam and ends to seal. Place lengthwise on prepared baking sheet, seam-side down, curving to make half a heart. Repeat with remaining dough, making other half of heart. Pinch rolls together at seams to seal. Cover with a dry towel. Let rise until doubled in bulk, about 1-1/2 hours. If seams of heart pull apart, gently pinch back together. **Preheat oven** to 350F (175C). Brush egg-white glaze over top of bread. Bake 30 to 40 minutes or until bread sounds hollow when tapped on top. Cool on a rack. Make Cherry Glaze. Drizzle over cooled coffeecake. Makes 1 coffeecake.

Cherry Glaze:
In a small bowl, combine powdered sugar, almond extract and vanilla extract. Stir in enough cherry-pie sauce to make a smooth, creamy glaze of drizzling consistency.

Tip   *Process lumpy powdered sugar in a food processor fitted with a metal blade to achieve smooth results.*

How to Make Cherry Valentine Bread

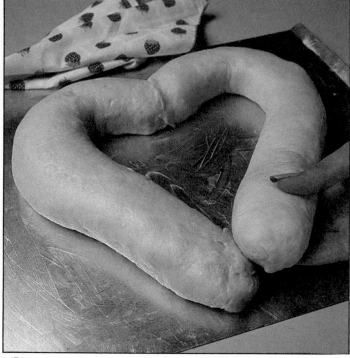

1/Place rolls, seam-side down, on baking sheet. Curve in heart shape.

2/Pinch rolls together at seams to seal. Let rise, then bake. Drizzle with Cherry Glaze.

Challah

This braided Jewish holiday bread is lightly textured and rich with eggs.

2 (1/4-oz.) pkgs. active dry yeast
   (2 tablespoons)
1 tablespoon sugar
1 cup warm water (110F, 45C)
2 tablespoons sugar
1-1/2 teaspoons salt
1/3 cup butter, melted
3 eggs, room temperature

1 egg yolk, room temperature
5 to 5-1/2 cups all-purpose or bread flour
3/4 cup golden raisins, if desired
Cornmeal
1 egg yolk blended with
   2 teaspoons cream for glaze
Sesame or poppy seeds, if desired

In large bowl of electric mixer, dissolve yeast and 1 tablespoon sugar in water. Let stand until foamy, 5 to 10 minutes. Add 2 tablespoons sugar, salt, butter, eggs, egg yolk and 2 to 2-1/2 cups flour. Beat at medium speed with electric mixer 2 minutes or, beat 200 vigorous strokes by hand. Stir in raisins, if desired, and enough remaining flour to make a soft dough. Turn out dough onto a lightly floured surface. Clean and grease bowl; set aside. **Knead dough** 8 to 10 minutes or until smooth and elastic. Place dough in greased bowl, turning to coat all sides. Cover with a slightly damp towel. Let rise in a warm place, free from drafts, until doubled in bulk, about 1 hour. Grease 1 large baking sheet for Six-Strand Braid and 2 large baking sheets for other braids. Sprinkle lightly with cornmeal; set aside. **Punch down dough;** knead 30 seconds. Braid as desired, page 73. Place shaped braids on prepared baking sheets. Cover with a dry towel. Let rise until doubled in bulk, about 1 hour. **Preheat oven** to 325F (165C). Brush egg-yolk glaze over tops of braids. Bake 25 minutes. Brush again with egg-yolk glaze. Sprinkle with sesame or poppy seeds if raisins are not used. Bake 10 to 20 minutes longer or until deep golden brown and bread sounds hollow when tapped on bottom. Cool on racks. Makes 1 large or 2 small braids.

Italian Easter Bread

Colorful Easter eggs nestle in the folds of this traditional Easter-bread wreath!

1 (1/4-oz.) pkg. active dry yeast
1 teaspoon sugar
1/4 cup warm water (110F, 45C)
1/3 cup milk, room temperature
1/4 cup sugar
1/4 cup butter, melted
2 eggs, room temperature
1/2 teaspoon anise seeds, crushed
3/4 teaspoon salt
2 teaspoons grated lemon peel
1 teaspoon vanilla extract
3-1/2 to 4 cups all-purpose or bread flour

1/2 cup golden raisins or
   chopped candied fruit, blotted dry
1/3 cup toasted chopped almonds
5 raw eggs in shells,
   each dyed a different color
1 egg white blended with
   2 teaspoons water for glaze
Frosting, see below
Colored sprinkles or
   jelly beans for decoration
Coconut Grass, opposite, if desired

Frosting:
1 cup powdered sugar
1/4 teaspoon almond extract

1 to 2 tablespoons milk

In large bowl of electric mixer, dissolve yeast and 1 teaspoon sugar in 1/4 cup water. Let stand until foamy, 5 to 10 minutes. Add milk, 1/4 cup sugar, butter, 2 eggs, anise seeds, salt, lemon peel, vanilla and 2 to 2-1/2 cups flour. Beat at medium speed with electric mixer 2 minutes or, beat 200 vigorous strokes by hand. Stir in enough remaining flour to make a soft dough. Turn out dough onto a lightly floured surface. Clean and grease bowl; set aside. **Knead dough** 6 to 8 minutes or until smooth and elastic. Place dough in greased bowl, turning to coat all sides. Cover with a slightly damp towel. Let rise in a warm place, free from drafts, until doubled in bulk, 1 to 1/2 hours. Grease a large baking sheet and outside of a custard cup. Invert greased custard cup onto center of prepared baking sheet; set aside. **Punch down dough;** knead 30 seconds. Pat or roll out dough to a large rectangle. Sprinkle raisins and almonds over surface. Knead until fruit and nuts are evenly distributed. Divide dough in half. Roll each half into a 24-inch rope. Loosely twist ropes together; pinch ends to seal. On prepared baking sheet, shape dough into a ring around inverted custard cup. Overlap ends; pinch lightly at sides to seal. At 5 equidistant points in twisted ring, gently separate ropes between twists. Carefully place raw colored eggs in separations, tucking eggs securely into dough. Eggs will touch baking sheet. Cover ring with a dry towel. Let rise until doubled in bulk, about 1 hour. **Preheat oven** to 350F (175C). Brush top of bread with eggwhite glaze. Do not brush glaze on eggs. Bake 30 to 35 minutes or until a skewer inserted in center of bread comes out clean. Cool on a rack. Prepare Frosting. Spoon Frosting over bread, between eggs. Decorate with colored sprinkles or jelly beans. If desired, create a nest in center of bread with Coconut Grass and additional jelly beans. Makes 1 loaf.

Frosting:
In a small bowl, combine powdered sugar and almond extract. Stir in enough milk to make a smooth, thick frosting of drizzling consistency.

 Use vegetable shortening or unsalted butter to grease baking pans. Salted butter causes some breads to stick to pans and may cause overbrowning at temperatures over 400F (205C).

Hot Cross Buns   Photo on page 147.

Baked on Good Friday, these spicy holiday buns are believed to have sacred protective powers.

2 (1/4-oz.) pkgs. active dry yeast
   (2 tablespoons)
1 teaspoon sugar
1/3 cup warm water (110F, 45C)
1-1/4 cups milk, room temperature
3 eggs, room temperature
1/2 cup butter, melted
1/3 cup sugar
2 teaspoons grated orange peel
1 teaspoon ground nutmeg
1/2 teaspoon ground cinnamon

1/4 teaspoon ground cloves
1-1/2 teaspoons salt
6-3/4 to 7-1/4 cups all-purpose
   or bread flour
1/2 cup finely chopped candied citron,
   orange peel, lemon peel or
   mixed candied fruit
1 cup currants
1 egg yolk blended with
   2 teaspoons water for glaze
Lemon Frosting, see below

Lemon Frosting:
1-1/2 cups powdered sugar
3 teaspoons lemon juice

3 to 5 teaspoons milk

In large bowl of electric mixer, dissolve yeast and 1 teaspoon sugar in 1/3 cup water. Let stand until foamy, 5 to 10 minutes. Add milk, eggs, butter, 1/3 cup sugar, 2 teaspoons orange peel, nutmeg, cinnamon, cloves, salt and 2-1/2 to 3 cups flour. Beat at medium speed with electric mixer 2 minutes or, beat 200 vigorous strokes by hand. Stir in enough remaining flour to make a soft dough. Turn out dough onto a lightly floured surface. Clean and grease bowl; set aside. **Knead dough** 10 to 12 minutes or until smooth and elastic. Place dough in greased bowl, turning to coat all sides. Cover with a slightly damp towel. Let rise in a warm place, free from drafts, until doubled in bulk, about 1 hour. Grease 2 large baking sheets; set aside. If candied fruit is moist, toss with 1 tablespoon flour; set aside. **Punch down dough;** knead 30 seconds. On a lightly floured surface, roll or pat out dough to a large rectangle. Sprinkle currants and candied fruit over surface. Knead dough until fruits are evenly distributed, adding additional flour, if necessary. Divide dough into fourths. Divide each fourth into 8 equal pieces, making a total of 32 pieces. Shape each piece into a smooth ball. Place balls about 1-1/2 inches apart on prepared baking sheets. Cover with a dry towel. Let rise until doubled in bulk, 45 to 60 minutes. **Preheat oven** to 375F (190C). With a razor blade, cut a shallow cross in top of each bun. Brush egg-yolk glaze over tops of buns. Bake 20 to 25 minutes or until deep golden brown. Cool on racks 10 minutes. Prepare Lemon Frosting. Pipe frosting into slashes in tops of buns or, use tip of a teaspoon to spoon frosting into slashes. Let frosting set 5 minutes. Serve warm. Makes 32 buns.

Lemon Frosting:
In a small bowl, combine powdered sugar and lemon juice. Stir in enough milk to make a smooth, thick frosting. Spoon into a pastry bag. Attach a tip with a round, 1/8-inch opening.

Coconut Grass

   Place 2 to 3 cups shredded coconut in a large jar or medium glass bowl with a lid. Add 2 to 4 drops green food coloring. Cover and shake until coconut reaches desired shade, adding more food coloring if necessary. Turn out coconut onto paper towels. Let stand 20 minutes for color to set. If desired, make 2 batches of coconut, 1 light green and 1 dark green. Let colors set before tossing together for realistic-looking Coconut Grass.

Easter-Basket Bread

Fill this edible Easter basket with Hot Cross Buns for a special Easter brunch.

1 recipe Basic White Bread dough,
   page 19, with changes given below
1 egg white blended with
   2 teaspoons water for glaze

Colored sprinkles, if desired
Jelly beans, if desired
Hot Cross Buns, page 145, or other rolls
Coconut Grass, page 145

Prepare Basic White Bread dough with following changes: Substitute 3/4 cup orange juice for 3/4 cup milk; increase sugar to 1/3 cup; add 1-1/2 teaspoons almond extract and 2 tablespoons grated orange peel. Prepare through first rising. Grease 2 large baking sheets and outside of a deep 2- or 2-1/2-quart soufflé dish; set aside. **Punch down dough;** knead 30 seconds. **To make basket handle:** Pinch off a piece of dough the size of a small orange. Cover remaining dough. Divide small piece of dough into thirds. On a lightly floured surface, roll each third into a 16-inch rope. Braid ropes, pinching ends to seal; cover and set aside. Divide remaining dough into 11 equal pieces. Cover 9 pieces of dough; set aside. Roll remaining 2 pieces into 28-inch ropes. **To make basket base:** On center of 1 prepared baking sheet, loosely coil 1 rope into a spiral. Continue spiral with remaining rope, pinching ends together. Tuck outside end under spiral; pinch to spiral to seal. Press dough spiral with palm of your hand, flattening so diameter is 1 inch larger than diameter of soufflé dish. Place prepared dish open-end up on center of dough spiral, leaving a 1/2-inch extension of dough on all sides; set aside. **To make basket side:** Roll remaining pieces of dough into 26-inch ropes. Braid 3 ropes; pinch ends together to seal. Repeat with remaining ropes, making 2 more braids. Lightly brush water on edge of dough spiral that extends beyond soufflé dish. Arrange 1 of 3 long braids around dish, on edge of dough spiral, stretching, if necessary, so ends touch. Tightly pinch ends to seal. Press braid tightly against dish. Lightly brush top of braid with water. Place another long braid on top of first braid, stretching, if necessary, so ends touch. Press against dish; pinch ends to seal. Lightly brush top with water. Repeat with remaining long braid. **To shape handle:** Measure diameter of dough basket. On second prepared baking sheet, shape reserved small braid into a U-shaped handle with space between ends equal to basket's diameter. Cover handle and basket with a dry towel. Let rise until bulk has increased by half, 30 to 45 minutes. If any seams pull apart, lightly pinch back together. **Preheat oven** to 350F (175C). Brush egg-white glaze over raised basket and handle. Place handle on top oven rack and basket on middle or lower rack. Bake 20 minutes. Remove basket and handle from oven. Brush handle with egg-white glaze; decorate with colored sprinkles, if desired. Return to oven; bake 5 minutes longer or until golden brown. Carefully remove handle from baking sheet; cool on a rack. Gently loosen dough from soufflé dish by running a knife between bread and dish. Remove dish. Brush inside of bread basket with egg-white glaze. With basket on baking sheet, place basket on top oven rack. Bake 20 to 30 minutes longer or until outside is golden brown and inside is pale golden. Five minutes before taking basket from oven, brush top braid of basket with egg-white glaze. Decorate with colored sprinkles, if desired. Bake final 5 minutes. Remove basket from baking sheet; cool on a rack. When basket and handle are completely cooled, insert a 4-inch wooden skewer halfway into center of each handle end. Attach handle to basket by inserting protruding skewer into basket rim. If necessary, use more wooden picks to secure handle in an upright position. If desired, place basket on a round platter. Surround with Coconut Grass and small clusters of jelly beans. Line basket with remaining Coconut Grass. Fill with Hot Cross Buns or your favorite rolls. Makes 1 large bread basket.

Note: The deeper your soufflé dish, the taller your basket can be. I used a 2-1/2-quart soufflé dish, 7 inches in diameter and 4 inches high.

Easter-Basket Bread filled with Hot Cross Buns, page 145.

Kulich   Photo on page 152.

This regal Russian Easter bread is crowned with a rose and served with Pashka, opposite.

3 tablespoons brandy or rum
1/2 cup raisins
1/2 cup chopped mixed candied fruit
1/2 teaspoon saffron threads
1 tablespoon brandy or rum
2 (1/4-oz.) pkgs. active dry yeast
  (2 tablespoons)
1 teaspoon sugar
1/3 cup warm water (110F, 45C)
1 cup whipping cream, room temperature
2/3 cup sugar
1/2 cup butter, melted
1 egg, room temperature

2 egg yolks, room temperature
2 teaspoons vanilla extract
1/2 teaspoon almond extract
1-1/2 teaspoons salt
1-1/2 teaspoons grated orange peel
1-1/2 teaspoons grated lemon peel
6-1/4 to 6-3/4 cups all-purpose or
  bread flour
1/2 cup toasted chopped almonds
Almond Icing, see below
1 small fresh rose or icing rose
Colored sprinkles, if desired
Pashka, opposite

Almond Icing:
1 egg white, room temperature
Pinch of salt
2 cups powdered sugar

1 teaspoon almond extract
1 tablespoon lemon juice

In a small bowl, combine 3 tablespoons brandy or rum, raisins and candied fruit. Cover; set aside overnight or 3 to 4 hours to soak. One hour before beginning bread, combine saffron and 1 tablespoon brandy or rum in a small bowl. Cover; set aside to soak. In large bowl of electric mixer, dissolve yeast and 1 teaspoon sugar in water. Let stand until foamy, 5 to 10 minutes. Pour brandy or rum not absorbed by fruit into yeast mixture. Blot fruit on paper towels; cover and set aside. To yeast mixture, add whipping cream, 2/3 cup sugar, butter, egg, egg yolks, vanilla, almond extract, salt, orange peel, lemon peel, saffron mixture and 2-1/2 to 3 cups flour. Beat at medium speed with electric mixer 3 minutes or, beat 300 vigorous strokes by hand. Stir in enough remaining flour to make a soft dough. Turn out dough onto a lightly floured surface. Clean and grease bowl; set aside. **Knead dough** 10 to 12 minutes or until smooth and elastic. Dough will feel buttery. Place dough in greased bowl, turning to coat all sides. Cover with a slightly damp towel. Let rise in a warm place, free from drafts, until doubled in bulk, 1 to 1-1/2 hours. Generously grease 2 (2-pound) coffee cans or 2 (3-pound) shortening cans. Cut and oil circles of waxed paper to fit bottoms of cans. **Punch down dough;** knead 30 seconds. Roll out dough to a large rectangle. Sprinkle with almonds and blotted fruit. Knead in fruit and nuts until evenly distributed. Divide dough in half. Shape into round balls. Place smooth-side up in prepared cans. Cover with a dry towel. Let rise until doubled in bulk, about 2 hours. **Preheat oven** to 375F (190C). Bake 20 minutes. Reduce oven heat to 325F (165C). Bake 35 to 45 minutes longer or until a skewer inserted in center comes out clean. If tops become too brown, cover lightly with foil. Let stand in cans 10 minutes. Turn out onto a rack to cool. Prepare Almond Icing. Drizzle over cooled loaves, letting icing drip down sides. Place rose in center of bread. Or, frost top and decorate with colored sprinkles or, with colored sprinkles, write **XV**, which means "Christ is risen." Let icing set until hard. Cut loaves horizontally, saving top slices as covers to keep bread from drying. Serve with Pashka. Makes 2 loaves.

Almond Icing:
In small bowl of electric mixer, beat egg white and salt until firm peaks form. Gradually beat in sugar, almond extract and lemon juice.

Pashka   Photo on page 152.

A deliciously creamy cheese mold—flavored with fresh orange peel and toasted almonds.

3 (8-oz.) pkgs. cream cheese,
  room temperature
3/4 cup butter, room temperature
2 egg yolks
2 tablespoons orange-flavored liqueur
1/3 cup whipping cream
1/2 teaspoon almond extract
1 teaspoon vanilla extract

1 tablespoon freshly grated orange peel
1/4 teaspoon salt
1 cup powdered sugar
3/4 cup toasted finely chopped almonds,
  if desired
Colored sprinkles, if desired
Fresh rosebuds or
  other flowers for decoration

Lightly oil 2 (1-pound) coffee cans or 3 (1-pound) vegetable or fruit cans. Line cans with 2 layers of cheesecloth, letting ends extend over rims; set aside. In large bowl of electric mixer, beat cream cheese and butter until smooth and creamy. Beat in egg yolks, orange liqueur, whipping cream, almond extract, vanilla, orange peel and salt until combined. Gradually beat in sugar until blended. Fold in almonds, if desired. Spoon mixture into prepared cans, filling each can about 1/3 full. Knock cans sharply on a firm surface to expel air bubbles. Spoon in remaining cheese mixture, filling cans evenly. Again knock cans sharply on a firm surface. Make a decorative swirl in tops of each. Cover tightly with foil; refrigerate overnight. To remove from cans, grasp ends of cheesecloth. Gently but firmly, pull Pashka from can; peel off cheesecloth. If desired, remove cheesecloth pattern from cheese by lightly rubbing with back of a spoon that has been dipped in water. Place molded cheese on a serving plate. If desired, decorate tops with colored sprinkles. Decorate plate with rosebuds or other flowers. Makes 2 or 3 cheese molds.

Cherry-Cordial Loaf

A beautiful loaf that tastes like chocolate-covered cherries—perfect for holiday gift giving.

3 cups all-purpose flour
1 tablespoon baking powder
1/2 teaspoon baking soda
1/2 teaspoon salt
1/4 cup sugar
1 (9-oz.) jar maraschino cherries
About 1/2 cup milk

1 egg, room temperature
1/4 cup brandy
2 tablespoons vegetable oil
2 teaspoons vanilla extract
1 cup miniature semisweet chocolate pieces
2 teaspoons sugar

Generously grease a 9" x 5" loaf pan; set aside. Preheat oven to 350F (175C). In a large bowl, combine flour, baking powder, baking soda, salt and 1/4 cup sugar; set aside. Drain liquid from cherries into a 1-cup liquid measuring cup. Add milk to make 1 cup; set aside. Blot cherries on paper towels. Finely chop enough cherries to make 1/2 cup. Cut remaining whole cherries in halves. Set aside to drain on paper towels. In a medium bowl, combine chopped cherries, liquid mixture, egg, brandy, oil and vanilla. Stir into flour mixture only until dry ingredients are moistened. Fold in chocolate pieces. Turn into prepared pan; smooth top. Sprinkle with 2 teaspoons sugar. Arrange cherry halves cut-side down in a row down center of batter. Press lightly into batter. Bake 65 to 70 minutes or until a wooden pick inserted in center comes out clean. Let stand in pan 10 minutes. Turn out of pan. Cool on a rack. Makes 1 loaf.

Gumdrop-Holly Wreath

A fun and festive bread sparkling with jewel-like pieces of gumdrops—perfect for gifts!

1 (1-lb.) pkg. small mixed gumdrops,
   spice or fruit-flavored
3 cups all-purpose flour
3-1/2 teaspoons baking powder
1 teaspoon salt
1/2 teaspoon ground cinnamon
1/4 teaspoon ground nutmeg

3/4 cup sugar
1 egg, room temperature
1-1/2 cups milk
2 tablespoons vegetable oil
1 teaspoon vanilla extract
3/4 cup chopped walnuts or pecans
Sugar Glaze, see below

Sugar Glaze:
1 cup powdered sugar
1/2 teaspoon vanilla extract

1 to 2 tablespoons milk

Dipping scissors in hot water to keep from sticking, cut 15 red gumdrops in half. Set aside top halves with 8 whole green gumdrops. Using brightest colors available, cut enough of remaining gumdrops into pea-size pieces to equal 1 cup; set aside. Grease and flour a 9-inch diameter, 3-inch-deep ring mold or springform pan with a center tube; set aside. **Preheat oven** to 350F (175C). In a large bowl, combine flour, baking powder, salt, cinnamon, nutmeg and sugar. Toss 1 cup cut gumdrops with flour mixture to coat and separate; set aside. In a medium bowl, lightly beat egg. Stir in milk, oil and vanilla. Stir into flour mixture only until dry ingredients are moistened. Stir in nuts. Turn into prepared pan. Use the back of a spoon to smooth top. Bake 50 to 60 minutes or until a wooden pick inserted in center comes out clean. Let stand in pan 10 minutes. Remove from pan; cool rounded-side up on a rack. Sprinkle sugar over work surface. On work surface, use a rolling pin to flatten 8 reserved green gumdrops. Cut into 15 leaf shapes; set aside. Prepare Sugar Glaze. Drizzle over cooled bread. Decorate top with 5 groupings of 3 red gumdrops for berries and 3 green-gumdrop leaves. Makes 1 loaf.

Sugar Glaze:
In a small bowl, combine powdered sugar and vanilla. Stir in enough milk to make a smooth, creamy glaze of drizzling consistency.

Before measuring syrupy sweeteners, lightly oil the measuring cup. Every drop of syrup will drain out effortlessly.

How to Make Gumdrop-Holly Wreath

1/After dipping scissors in hot water, cut 15 red gumdrops in half. Reserve red tops and 8 whole green gumdrops.

2/Flatten reserved green gumdrops with rolling pin. Cut into 15 leaf shapes. Arrange cut gumdrops on glazed loaf in clusters of berries and leaves.

Panettone

Italian fruit loaf—traditionally served at Christmas and other special celebrations.

3 (1/4-oz.) pkgs. active dry yeast
  (3 tablespoons)
1 teaspoon sugar
1/2 cup warm water (110F, 45C)
1/4 cup honey
6 egg yolks, room temperature
1/2 cup butter, melted
1-1/2 teaspoons salt
1-1/2 teaspoons vanilla extract
2 teaspoons freshly grated orange peel

2 teaspoons anise seeds, crushed
3-1/2 to 4 cups all-purpose flour
1/3 cup toasted pine nuts or
  slivered almonds
1/3 cup finely chopped citron
1/3 cup dark raisins
1/3 cup golden raisins
1 egg white blended with
  2 teaspoons water for glaze

In large bowl of electric mixer, dissolve yeast and sugar in 1/2 cup water. Let stand until foamy, 5 to 10 minutes. Add honey, egg yolks, butter, salt, vanilla, orange peel, anise seeds and 1-1/2 to 2 cups flour. Beat at medium speed with electric mixer 2 minutes or, beat 200 vigorous strokes by hand. Stir in pine nuts or almonds, citron, raisins and enough remaining flour to make a soft dough. Turn out dough onto a lightly floured surface. Clean and grease bowl; set aside. **Knead dough** 8 to 10 minutes or until smooth and elastic, adding very little flour. Dough will be soft, moist and slightly sticky. Place dough in greased bowl, turning to coat all sides. Cover with a slightly damp towel. Let rise in a warm place, free from drafts, until doubled in bulk, about 2 hours. Generously grease 2 (1-quart) soufflé dishes or 2 (1-pound) coffee cans; set aside. **Punch down dough;** knead 30 seconds. Shape dough into 2 smooth balls. Place smooth-side up in prepared dishes or cans. Cover with a dry towel. Let rise until doubled in bulk, about 1 hour. **Preheat oven** to 350F (175C). Brush tops of loaves with egg-white glaze. Bake 35 to 40 minutes or until bread sounds hollow when tapped on top. Carefully turn out on a rack to cool. Makes 2 loaves.

Dresden Stollen

This rum-spiked, fruit-laden bread originated in Dresden and is a German Christmas tradition.

1 cup coarsely chopped mixed candied fruit
1/2 cup golden raisins
1/2 cup currants
1/4 cup finely chopped candied orange peel
1/4 cup finely chopped citron
1/2 cup dark rum or brandy
2 (1/4-oz.) pkgs. active dry yeast
  (2 tablespoons)
1 tablespoon brown sugar
1-1/4 cups warm milk (110F, 45C)
5-1/2 to 6 cups all-purpose or bread flour
2 to 3 tablespoons all-purpose
  or bread flour

3/4 cup packed brown sugar
2 eggs, room temperature
1 cup butter, melted
Grated peel of 1 large lemon
1 teaspoon vanilla extract
1 teaspoon almond extract
1 teaspoon salt
1 cup toasted chopped almonds
Melted butter
Granulated sugar
20 to 25 candied-cherry halves, if desired
Powdered sugar

In a medium bowl, combine 1 cup candied fruit, raisins, currants, orange peel, citron and rum or brandy. Cover; set aside overnight or 3 to 4 hours to soak. In large bowl of electric mixer, dissolve yeast and 1 tablespoon brown sugar in milk. Let stand until foamy, 5 to 10 minutes. Add 1 to 1-1/2 cups flour. Beat at medium speed with electric mixer 3 minutes or, 300 vigorous strokes by hand. Cover tightly with plastic wrap. Let sponge rise in a warm place, free from drafts, until light and bubbly, about 15 minutes. Drain liquid off fruit; reserve liquid. Toss drained fruit with 2 to 3 tablespoons flour; set aside. **Stir down sponge.** Add 3/4 cup brown sugar, eggs, 1 cup butter, lemon peel, vanilla, almond extract, salt, liquid from fruit and enough remaining flour to make a soft dough. Turn out dough onto a lightly floured surface. Clean and grease bowl; set aside. **Knead dough** 8 to 10 minutes or until smooth and elastic. Dough will be soft and buttery. On a generously floured surface, pat or roll out dough to a large rectangle, 1/2 inch thick. Sprinkle floured fruit and nuts over surface. Knead in fruit and nuts until evenly distributed. Place dough in greased bowl, turning to coat all sides. Cover with a slightly damp towel. Let rise in a warm place, free from drafts, until doubled in bulk, about 1-1/2 hours. Grease 2 large baking sheets; set aside. Butter 2 (15-inch) lengths of waxed paper; set aside. **Punch down dough;** knead 30 seconds. Divide dough in half. Shape each half into a 12" x 8" oval, 1/2 to 3/4 inch thick. Brush with melted butter; sprinkle lightly with granulated sugar. Fold dough almost in half lengthwise, letting 1 to 1-1/2 inches of bottom dough extend beyond edge of top dough. Place folded dough on prepared baking sheets. Press fold gently. Lightly press top edge into bottom layer to seal. Cover with buttered waxed paper. Let rise until bulk is increased by half, about 60 minutes. **Preheat oven** to 350F (175C). If desired, gently tuck candied-cherry halves into dough where bottom edge extends beyond top edge. Brush loaves with melted butter. Bake 35 to 45 minutes or until a skewer inserted in center comes out clean. If tops become too brown, cover lightly with foil. Cool baked loaves on racks. As loaves cool, brush 2 to 3 more times with melted butter. When cool, generously sprinkle with powdered sugar. Cut in thin slices. Makes 2 loaves.

Clockwise from right: Swedish Limpa, page 54; Dresden Stollen, above; Khachapuri, page 30; Pashka, page 149; and Kulich, page 148.

Candy-Cane Bread

Chunks of peppermint candy dot this bread—it's too good to hang on the tree!

1 recipe Basic Sweet Yeast Dough, page 59
1 cup coarsely crushed peppermint candy
1 egg white blended with 2 to 6 drops red
    food coloring

Coarse red decorating sugar, if desired
Peppermint Glaze, see below
1/3 to 1/2 cup finely crushed peppermint
    candy

Peppermint Glaze:
1 cup powdered sugar
1 to 2 drops peppermint extract

1 to 2 tablespoons milk

Prepare Basic Sweet Yeast Dough through first rising. Grease 2 large baking sheets; set aside. **Punch down dough;** knead 30 seconds. On a lightly floured surface, roll or pat out dough to a large rectangle. Sprinkle with 1 cup coarsely crushed candy. Fold dough over candy, then knead to distribute evenly. Work quickly to avoid melting candy. Divide dough into 4 equal pieces. Roll each piece into a 22-inch rope. Tightly twist 2 ropes together; pinch ends to seal. Repeat with remaining 2 ropes. Place twisted ropes on prepared baking sheets, curving like candy canes. Cover with a dry towel. Let rise in a warm place, free from drafts, until doubled in bulk, about 1 hour. **Preheat oven** to 350F (175C). Carefully brush every other section of twists with red egg-white mixture. If desired, sprinkle coarse red sugar over red sections of twists. Bake 25 to 35 minutes or until bread sounds hollow when tapped on top. Cool on racks. Drizzle Peppermint Glaze over white sections of twists. Sprinkle with finely crushed candy. Makes 2 loaves.

Peppermint Glaze:
In a small bowl, combine powdered sugar and peppermint extract. Stir in enough milk to make a smooth, creamy glaze of drizzling consistency.

 Tip *Rotating loaves of bread during baking, front to back and top to bottom shelves, provides more even baking and browning.*

How to Make Candy-Cane Bread

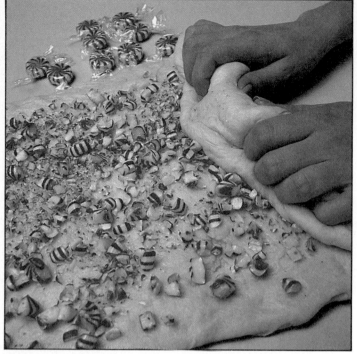

1/Sprinkle 1 cup crushed candy over dough. Fold dough over candy, then knead to distribute evenly.

2/Twist 2 ropes tightly; pinch ends to seal. Place twisted ropes on baking sheets, curving like candy canes.

3/Carefully brush every other section with red egg-white mixture. Sprinkle red sections with coarse red sugar.

4/Drizzle Peppermint Glaze over white sections of twists. Sprinkle with finely crushed candy.

Eggnog Christmas-Tree Bread

Eggnog-flavored, this festive pull-apart bread has a surprise inside each piece!

2 (1/4-oz.) pkgs. active dry yeast
   (2 tablespoons)
1 teaspoon sugar
1/3 cup warm water (110F, 45C)
1-1/2 cups dairy or homemade eggnog,
   not canned, room temperature
2 eggs, room temperature
1/2 teaspoon rum flavoring
1 teaspoon vanilla extract
1/2 cup butter, melted
1/2 cup sugar

2 teaspoons salt
1/4 teaspoon ground cardamom, if desired
1/2 teaspoon ground nutmeg
1/4 teaspoon ground cinnamon
5-1/2 to 6 cups all-purpose or bread flour
32 whole maraschino cherries, blotted dry
1 egg white blended with
   1 tablespoon water for glaze
Eggnog Icing, see below
16 maraschino cherries, halved, blotted dry
Candied fruit for decoration, if desired

Eggnog Icing:
1 cup powdered sugar
Pinch of salt
1 teaspoon butter, room temperature

2 drops rum flavoring
1 to 2 tablespoons dairy eggnog

Grease 2 large baking sheets; set aside. In large bowl of electric mixer, dissolve yeast and 1 teaspoon sugar in 1/3 cup water. Let stand until foamy, 5 to 10 minutes. Add eggnog, eggs, rum flavoring, vanilla, butter, 1/2 cup sugar, salt, cardamom, nutmeg, cinnamon and 2 to 2-1/2 cups flour. Beat at medium speed with electric mixer 2 minutes or, beat 200 vigorous strokes by hand. Stir in enough remaining flour to make a soft dough. Turn out dough onto a lightly floured surface. **Knead dough** 4 to 6 minutes or until smooth. Divide dough in half. Cover half; set aside. Divide remaining dough into 16 equal pieces. Reserve 1 piece to make top and base of Christmas tree. Flatten remaining pieces into 2-inch circles. Place a cherry in center of each circle. Bring edges together over cherries; pinch firmly to seal. Beginning 3 inches from 1 end of a prepared baking sheet, arrange balls seam-side down in graduated rows of 5, 4, 3, 2 and 1 to make a Christmas tree. Pinch off two-thirds of reserved piece of dough for tree trunk; use remaining dough to make a tree-top decoration. Repeat with reserved half of dough. Butter 2 (18-inch) lengths of waxed paper. Place over loaves. Let rise in a warm place, free from drafts, until doubled in bulk, about 1 hour. **Preheat oven** to 375F (190C). Brush egg-white glaze over tops of trees. Bake 20 to 25 minutes or until golden brown. To avoid breaking baked trees, carefully use 2 metal spatulas to remove from baking sheets. Cool 20 minutes on racks. Pipe or drizzle with Eggnog Icing. Place a maraschino-cherry half or piece of candied fruit on center of each ball. Let icing set 5 minutes. Makes 2 loaves.

Eggnog Icing:
In a small bowl, combine powdered sugar, salt, butter and rum flavoring. Stir in enough eggnog to make a smooth, creamy glaze of drizzling consistency.

Variation
Brush raised dough with egg-white glaze. Sprinkle red-colored sugar lightly on top and heavily in crevices to define segments. If desired, place a maraschino-cherry half or a piece of candied fruit on center of each segment. Bake as directed.

Pumpkin-Praline Rolls

Perfect for Thanksgiving. Spread with whipped cream cheese, then listen to the raves!

1/2 cup raisins
2 tablespoons rum or orange juice
2 (1/4-oz.) pkgs. active dry yeast
  (2 tablespoons)
1 teaspoon brown sugar
1/3 cup warm water (110F, 45C)
1/3 cup packed brown sugar
2 eggs, room temperature
2 tablespoons vegetable oil
3/4 cup mashed cooked pumpkin or
  canned pumpkin

1-1/2 teaspoons salt
1-1/2 teaspoons ground cinnamon
3/4 teaspoon ground nutmeg
1/4 teaspoon ground ginger
2-3/4 to 3-1/4 cups all-purpose or
  bread flour
1/2 cup toasted chopped pecans
Praline Topping, see below
24 to 28 pecan halves

Praline Topping:
1/2 cup packed brown sugar
1/2 teaspoon ground cinnamon

2 tablespoons cold butter
1/2 cup finely chopped pecans

In a small bowl, combine raisins and rum or orange juice. Cover; let soak overnight or 3 to 4 hours. In large bowl of electric mixer, dissolve yeast and 1 teaspoon brown sugar in water. Let stand until foamy, 5 to 10 minutes. Add 1/3 cup brown sugar, eggs, oil, pumpkin, salt, cinnamon, nutmeg, ginger and 1-1/2 to 2 cups flour. Beat at medium speed with electric mixer 4 minutes or, beat 400 vigorous strokes by hand. Stir in pecans, raisin mixture and enough remaining flour to make a stiff batter. Cover with a slightly damp towel. Let rise in a warm place, free from drafts, until doubled in bulk, about 1 hour. Grease 24 muffin cups; set aside. Prepare Praline Topping; set aside. **Stir down batter.** Spoon into prepared muffin cups, filling half full. Butter your fingers and 2 (14-inch) lengths of waxed paper. Smooth tops of batter with your buttered fingers. Sprinkle 1 heaping teaspoon Praline Topping into each muffin cup. Press lightly into dough with back of a spoon. Press 1 pecan half into top of each. Cover lightly with buttered waxed paper. Let rise until doubled in bulk, about 30 minutes. **Preheat oven** to 375F (190C). Bake 15 to 20 minutes or until golden brown. Cool on racks 5 minutes. Makes 24 to 28 rolls.

Praline Topping:
In a medium bowl, combine brown sugar and cinnamon. Use a pastry cutter or 2 knives to cut in butter until mixture resembles coarse crumbs. Stir in pecans.

Tip *To "speed-soak" raisins or currants, combine fruit with soaking liquid in a medium bowl. Cover and microwave on HIGH 30 seconds. Let stand 5 minutes.*

Yummy-Yam Bread

Omit the Raisin-Nut Filling and you have a fragrant, spicy bread for turkey sandwiches.

2 (1/4-oz.) pkgs. active dry yeast
   (2 tablespoons)
1 teaspoon brown sugar
2/3 cup warm water (110F, 45C)
1/3 cup packed brown sugar
1 cup mashed canned yams or pumpkin
1/4 cup butter, melted
3 eggs, room temperature
1-1/2 teaspoons ground cinnamon
1/2 teaspoon ground allspice

1/2 teaspoon ground ginger
1/4 teaspoon ground cloves
2 teaspoons freshly grated orange peel
2 teaspoons salt
5-3/4 to 6-1/4 cups all-purpose or bread flour
Raisin-Nut Filling, see below
3 tablespoons brown sugar
1/4 teaspoon ground cinnamon
2 tablespoons butter, melted

Raisin-Nut Filling:
1/2 cup packed brown sugar
1 teaspoon ground cinnamon
1/4 teaspoon ground nutmeg

1/4 teaspoon ground ginger
1/2 cup finely chopped walnuts or pecans
1/3 cup raisins

In large bowl of electric mixer, dissolve yeast and 1 teaspoon brown sugar in water. Let stand until foamy, 5 to 10 minutes. Add 1/3 cup brown sugar, yams or pumpkin, 1/4 cup butter, eggs, 1-1/2 teaspoons cinnamon, allspice, ginger, cloves, orange peel, salt and 1-1/2 to 2 cups flour. Beat at medium speed with electric mixer 2 minutes or, beat 200 vigorous strokes by hand. Stir in enough remaining flour to make a soft dough. Turn out dough onto a lightly floured surface. Clean and grease bowl; set aside. **Knead dough** 10 to 12 minutes or until smooth and elastic. Place dough in greased bowl, turning to coat all sides. Cover with a slightly damp towel. Let rise in a warm place, free from drafts, until doubled in bulk, about 1 hour. Grease 2 (2-quart) soufflé or casserole dishes; set aside. **Punch down dough;** knead 30 seconds. Divide dough in half. Divide each half into 24 pieces. Flatten each piece into a circle about 3 inches in diameter. Place 1 teaspoon Raisin-Nut Filling in center of each circle. Pinch edges together tightly to seal. Arrange balls of dough seam-side down in prepared dishes. In each dish, make 2 layers, each with 8 balls around outside edge and 4 balls in center of dish. Cover with a dry towel. Let rise until doubled in bulk, about 1 hour. Combine 3 tablespoons brown sugar and 1/4 teaspoon cinnamon; set aside. **Preheat oven** to 375F (190C). Sprinkle half of cinnamon-sugar mixture over each loaf; drizzle with 1 tablespoon melted butter. Bake 40 to 45 minutes or until a wooden pick inserted in center comes out clean. Carefully remove from dishes. Cool on racks. Makes 2 loaves.

Raisin-Nut Filling:
In a small bowl, combine all ingredients.

Variation

Savory Yummy-Yam Bread: Omit Raisin-Nut Filling. After first rising, punch down dough; shape into 2 loaves. Before baking, slash tops of loaves as desired. Brush with melted butter. Bake 30 to 35 minutes.

Jack-O-Lantern Bread

A perfect bread for Halloween parties!

1 recipe Yummy-Yam Bread, opposite,
    with changes given below
Jack-O-Lantern Frosting, see below

Raisins, whole cloves, whole allspice or
    toasted hulled pumpkin seeds

Jack-O-Lantern Frosting:
1 (16-oz.) pkg. powdered sugar
3/4 teaspoon ground cinnamon
1 teaspoon vanilla extract

6 to 8 tablespoons orange juice
Orange food coloring

Prepare Yummy-Yam Bread dough with following changes: Substitute mashed pumpkin for mashed yams; increase brown sugar to 2/3 cup; add 1 cup raisins. Prepare through first rising, adding more flour, if needed. Grease 2 (1-1/2- or 2-quart) soufflé dishes; set aside. **Punch down dough;** knead 30 seconds. Divide dough in half. Shape each half into a smooth ball; place in prepared dishes. Cover with a dry towel. Let rise until doubled in bulk, about 1 hour. **Preheat oven** to 375F (190C). Bake 35 to 45 minutes or until bread sounds hollow when tapped on bottom. Remove from dishes. Cool on racks. Prepare Jack-O-Lantern Frosting. Spread half of frosting over top and side of each loaf. Use raisins, cloves, allspice, or pumpkin seeds to make a Jack-O-Lantern face in frosting. Let frosting set 15 minutes. Makes 2 loaves.

Jack-O-Lantern Frosting:
In a medium bowl, combine powdered sugar, cinnamon and vanilla. Stir in 6 tablespoons orange juice and food coloring. Stir in enough of remaining orange juice, 1/2 teaspoon at a time, to make a thick, creamy frosting.

Pumpkin-Seed & Date Bread

A deliciously wholesome pumpkin-wheat bread — rich with yogurt, dates and oatmeal.

1-1/4 cups raw hulled pumpkin seeds
3 cups all-purpose flour
3/4 cup finely snipped or chopped dates
2-1/2 teaspoons baking powder
1 teaspoon baking soda
1-1/2 teaspoons salt
1 cup regular or quick-cooking rolled oats
1-1/2 teaspoons ground cinnamon

3/4 teaspoon ground ginger
3/4 teaspoon ground nutmeg
4 eggs, room temperature
1 cup packed brown sugar
1/2 cup vegetable oil
1/2 cup plain yogurt, room temperature
1 (16-oz.) can pumpkin
Grated peel of 1 medium lemon

In a large skillet over medium heat, toast pumpkin seeds until they begin to make popping sounds and start to turn golden brown; set aside to cool. Grease 2 (8" x 4") loaf pans; set aside. **Preheat oven** to 350F (175C). In a large bowl, combine flour and dates. Use your fingers to separate dates and coat with flour. Stir in baking powder, baking soda, salt, oats, cinnamon, ginger and nutmeg until combined; set aside. In a medium bowl, lightly beat eggs. Stir in brown sugar, oil, yogurt, pumpkin and lemon peel. Stir into flour mixture only until dry ingredients are moistened. Stir in 1 cup toasted pumpkin seeds. Turn into prepared pans. Smooth tops; sprinkle 2 tablespoons toasted pumpkin seeds over top of each loaf. Lightly press into surface with back of a spoon. Bake 60 to 70 minutes or until a wooden pick inserted in center comes out clean. Let stand in pan 10 minutes. Turn out onto a rack to cool. Makes 2 loaves.

Griddle & Fried Breads

Imagine small breads, hot off the griddle or plucked from a sizzling bath of hot oil, all fragrant and savory. What could be more enticing? There's something magical about griddle and fried breads. Maybe it's being able to watch them change from dough or batter into their full-blown, golden-brown glory.

Take the doughnut for example. Many people resist making their own doughnuts because they think frying in deep fat produces greasy results. Nonsense! All you need are a few frying basics. First of all, you don't need a deep-fat fryer. Any deep, heavy pot will do. Temperature is the most important factor in frying breads. A candy or deep-fry thermometer will help you keep the oil at the necessary 370F to 375F (190C). When the shaped dough is lowered into hot oil, several things happen. Heat activates the carbon dioxide, causing the bread to puff up almost immediately. Starch in the dough stiffens, strengthening the structure. The surface begins to brown, signaling doneness. Remember to fry only a few pieces at a time. Crowding quickly lowers oil temperature and causes uneven frying.

Now that you see how simple it is to fry breads, be sure and try savory Hungarian Langos. My first taste of this delicious fried bread made with mashed potatoes was at a tiny Hungarian restaurant in Los Angeles. The owner brought the steaming-hot puffs out on a large platter with a bowl of cut garlic cloves in the center. We rubbed the golden, rectangular breads vigorously with the garlic as he instructed. The flavor was so sensational, I nearly fainted with pleasure! We quickly ordered another platter of langos and bowls of thick Hungarian soup to complete our dinner—a truly choice meal!

English Muffins and Crumpets have delighted the British for centuries. Both breads require a second toasting after their initial baking. One is split, the other is not; one begins as dough, the other as batter. Each one is delicious and both reach their ultimate glory when accompanied by lots of sweet butter and fresh jam or marmalade.

Scottish Griddle Scones

Split these scones while hot and spread with Strawberry Devonshire Cream. Heavenly!

2 cups all-purpose flour
1 tablespoon baking powder
1/2 teaspoon salt
6 tablespoons cold butter,
  cut in 10 pieces

2 eggs, room temperature
2 tablespoons honey
1/2 cup whipping cream
Honey, jam or Strawberry Devonshire Cream,
  below

In a large bowl, combine flour, baking powder and salt. Use a pastry cutter or 2 knives to cut in butter until mixture resembles coarse crumbs; set aside. In a medium bowl, lightly whisk eggs, 2 tablespoons honey and whipping cream until blended. Stir into flour mixture only until dry ingredients are moistened. **To prepare in food processor:** Fit processor with metal blade. Place flour, baking powder, salt and butter in work bowl. Turn machine on and off only until mixture resembles coarse crumbs. Add eggs, 2 tablespoons honey and whipping cream. Process only until blended. Turn out dough onto a generously floured surface. Flour your hands. Gently pat or press dough only until it holds together. Cut dough in half. Pat each half into a circle about 1/2 inch thick. Lightly dust flour over tops of circles. With a floured knife, cut each circle into quarters. Preheat an ungreased griddle or skillet over medium-low heat. Gently place scones on hot griddle. When bottoms are lightly browned and scones rise slightly, about 13 minutes, turn and brown other side, 7 to 10 minutes. Serve hot with honey, jam or Strawberry Devonshire Cream. To preserve their tender texture, pull scones apart with your fingers. Do not cut with a knife. Makes 8 scones.

Variations

Orange Griddle Scones: Add 1 tablespoon freshly grated orange peel. Serve with Citrus-Honey Butter, page 46.
Oven-Baked Scones: Lightly grease a large baking sheet; set aside. Preheat oven to 425F (220C). Place quartered scones 2 inches apart on prepared baking sheet. Bake 12 to 15 minutes or until golden brown.

Strawberry Devonshire Cream

Serve on hot waffles, pancakes or scones.

1/2 cup whipping cream, chilled
2 tablespoons brown sugar

1/2 cup dairy sour cream, room temperature
1 cup diced fresh strawberries

In small bowl of electric mixer, combine whipping cream and brown sugar; let stand 2 to 3 minutes. Whip cream mixture until firm peaks form. Gently fold in sour cream and strawberries. Spoon into a medium serving dish. Cover and refrigerate. Serve cold. Makes about 2-1/2 cups.

Tip *A food processor fitted with a metal blade makes quick work of cutting butter into biscuit dough. Process only to the point where mixture resembles coarse crumbs. Overprocessing creates tough biscuits.*

Danish Aebleskivers

This Danish delicacy can be served as breakfast, dessert or a snack.

1 (1/4-oz.) pkg. active dry yeast
  (1 tablespoon)
1 teaspoon granulated sugar
1/4 cup warm water (110F, 45C)
5 eggs, separated, room temperature
1-3/4 cups half and half
3-1/2 cups all-purpose flour
1/4 cup granulated sugar

2/3 cup butter, melted
1/2 teaspoon salt
1/4 teaspoon ground cardamom
Grated peel of 1/2 large lemon
Melted butter for frying
Powdered sugar
Quick & Fresh Applesauce,
  below, or preserves

In large bowl of electric mixer, dissolve yeast and 1 teaspoon granulated sugar in water. Let stand until foamy, 5 to 10 minutes. In small bowl of electric mixer, beat egg whites until stiff but not dry; set aside. To foamy yeast mixture, add egg yolks, half and half, flour, 1/4 cup granulated sugar, 2/3 cup butter, salt, cardamom and lemon peel. Beat with electric mixer at medium speed, only until batter is smooth. Fold in beaten egg whites. Cover with a slightly damp towel. Let rise in a warm place, free from drafts, until doubled in bulk, about 1 hour. Preheat aebleskiver pan over medium-high heat. Pour about 1/2 tablespoon melted butter into each indentation. Spoon in batter almost to top of each indentation. Cook until aebleskivers are browned on bottom. Use 2 forks or a metal skewer to turn; brown other side. Drain briefly on paper towels. To serve, sprinkle with powdered sugar. Serve immediately with Quick & Fresh Applesauce or your favorite preserves. Leftovers may be frozen and reheated 10 minutes in a 350F (175C) oven. Makes about 40 Aebleskivers.

Variation

If an aebleskiver pan is not available, place a large heavy skillet over medium heat. Add melted butter until 1/4 inch deep. Carefully drop mounds of batter into hot butter by tablespoonfuls. Fry until browned, turning once.

Quick & Fresh Applesauce

Delightful with pancakes, waffles and irresistible Aebleskivers, above!

4 crisp, tart red apples, unpeeled
1/4 cup orange juice
1/4 cup sugar

1 teaspoon grated orange peel
1/4 teaspoon ground cinnamon
1/4 teaspoon ground allspice

Remove cores from apples; cut cored apples into eighths. Place in cold, salted water to prevent discoloration. Soak 5 minutes; blot on paper towels. Combine all ingredients in a blender or food processor fitted with a metal blade. Use on and off pulses to process until apples are texture you desire. Spoon into a medium serving dish. Serve at room temperature. Makes about 3 cups.

English Muffins

Cook half of the dough as English muffins and the other half as English-muffin bread!

2 (1/4-oz.) pkgs. active dry yeast
   (2 tablespoons)
1 teaspoon sugar
1 cup warm water (110F, 45C)
1 cup milk, room temperature
1/4 cup honey

1/4 cup butter, melted
1-1/2 teaspoons salt
5-1/2 to 6 cups all-purpose or
   bread flour
Cornmeal

In large bowl of electric mixer, dissolve yeast and sugar in water. Let stand until foamy, 5 to 10 minutes. Add milk, honey, butter, salt and 2 to 2-1/2 cups flour. Beat at medium speed with electric mixer 2 minutes or, beat 200 vigorous strokes by hand. Stir in enough remaining flour to make a soft dough. Turn out dough onto a lightly floured surface. Clean and grease bowl; set aside. Knead dough 6 to 8 minutes or until smooth and elastic. Place dough in greased bowl, turning to coat all sides. Cover with a slightly damp towel. Let rise in a warm place, free from drafts, until slightly more than doubled in bulk, about 1 hour. Generously sprinkle cornmeal over 2 ungreased baking sheets; set aside. **Do not punch down dough.** On a lightly floured surface, roll out dough until 1/2 inch thick. Use a 3-inch cutter to cut dough into rounds. Place on prepared baking sheets. Gather up remaining dough; reroll and cut into rounds. Generously sprinkle cornmeal over tops of rounds. Lightly press cornmeal into surface of each round. Cover rounds with waxed paper. Let rise until doubled in bulk, 30 to 45 minutes. **Preheat a griddle** or large heavy skillet over medium-high heat or, preheat electric griddle or skillet to 325F (165C). Sprinkle cornmeal over griddle. Do not grease. Bake muffins on hot griddle or skillet, 8 to 12 minutes on each side or until evenly browned. Cool to room temperature on racks. Use 2 forks to split muffins. Toast before serving. Makes about 20 English muffins.

Variations

Whole-Wheat English Muffins: Substitute 2-1/2 cups whole-wheat flour for 2-1/2 cups all-purpose or bread flour. Add 1/2 cup toasted wheat germ. Add 1 cup raisins, if desired.

Cinnamon-Raisin English Muffins: Add 1 teaspoon ground cinnamon, 1/2 teaspoon ground nutmeg, 1 teaspoon vanilla extract and 1 cup raisins.

Sourdough English Muffins: Reduce water and flour by 3/4 cup each. Add 1 cup sourdough starter.

English-Muffin Bread: Grease 2 (8" x 4") loaf pans; generously sprinkle cornmeal over bottoms and sides. Preheat oven to 375F (190C). After first rising, punch down dough; divide in half. Shape into loaves. Generously sprinkle cornmeal over tops. Press into surface of each loaf. Place in prepared pans. Cover with a dry towel. Let rise in a warm place, free from drafts, until doubled in bulk, about 45 minutes. Slash tops as desired. Bake 30 to 35 minutes or until bread sounds hollow when tapped on bottom. Remove from pans. Cool on racks. Makes 2 loaves.

 Buy inexpensive metal salt shakers. Fill with flour and use to dust work surface with flour while kneading dough.

Hungarian Langos

Hungarians rub this puffy fried bread with cut garlic cloves and serve it with hearty soups.

1 (1/4-oz.) pkg. active dry yeast
  (1 tablespoon)
2 teaspoons sugar
1/4 cup warm water (110F, 45C)
1 cup milk, room temperature
1 egg yolk, room temperature
1/2 cup mashed cooked potatoes
1/4 cup butter, melted

1 medium garlic clove, crushed
2 teaspoons salt
3/4 teaspoon ground ginger
4 to 4-1/2 cups all-purpose or bread flour
Peanut oil or vegetable oil for frying
6 garlic cloves, halved
Salt

In large bowl of electric mixer, dissolve yeast and sugar in water. Let stand until foamy, 5 to 10 minutes. Add milk, egg yolk, potatoes, butter, 1 crushed garlic clove, 2 teaspoons salt, ginger and 1 to 1-1/2 cups flour. Beat at medium speed with electric mixer 2 minutes or, beat 200 vigorous strokes by hand. Stir in enough remaining flour to make a soft dough. Turn out dough onto a lightly floured surface. Clean and grease bowl; set aside. **Knead dough** 6 to 8 minutes or until smooth and elastic. Dough will be slightly tacky, but not sticky. Place dough in greased bowl, turning to coat all sides. Cover with a slightly damp towel. Let rise in a warm place, free from drafts, until doubled in bulk, 45 to 60 minutes. **Punch down dough;** knead 30 seconds. Cover and let stand 10 minutes. On a lightly floured surface, roll out dough to a 24" x 6" rectangle, about 1/2 inch thick. Cut into 12 (4" x 3") rectangles. If dough shrinks after cutting, roll each piece to a 4" x 3" rectangle. With a sharp, pointed knife, make 3 parallel lengthwise slashes 2 inches long and evenly spaced in center of each rectangle, cutting all the way through dough. Cover with a dry towel; let stand 20 minutes. Pour oil 2 inches deep in a large heavy skillet. Heat oil to 370F (190C) or until a 1-inch cube of bread turns golden brown in 50 seconds. Use a metal spatula to lift dough from work surface. Carefully place dough in hot oil. Fry bread pieces, a few at a time, until puffed and golden brown on both sides. Do not crowd. Use a slotted spoon to remove cooked breads from oil. Drain on paper towels. Keep fried langos in warm oven while frying remaining dough. Serve warm with cut garlic cloves. Rub cut garlic over surface of langos; sprinkle with salt. Makes 12 langos.

Variation

Sweet Langos: Increase sugar to 1/4 cup. Omit garlic; decrease salt to 1/2 teaspoon. To serve for breakfast, do not rub with garlic. Dust with powdered sugar. Serve with jam or honey.

Tip *Gather recipe ingredients the night before for speedily assembled breads the next morning.*

Hungarian Langos with fresh garlic

Cake Doughnuts

Chilling the dough keeps these rich, tender morsels from absorbing too much oil.

3 cups all-purpose flour
1 tablespoon baking powder
1/2 teaspoon salt
2/3 cup granulated sugar
1/2 teaspoon ground nutmeg
1 teaspoon grated lemon peel
2 eggs

1/3 cup butter, melted
2 teaspoons vanilla extract
1/2 cup milk
Peanut oil or vegetable oil for deep-frying
Granulated or powdered sugar
Glaze of choice, if desired, opposite

In a large bowl, combine flour, baking powder, salt, 2/3 cup granulated sugar, nutmeg and lemon peel; set aside. In a medium bowl, lightly beat eggs. Stir in butter, vanilla and milk. Stir into flour mixture only until dry ingredients are moistened. Cover tightly with plastic wrap; refrigerate 1 hour. Lightly flour a large baking sheet; set aside. On a generously floured surface, roll out refrigerated dough until 1/2 inch thick. Cut with a floured 2-1/2- to 3-inch doughnut cutter. Or cut with a 3-inch biscuit cutter and a 1-inch canapé cutter for center. Arrange cut-out dough on floured baking sheet. Cover with a dry towel. Refrigerate until ready to cook, but no longer than 2 hours. Pour oil for deep-frying 2 to 3 inches deep in a large deep skillet, 4-quart saucepan or a deep-fat fryer. **Heat oil** to 370F (190C) or until a 1-inch cube of bread turns golden brown in 50 seconds. Fry doughnuts and doughnut holes a few at a time until golden brown on both sides, 2 to 3 minutes. Use a slotted spoon to remove cooked doughnuts from oil. Drain on paper towels. Coat with granulated sugar while warm or, cool and dip in powdered sugar or glaze of your choice. Serve warm or at room temperature. Cake doughnuts do not keep well. Serve same day made or, before dipping in glaze, freeze on day they are made. To reheat, place frozen doughnuts on an ungreased baking sheet. Lightly cover with foil. Heat 10 to 15 minutes in a preheated 350F (175C) oven. Makes about 18 doughnuts and 18 doughnut holes.

Variations

Gingerbread Doughnuts: Substitute 2/3 cup packed brown sugar for 2/3 cup granulated sugar. Substitute 1 tablespoon molasses for vanilla. Add 2 teaspoons ground ginger. Add 1 tablespoon minced crystallized ginger, if desired. Glaze with Spicy Glaze, opposite, substituting 1 teaspoon ground ginger for 1/2 teaspoon each ground cinnamon and ground nutmeg or, glaze with Maple Glaze, opposite.
Chocolate Doughnuts: Add 1/3 cup unsweetened cocoa powder. Increase granulated sugar to 1 cup. Glaze with Chocolate Glaze, opposite.
Spiced Doughnuts: Add 1-1/2 teaspoons ground cinnamon, 1/2 teaspoon ground allspice and 1/4 teaspoon ground cloves. Glaze with Spicy Glaze, opposite.

 To sugar-coat doughnuts, place sugar in a plastic or paper bag. Add doughnuts 1 or 2 at a time; shake gently. If using a plastic bag, let doughnuts cool 5 minutes before sugar-coating. Heat from doughnuts could melt a hole in the plastic bag!

Raised Doughnuts

Freeze some of these easy, delicious doughnuts and reheat them for a morning treat.

Basic Sweet Yeast Dough, page 59   **Granulated or powdered sugar**
Peanut oil or vegetable oil for deep-frying   **Glaze of choice, if desired, below**

Lightly flour a large baking sheet; set aside. Prepare Basic Sweet Yeast Dough through first rising. **Punch down dough;** roll out until 1/2 inch thick. Cut dough with a floured 2-1/2- to 3-inch doughnut cutter. Or, cut with a 3-inch biscuit cutter and a 1-inch canapé cutter for center. Place doughnuts and doughnut holes on prepared baking sheet. Cover with a dry towel. Let rise in a warm place, free from drafts, until doubled in bulk, 30 to 45 minutes. Or, cover tightly with plastic wrap. Let rise in refrigerator until next morning. Pour oil for deep-frying 3 inches deep in a large deep skillet, 4-quart saucepan or a deep-fat fryer. **Heat oil** to 370F (190C) or until a 1-inch cube of bread turns golden brown in 50 seconds. Fry doughnuts and doughnut holes a few at a time until golden brown on both sides, 3 to 4 minutes. Use a slotted spoon to remove fried doughnuts and holes from oil. Drain on paper towels. Coat with granulated sugar while warm or, cool and dip in powdered sugar or glaze of your choice. Cool on racks at least 10 minutes before serving. Unglazed doughnuts may be frozen. To reheat, place frozen doughnuts on an ungreased baking sheet. Lightly cover with foil. Heat 10 to 15 minutes in a preheated 350F (175C) oven. Makes 12 to 14 doughnuts and doughnut holes.

Variations

Spicy Raisin Doughnuts: To Basic Sweet Yeast Dough recipe, add 1 teaspoon grated lemon peel, 1 teaspoon ground cinnamon, 1/2 teaspoon ground nutmeg and 3/4 cup raisins. In a small bowl, combine 1 cup sugar and 1 teaspoon ground cinnamon. Dip fried doughnuts and doughnut holes in sugar mixture.

Jelly Doughnuts: Roll out dough until 1/4 inch thick. Cut dough with a floured 3-inch biscuit cutter. Place 1 teaspoon jelly or jam or 1/2 teaspoon each of jam and softened cream cheese in center of half of dough rounds. Lightly brush edges with unbeaten egg white. Place an unfilled dough round over each filled round. Pinch edges to seal.

Nut-Coated Doughnuts: Dip tops of fried doughnuts into desired glaze, then into a bowl of finely chopped walnuts, pecans or almonds.

Doughnut Glazes

Sugar Glaze: In a small saucepan, combine 2 cups sugar and 1-1/2 cups water. Bring to a boil over medium-high heat. Boil 4 minutes without stirring. Cool 15 minutes; stir in 1 teaspoon vanilla extract.

Orange Glaze: In a small bowl, combine 1 cup powdered sugar, 1/4 teaspoon ground nutmeg and 1 teaspoon grated orange peel. Stir in 1 to 2 tablespoons orange juice to make a smooth creamy glaze.

Maple Glaze: In a small bowl, combine 1 cup powdered sugar, 1/2 teaspoon maple flavoring and 3 to 4 tablespoons pure maple syrup, making a smooth creamy glaze.

Chocolate Glaze: In top of a double boiler, melt 4 ounces semisweet chocolate and 1/3 cup butter over simmering water. Remove from heat. Stir in 1-1/2 cups powdered sugar, 2 teaspoons vanilla extract and 3 to 4 tablespoons hot water, making a smooth creamy glaze.

Spicy Glaze: In a small bowl, combine 1 cup powdered sugar and 1/2 teaspoon each ground cinnamon and ground nutmeg. Stir in 1 to 2 tablespoons milk, making a smooth creamy glaze.

How to Make Crumpets

1/Spoon batter into rings, 1/2 inch deep. Cook over medium heat about 7 minutes or until surface appears dry and forms a thin skin.

2/Remove rings. Turn crumpets; lightly brown other side, about 3 minutes. To serve, toast without splitting.

Crumpets

Toast these moist, chewy English tea biscuits and serve with sweet butter and marmalade.

1 (1/4-oz.) pkg. active dry yeast (1 tablespoon)	**2 tablespoons butter, melted**
1 teaspoon sugar	**1-1/4 teaspoons salt**
3/4 cup warm water (110F, 45C)	**1-1/4 cups all-purpose flour**
1/2 cup milk, room temperature	**1/2 teaspoon baking soda**
	1 tablespoon hot water

In large bowl of electric mixer, dissolve yeast and sugar in 3/4 cup water. Let stand until foamy, 5 to 10 minutes. Add milk, butter, salt and flour. Beat at medium speed with electric mixer 4 minutes or, beat 400 vigorous strokes by hand. Cover with a slightly damp towel. Let rise in a warm place, free from drafts, until doubled in bulk, about 1-1/2 hours. In a small bowl, stir soda into 1 tablespoon hot water. Stir into batter; beat until thoroughly blended. Cover with a slightly damp towel. Let rise again until doubled in bulk, about 1 hour. Lightly grease a griddle or skillet and crumpet or muffin rings or use 7-ounce tuna cans with tops and bottoms removed. Arrange rings on griddle, not touching. **Preheat griddle** over medium heat until a drop of water sizzles on surface. Spoon batter into rings, 1/2 inch deep. Cook over medium heat about 7 minutes or until surface appears dry and forms a thin skin. Remove rings. Turn crumpets; lightly brown other side, about 3 minutes. Repeat with remaining batter. Serve warm or, cool on racks. To serve, toast without splitting. Makes 10 to 12 crumpets.

Variations

Spiced Crumpets: Reduce salt to 1/2 teaspoon. Add 1-1/2 tablespoons sugar and 1/4 teaspoon each of ground cinnamon and ground nutmeg.
Whole-Wheat Crumpets: Substitute 1/2 cup whole-wheat flour for 1/2 cup all-purpose flour. Add 1 tablespoon honey and 3 tablespoons wheat germ.

Pain Perdu

Better known as French toast, try whole-grain breads for a delightful taste treat!

3 eggs, room temperature
2/3 cup half and half
1/4 cup honey
1/3 cup rum, brandy, milk or orange juice
1/2 teaspoon ground cinnamon
1/2 teaspoon ground nutmeg

1/8 teaspoon salt
8 slices white or whole-grain bread,
   1/2 to 3/4 inch thick
About 1/4 cup butter
Powdered sugar
Honey, jam or syrup

Preheat oven to 350F (175C). In a medium, shallow bowl, lightly beat eggs. Stir in half and half; honey; rum, brandy, milk or orange juice; cinnamon; nutmeg and salt; set aside. Cut crusts from bread, if desired. Cut each slice in half diagonally; set aside. Melt butter in a large skillet over medium-high heat. Dip each piece of bread in egg mixture, turning to coat both sides. Fry coated bread in melted butter until golden brown on both sides. Remove from pan; blot on paper towels. Keep warm in oven until all pieces are fried. Serve immediately. Sprinkle with powdered sugar or serve with honey, jam or your favorite syrup. Makes 4 to 6 servings.

Variations

Orange French Toast: Substitute 2/3 cup orange juice for 2/3 cup half and half. Add 1 tablespoon grated orange peel. Serve with melted orange marmalade.
Peanut-Butter French Toast: Blend 1/3 cup peanut butter into egg mixture. Serve with melted peanut butter.
Baked French Toast: Preheat oven to 450F (230C). Place 1/4 cup unsalted butter in each of 2 (15" x 10") jelly-roll pans or baking sheets with raised sides. Place pans in oven until butter melts. Dip bread slices in egg mixture as directed. Arrange 8 half slices on each jelly-roll pan. Bake 5 minutes. Turn slices over; bake 5 minutes longer or until golden brown.

Hot Buttered Rum Syrup

Wonderful on blustery winter mornings served over French toast, waffles or pancakes!

1 cup sugar
1/3 cup water
1 large cinnamon stick, broken in half

1/3 cup cold butter, cut into 4 pieces
2 to 3 tablespoons rum

Combine sugar, water and cinnamon stick in small saucepan; bring to a boil over high heat. Continue to boil, without stirring, 2 minutes. Remove from heat. Add butter; stir briskly until melted. Stir in rum until blended. Pour into a small pitcher. Serve warm or at room temperature. Makes about 1-1/4 cups.

Sour-Cream Waffles

Use your imagination to vary the flavor of these rich waffle sensations!

3 eggs, separated, room temperature
1-1/2 cups all-purpose flour
2 teaspoons baking powder
1/2 teaspoon baking soda
1/4 teaspoon salt
2 tablespoons granulated sugar
3/4 cup dairy sour cream, room temperature

3/4 cup milk, room temperature
2/3 cup butter, melted
1/2 teaspoon vanilla extract
Syrup, honey, preserves or other spread,
   if desired
Fresh fruit and powdered sugar, if desired

Follow manufacturer's directions for preheating and greasing waffle iron. In a medium bowl, beat egg whites until stiff but not dry; set aside. In a large bowl, combine flour, baking powder, baking soda, salt and granulated sugar; set aside. In a medium bowl, lightly beat egg yolks. Stir in sour cream, milk, butter and vanilla extract. Stir into flour mixture only until dry ingredients are moistened. Gently fold in beaten egg whites. Bake according to manufacturer's directions. Serve with syrup, honey, preserves or your favorite spread, if desired. Or, spoon fresh fruit on top, then sprinkle with powdered sugar. Makes 4 to 8 waffles.

Variations

Gingerbread Waffles: Add 3/4 teaspoon ground ginger, 1/4 teaspoon each ground cinnamon and ground allspice and 2 tablespoons molasses. Stir in 2 teaspoons minced crystallized ginger, if desired.
Cornmeal Waffles: Omit vanilla. Reduce granulated sugar to 1 tablespoon. Substitute 3/4 cup cornmeal for 3/4 cup all-purpose flour. Stir in 2 tablespoons diced green chilies, if desired.
Luau Waffles: Add 1 (8-ounce) can crushed pineapple, well drained and blotted on paper towels. Add 1/2 cup flaked coconut.
Whole-Wheat Waffles: Substitute 3/4 cup whole-wheat flour for 3/4 cup all-purpose flour. Add 1/4 cup wheat germ.
Bran Waffles: Add 1/2 cup bran flakes and 2 teaspoons molasses.
Ham & Cheese Waffles: Omit vanilla. Reduce granulated sugar to 2 teaspoons. Add 1 cup (4 ounces) shredded Cheddar cheese and 1/2 cup diced cooked ham.
Spiced Nut Waffles: Add 1/2 cup finely chopped walnuts or pecans, 1/2 teaspoon ground cinnamon and 1/4 teaspoon each ground nutmeg and ground allspice.
Sourdough Waffles: Substitute 1 cup sourdough starter for 3/4 cup flour and 3/4 cup milk.

Cranberry-Orange Syrup

A nice change from the ordinary!

1 cup cranberry juice
1 cup sugar

2 tablespoons thawed frozen-
   orange-juice concentrate

Combine all ingredients in a small saucepan. Bring to a rolling boil over high heat. Without stirring, continue to boil 5 minutes. Serve slightly warm. Makes about 1 cup.

Variation

Substitute 1 cup of any clear fruit juice for cranberry juice.

Ron's Cream Pancakes

These feather-light pancakes—flavored with lemon and vanilla—are my husband's favorite.

2 eggs, separated, room temperature
1 cup all-purpose flour
1 teaspoon baking powder
1/4 teaspoon salt
1/3 cup powdered sugar

1 cup half and half, room temperature
1 teaspoon vanilla extract
1-1/2 teaspoons freshly grated lemon peel
Powdered sugar, honey, syrup or jam

Lightly grease a large griddle or skillet. Preheat griddle over medium heat until a drop of water bounces across surface or, preheat electric griddle or skillet to 425F (220C). In a medium bowl, beat egg whites until stiff but not dry; set aside. In a large bowl, combine flour, baking powder, salt and 1/3 cup powdered sugar; set aside. In a medium bowl, lightly beat egg yolks. Stir in half and half, vanilla and lemon peel. Stir into flour mixture only until dry ingredients are moistened. Gently fold in beaten egg whites. Cook on preheated griddle until bottoms are golden brown and bubbles begin to break through surface. Turn and cook other side until golden brown. Sprinkle with powdered sugar or, serve with honey, syrup or your favorite jam. Makes 12 to 16 pancakes.

Variations

Zucchini-Cheese Pancakes: Reduce sugar to 1 tablespoon. Toss 1/2 cup grated zucchini and 1/2 cup (2 ounces) shredded Cheddar cheese with flour mixture.

Whole-Wheat Pancakes: Substitute 1/2 cup whole-wheat flour for 1/2 cup all-purpose flour. Add 2 tablespoons wheat germ.

Spicy Orange Pancakes: Substitute 1 cup orange juice for half and half. Substitute 2 teaspoons grated orange peel for lemon peel. Add 1/2 teaspoon each of ground nutmeg and ground cinnamon. Stir in 1/3 cup finely chopped mandarin oranges, if desired.

Eggnog Pancakes: Omit lemon peel. Substitute 1 cup dairy eggnog for half and half. Add 1/2 teaspoon ground nutmeg and 1/4 teaspoon each ground cinnamon and rum extract.

Banana Pancakes: Immediately after pouring batter onto griddle, place 4 or 5 thin banana slices on each pancake.

Sunflower-Seed Pancakes: Reduce sugar to 1 tablespoon. Add 1/2 cup raw hulled sunflower seeds.

Buckwheat Pancakes: Omit sugar. Add 2 tablespoons pure maple syrup and 1/2 teaspoon maple flavoring. Substitute 1/4 cup buckwheat flour for 1/4 cup all-purpose flour.

Sourdough Pancakes: Reduce sugar to 1 tablespoon. Substitute 1 cup sourdough starter for 3/4 cup flour and 3/4 cup half and half.

Bourbon-Pecan Pancakes: Substitute 1/4 cup bourbon for 1/4 cup half and half. Add 1/2 cup finely chopped pecans.

Tip *Homemade syrups thicken as they cool. If syrups begin to form sugar crystals, reheat gently until crystals dissolve. Serve syrups warm to intensify flavor. Refrigerate syrups containing butter; warm before serving.*

Blueberry-Orange Yeast Cakes

Fit for a king! Serve these elegant, light pancakes with Honey-Berry Butter, page 46.

1 (1/4-oz.) pkg. active dry yeast
   (1 tablespoon)
1/2 cup warm orange juice (110F, 45C)
5 eggs, separated, room temperature
1-1/2 cups milk, room temperature
Grated peel of 1 large orange
2/3 cup butter, melted

3 tablespoons sugar
1 teaspoon salt
1 teaspoon vanilla extract
3-1/2 cups all-purpose flour
1/4 teaspoon cream of tartar
1 to 1-1/2 cups fresh or
   frozen blueberries, not thawed

In large bowl of electric mixer, dissolve yeast in orange juice. Let stand until foamy, 5 to 10 minutes. In small bowl of electric mixer, beat egg whites with cream of tartar until stiff but not dry; set aside. Add milk, egg yolks, orange peel, butter, sugar, salt, vanilla and flour to foamy yeast mixture. Beat at medium-low speed only until flour is moistened and batter is almost smooth. Fold in beaten egg whites. Cover with a slightly damp towel. Let rise in a warm place, free from drafts, until doubled in bulk, about 1 hour. Lightly grease a griddle or skillet. Preheat to 425F (220C) or until a drop of water bounces across surface. Stir down batter. Fold in fresh or frozen blueberries. To make each pancake, pour about 1/4 cup batter onto preheated griddle. Cook until bottom is golden brown and bubbles begin to break through surface. Turn; cook other side until golden brown. Makes 35 to 40 pancakes.

Spiced Honey-Butter Syrup

Lightly spiced and buttery good!

1 cup honey
1/4 cup butter
1/2 teaspoon ground cinnamon

1/4 teaspoon ground ginger
1 teaspoon vanilla extract

In a small saucepan, combine honey, butter, cinnamon and ginger. Stirring occasionally, cook over medium heat until butter melts and mixture is warmed through. Remove from heat; stir in vanilla. Pour into a small pitcher. Makes about 1-1/4 cups.

Variation

Honey-Almond Syrup: Substitute 3/4 to 1 teaspoon almond extract for vanilla extract.

Tip *For pretty butter: Create butter curls with a butter curler; butter balls with a melon baller; butter molds with decorative butter or candy molds; or use a pastry bag with a large star tip to pipe butter into pretty glass bowls.*

Index

A

Aebleskivers, Danish 162
All-Wheat Bread 39
Almond Bread, Amaretto- 82
Almond Filling 103
Almond Filling, Crunchy- 105
Almond Loaf, Nutmeg- 149
Almond-Raisin Bagels 92
Almond Syrup, Honey- 172
Altitude Adjustments, High- 15
Amaretto-Almond Bread 82
Amaretto Butter 82
Amaretto-Nut Butter 82
Ambrosia Muffins, Lemon- 109
Anadama Bread 41
Anadama Bread, Cheddar 41
Anadama Bread, Raisin 41
Apple Bread, Oatmeal- 56
Apple Filling, Spiced- 103
Apple Muffins, Candied- 108
Apple-Streusel Bread, Dutch 135
Apple Twist, Caramel- 129
Applesauce, Quick & Fresh 162
Apricot & Chocolate-Chip Bread 132
Apricot Boston-Brown Bread 138
Apricot Bread, Banana- 130
Apricot Bread, Danish 80
Apricot Filling 105
Apricot-Nectar Bread 132
Apricot-Orange Bread 132
Apricot-Raisin Bread 132
Austrian Guglhupf 78-79
Avocado-Orange Bread, California 131

B

Babka, Polish Cheese 63
Bacon Bread, Peanut-Butter & 83
Bagels 92-93
Baguettes, Roquefort 29
Baked Brown Bread 138
Baked French Toast 169
Baking and Cooling 14
Banana & Bran Muffins, Maple- 109
Banana-Apricot Bread 130
Banana Bread, Blueberry- 130
Banana Bread, Old-Fashioned 130
Banana Bread, Raisin- 130
Banana Bread, Whole-Wheat 130
Banana-Daiquiri Bread 130
Banana Gingerbread 139
Banana Pancakes 171
Basic Sourdough Starter 24
Basic Sweet Yeast Dough 59
Basic White Bread 19, 22, 98
Basket Bread, Easter- 146-147
Baskets, Toast 56-57
Batter Breads 74-85
Beer & Rye Bread 55
Beer-Rye Bagels 92
Beer Sticks 98-99
Berry Butter, Honey- 46
Biscuits
    Butter 113
    Buttermilk-Yeast 87
    Chili-Cheese 87
    Double-Butter 87
    Easy Cream 113
    Ham & Cheese Drop 112
    Herbed Cheese 113
    Onion 113

    Raisin-Nut 113
    Rye 113
    Seeded 113
    Sesame-Yeast 87
    Sherried Tea 114-115
    Sugar 'N Spice 87
    Sunflower-Seed 113
    Whole-Wheat 113
Black Bread, Russian 52
Blender Butter 42
Blueberries 'N Cheese Coffeecake 137
Blueberry-Banana Bread 130
Blueberry Bread, Ginger-Peachy 136
Blueberry Muffins, Lemon- 108
Blueberry-Orange Yeast Cakes 172
Blueberry-Streusel Muffins 108
Blueberry-Yogurt Bread 75
Boston Brown Bread 138
Boston Brown Bread, Apricot 138
Bourbon-Pecan Pancakes 171
Braided Stuffing Bread 141
Braiding Dough 73
Bran Bread, Honey- 119
Bran Bread, Molasses- 44-45, 49, 98
Bran Brown Bread 119
Bran Buns, Wheat- 94-95
Bran Muffins, Maple-Banana & 109
Bran Waffles 170
Bread Basics 4-17
Bread Ingredients 5-8
Bread Talk 9-14
Breadsticks Italiano 99
Breadsticks, Speedy 32
Brioche 20-22
Brioche à Tête 20
Brioche au Fromage 20
Brioche, Lemon-Pecan 20
Brioches, Petites 20
Brittlebread, Scandinavian 116
Bromate, see Potassium Bromate
Brown Bread, Baked 138
Brown Bread, Boston 138
Brown Bread, Bran 119
Buckwheat Pancakes 171
Buns, Rolls & 90-91, 98
Buns, see Rolls & Buns
Butter Biscuits 113
Butters
    Amaretto 82
    Amaretto-Nut 82
    Blender 42
    Cheddar 85
    Citrus-Honey 46
    Ginger-Peachy 136
    Homemade 42
    Honey 46
    Honey-Berry 46
    Maple 48
    Molasses 48
    Sesame 53
    Spirited 82
    Sunflower-Seed 53
Butterflake Bread 26, 98
Buttermilk-Wheat Bread 43
Buttermilk-Yeast Biscuits 87
Butter-Top Bread 19

C

Cake Doughnuts 166
California Avocado-Orange Bread 131

Candied-Apple Muffins 108
Candy-Cane Bread 154-155
Caramel-Apple Twist 129
Carrot-Raisin Bread, Wheaty 50
Challah 143
Cheddar Butter 85
Cheese Breads & Coffeecakes
    Blueberries 'N Cheese Coffeecake 137
    Cheddar Anadama Bread 41
    Cheddar-Cheese Bagels 92
    Cheddar-Pear Coffeecake 61
    Cheese Croutons 57
    Cheesy-Dill Rye Bread 53
    Cheesy Sunflower Cornbread 126
    Chili-Cheese Biscuits 87
    Dill-Cheese Bread 83
    Garlic-Cheese Bread 31
    Green-Chili & Cheese Bread 85
    Ham & Cheese Drop Biscuits 112
    Herbed Cheese Biscuits 113
    Italian Cheese Crescents 114-115
    Khachapuri 30-31
    Nutty Double-Cheese Bread 122
    Olive-Cheese Bread 123
    Polish Cheese Babka 63
    Poppy-Cheddar Bread 121
    Poppy-Parmesan Bread 121
    Pull-Apart Cheese Ring 122
    Quick Cheese Pastries 97
    Ricotta-Orange Ring 64
    Swiss Onion Bread 33
    Zucchini-Cheese Bread 120
    Zucchini-Cheese Pancakes 171
Cheese Filling, Cherry- 103
Cheese Filling, Currant- 105
Cheese Filling, Herb- 103
Cheese Filling, Sweet 103
Cheese Spread, Prune- 94
Cherry-Cheese Filling 103
Cherry-Cordial Loaf 149
Cherry Valentine Bread 142-143
Chili-Cheese Biscuits 87
Chive Rolls, Potato- 44-45, 96, 98
Chocolat, Petits Pains au 102
Chocolate-Chip Bread, Apricot & 132
Chocolate Doughnuts 166
Chocolate-Streusel Coffeecake 134
Christmas-Tree Bread, Eggnog 156
Cinnamon Bread, Old-Fashioned 62
Cinnamon-Honey Butter 46
Cinnamon-Nut Rolls 88
Cinnamon-Nut Strips 65
Cinnamon-Raisin English Muffins 163
Cinnamon Rolls, Grandmother's 88, 98
Citrus-Honey Butter 46
Classic Croissants 44-45, 100-101
Classic French Bread 22-23
Cloverleaf Rolls 90
Cocktail Bagels 93
Cocktail-Bagel Spreads 93
Coconut Grass 145
Coffeecakes, Sweet Quick Breads & 128-139
Coffeecakes, Sweet Yeast Breads & 58-73
Coffeecakes
    Austrian Guglhupf 78-79
    Blueberries 'N Cheese Coffeecake 137
    Caramel-Apple Twist 129
    Cheddar-Pear Coffeecake 61
    Cherry Valentine Bread 142

Index

Chocolate-Streusel Coffeecake 134
Cookie-Filled Coffeecake 59
French Mocha Ring 60
Marzipan Coffee Ring 70-71
Peaches 'N Cream Coffeecake 76-77
Polish Cheese Babka 63
Raspberry-Ripple Coffeecake 132-133
Ricotta-Orange Ring 64
Sally Lunn 79
Cooling and Baking 14
Corn-Kernel Batter Bread 84
Cornbreads
Cheesy Sunflower Cornbread 126
Herbed Cornbread 126
High-Rise Cornbread 40
Mexican-Cornbread Ring 124-125
Nutty Pumpkin Cornbread 124
Peanut-Butter & Sausage Cornbread 126
Sweet Cornbread 126
Traditional Cornbread 126
Cornmeal Waffles 170
Cracked-Wheat Bread 36
Crackers
Scandinavian Brittlebread 116
Toasted-Oat Crisps 117
Cranberry-Orange Syrup 170
Cream Filling, Rum- 105
Cream, Strawberry Devonshire 161
Cream, Whipped Ginger 70
Cream-Cheese Spread, Lox & 93
Cream-Cheese Spread, Orange & 94-95
Creamy Lemon Loaf 127
Creamy Maple Spread 43
Croissant Fillings 103
Croissants 100-103
Croissants & Danish Pastries, Freezing 106
Croutons 57
Crumpets 168
Crunchy Onion Sticks 113
Crunchy-Almond Filling 105
Crust, The Upper 15
Currant-Cheese Filling 105

D
Daiquiri Bread, Banana- 130
Danish Aebleskivers 162
Danish Apricot Bread 80
Danish Pastries 104-106
Danish Pastries, Freezing Croissants & 106
Danish-Pastry Fillings 105
Danish Pastry, Quick 104
Danish-Pastry Shapes 106
Danish Prune Bread 80-81
Date Bread, Ginger- 139
Date Bread, Pumpkin-Seed & 159
Date Bread, Whole-Earth 44-46
Diet Bread, Salt-Free 19
Dill-Cheese Bread 83
Dill Rye Bread, Cheesy- 53
Dilly-Rye Bread 53
Double-Butter Biscuits 87
Dough, Storing & Freezing Unbaked 55
Doughnut Glazes 167
Doughnuts
Cake 166
Chocolate 166
Gingerbread 166
Jelly 167
Nut-Coated 167
Raised 167

Spiced 166
Spicy Raisin 167
Dresden Stollen 152-153
Dutch Apple-Streusel Bread 135

E
Easter-Basket Bread 146-147
Easter Bread, Italian 144
Easy Cream Biscuits 113
Egg Bagels 92
Egg Bread, Mama's 27, 98
Eggnog Christmas-Tree Bread 156
Eggnog Pancakes 171
English Muffins 163
English-Muffin Bread 163

F
Fennel Sticks 99
Festive & Holiday Breads 140-159
Fillings, Croissant 103
Fillings, Danish-Pastry 105
Flour 5
Flours, Meals & Grains, Special 6
Freezing & Storing Bread 54
Freezing & Storing Unbaked Dough 55
Freezing Croissants & Danish Pastries 106
French Bread, Classic 22-23
French Bread, Peasant 27
French Bread, Wheat 23
French Mocha Ring 60
French Toast, Baked 169
French Toast, see Pain Perdu 169
Fried Bread 40
Fried Breads, Griddle & 160-172
Fried Croutons 57
Fruit or Nut Bread 19
Fruited-Wheat Bread 69

G
Griddle & Fried Breads 160-172
Garlic Croutons 57
Garlic-Cheese Bread 31
Ginger Cream, Whipped 70
Ginger-Date Bread 139
Ginger-Orange Spread 94
Ginger-Peachy Blueberry Bread 136
Ginger-Peachy Butter 136
Gingerbread
Banana Gingerbread 139
Gingerbread Doughnuts 166
Gingerbread Waffles 170
Twice Gingerbread 139
Glazes, Doughnut 167
Graham Loaf, Honey- 139
Grain Bread, Malted Multi- 37
Grains, Special Flours, Meals & 7
Grandma's Oatmeal Bread 44-45, 47
Grandmother's Cinnamon Rolls 88, 98
Grass, Coconut 145
Green-Chili & Cheese Bread 85
Griddle Scones, Orange 161
Griddle Scones, Scottish 161
Ground-Nut Filling 105
Guglhupf, Austrian 78-79
Gumdrop-Holly Wreath 150-151

H
Ham & Cheese Drop Biscuits 112
Ham & Cheese Waffles 170
Hamburger Buns 91
Hand-Print Rolls 91

Hawaiian Sweet Bread 75
Herb Bread 19
Herbed Cheese Biscuits 113
Herb-Cheese Filling 103
Herbed Cornbread 126
Herbed Mushroom Bread 32
High-Altitude Adjustments 15
High-Rise Cornbread 40
Holiday Breads, Festive & 140-159
Holly Wreath, Gumdrop- 150-151
Homemade Butter 42
Hominy Honeys 110, 114
Honey-Almond Syrup 172
Honey-Berry Butter 46
Honey-Bran Bread 119
Honey Butter 46
Honey Butter, Cinnamon- 46
Honey Butter, Citrus- 46
Honey-Butter Syrup, Spiced 172
Honey-Graham Loaf 139
Hot Buttered Rum Syrup 169
Hot Cross Buns 145, 147
Hot-Dog Buns 91
How to Make Yeast Dough 9
Hungarian Langos 164-165

I
Ingredients, Bread 5-8
Irish Soda Bread 127
Italian Cheese Crescents 114-115
Italian Easter Bread 144
Italian-Sausage Bread 84
Italiano, Breadsticks 99

J
Jack-O-Lantern Bread 159
Jelly Doughnuts 167

K
Kaymak 52
Khachapuri 30-31, 152
Kneading and Mixing 9
Knot-Shape Rolls 90
Kugelhopf, see Austrian Guglhupf
Kulich 148, 152

L
Little Quick Breads 107-117
Little Yeast Breads 86-106
Langos, Hungarian 164-165
Langos, Sweet 164
Leavening Agents 7
Lemon-Ambrosia Muffins 109
Lemon-Blueberry Muffins 108
Lemon Loaf, Creamy 127
Lemon-Pecan Brioche 20
Limpa, Swedish 54, 152
Liquids 8
Lox & Cream-Cheese Spread 93
Luau Waffles 170
Lunn, Sally 79

M
Malted Multi-Grain Bread 37
Mama's Egg Bread 27, 98
Maple-Banana & Bran Muffins 109
Maple Butter 48
Maple-Pecan Popovers 112
Maple-Pecan Sticky Buns 89
Maple Spread, Creamy 43
Marzipan Coffee Ring 70-71
Meals & Grains, Special Flours 7

Index

Melba Toast 23
Mexican-Cornbread Ring 124-125
Mixing and Kneading 9
Molasses Butter 48
Molasses-Bran Bread 44-45, 49, 98
Monkey Bread 19
Muffin Bread, English- 163
Muffins
  Blueberry-Streusel 108
  Candied-Apple 108
  Cinnamon-Raisin English 163
  English 163
  Hominy Honeys 110, 114
  Lemon-Ambrosia 109
  Lemon-Blueberry 108
  Maple-Banana & Bran 109
  Open Sesames 110
  Sourdough English 163
  Whole-Wheat English 163
Multi-Grain Bread, Malted 37
Mushroom Bread, Herbed 32
Mushroom Spread, Nutty 93

N
Nut Biscuits, Raisin- 113
Nut Butter, Amaretto- 82
Nut-Coated Doughnuts 167
Nut Filling, Ground- 105
Nut or Fruit Bread 19
Nut Rolls, Cinnamon- 88
Nut Sticky Buns, Raisin- 89
Nut Strips, Cinnamon 65
Nut Waffles, Spiced 170
Nutmeg-Almond Loaf 149
Nutty Double-Cheese Bread 122
Nutty Mushroom Spread 93
Nutty Pumpkin Cornbread 124

O
Oatmeal Breads
  Grandma's Oatmeal Bread 44-45, 47
  Oatmeal-Apple Bread 56
  Oatmeal Bread with Raisins or Nuts 47
  Oatmeal Honor Rolls 96
  Toasted-Oat Crisps 117
  Wheat & Oatmeal Bread 47
Old-Fashioned Banana Bread 130
Old-Fashioned Cinnamon Bread 62
Olive-Cheese Bread 123
Onion Breads
  Crunchy Onion Sticks 113
  Onion Bagels 92
  Onion Biscuits 113
  Onion Buns 91
  Swiss Onion Bread 33
Open Sesames 110
Orange & Cream-Cheese Spread 94-95
Orange Bread, Apricot- 132
Orange Bread, California Avocado- 131
Orange French Toast 169
Orange Griddle Scones 161
Orange Pancakes, Spicy 171
Orange-Pecan Spirals 114, 116-117
Orange Ring, Ricotta- 64-65
Orange Spread, Ginger- 94
Orange Syrup, Cranberry- 170
Orange Yeast Cakes, Blueberry- 172
Oval Rolls 91
Overnight Sweet Dough 59

P
Pain Perdu 169
Pan Rolls 91
Pancakes
  Banana Pancakes 171
  Blueberry-Orange Yeast Cakes 172
  Bourbon-Pecan Pancakes 171
  Buckwheat Pancakes 171
  Eggnog Pancakes 171
  Ron's Cream Pancakes 171
  Sourdough Pancakes 171
  Spicy Orange Pancakes 171
  Sunflower-Seed Pancakes 171
  Whole-Wheat Pancakes 171
  Zucchini-Cheese Pancakes 171
Panettone 151
Parker-House Rolls 90
Parmesan Bread, Poppy- 121
Parmesan Popovers 112
Pashka 149, 152
Pastries, Danish 104-106
Pastries, Quick Cheese 97
Peaches 'N Cream Coffeecake 76-77
Peachy Blueberry Bread, Ginger- 136
Peachy Butter, Ginger- 136
Peanut-Butter & Bacon Bread 83
Peanut-Butter & Sausage Cornbread 126
Peanut-Butter French Toast 169
Pear Coffeecake, Cheddar- 61
Peasant French Bread 27
Pecan Pancakes, Bourbon- 171
Pecan Spirals, Orange- 114, 116-117
Pecan Sticky Buns, Maple- 89
Pepper Sticks 99
Pepperoni-Pizza Bread 121
Petites Brioches 20
Petits Pains au Chocolat 102
Piña-Colada Bread 131
Pita Bread 34
Pita Petals 34
Pizza Bread, Pepperoni- 121
Pizza Crisps 50-51
Polish Cheese Babka 63
Popovers 112
Poppy-Cheddar Bread 121
Poppy-Parmesan Bread 121
Poppy-Swirl Loaves 66-67
Potassium Bromate 5
Potato-Chive Rolls 44-45, 96, 98
Potatoes-au-Gratin Bread 28-29
Potato Sourdough Starter 24
Praline Rolls, Pumpkin 157
Praline-Rum Rolls 111
Problems, see What Went Wrong 16-17
Proofing Yeast 9
Prune Bread, Danish 80-81
Prune-Cheese Spread 94
Prune Filling 105
Pudding Bread, Rice- 137
Pull-Apart Cheese Ring 122
Pumpkin Cornbread, Nutty 124
Pumpkin-Praline Rolls 157
Pumpkin-Seed & Date Bread 159
Punching Down and Shaping 13

Q
Quick Breads, Little 107-117
Quick Breads, Savory 118-127
Quick & Fresh Applesauce 162
Quick Cheese Pastries 97

Quick Croissants 102
Quick Danish Pastry 104
Quick Sourdough Bread 25

R
Rais'n-Shine Bread 68
Rais'n-Shine Bread, Wheaty 68
Raised Doughnuts 167
Raisin Anadama Bread 41
Raisin-Banana Bread 130
Raisin Bread, Apricot- 132
Raisin Bread, Wheaty Carrot- 50
Raisin Doughnuts, Spicy 167
Raisin English Muffins, Cinnamon- 163
Raisin-Nut Biscuits 113
Raisin-Nut Sticky Buns 89
Raspberry-Ripple Coffeecake 132-133
Rice-Pudding Bread 137
Ricotta-Orange Ring 64-65
Ring, Marzipan Coffee 70-71
Rise, Setting Dough to 11
Rolls & Buns 90-91, 98
  Cinnamon-Nut Rolls 88
  Croissants 100-103
  Grandmother's Cinnamon Rolls 88, 98
  Hot Cross Buns 145, 147
  Hungarian Langos 164-165
  Italian Cheese Crescents 115
  Maple-Pecan Sticky Buns 89
  Oatmeal Honor Rolls 96
  Orange-Pecan Spirals 116-117
  Petites Brioches 20
  Popovers 112
  Potato-Chive Rolls 44-45, 96, 98
  Praline-Rum Rolls 111
  Pumpkin Praline Rolls 157
  Quick Croissants 102
  Raisin-Nut Sticky Buns 89
  Wheat-Bran Buns 94-95
  Whole-Wheat Croissants 102
Ron's Cream Pancakes 171
Roquefort Baguettes 29
Round Rolls 91
Rum Rolls, Praline- 111
Rum Syrup, Hot Buttered 169
Rum-Cream Filling 105
Russian Black Bread 52
Rye Breads
  Beer & Rye Bread 55
  Cheesy-Dill Rye Bread 53
  Dilly-Rye Bread 53
  Rye Biscuits 113
  Swedish Limpa 54
Rye Breads, Whole-Grain & 35-57
Rye Sourdough Starter 24

S
Saffron Bread 19
Sally Lunn 79
Salt-Free Diet Bread 19
San Francisco Sourdough Bread 22, 25
Sausage Bread, Italian- 84
Sausage Cornbread, Peanut-Butter & 126
Savory Quick Breads 118-127
Savory Stuffing Bread 141
Savory Yummy-Yam Bread 158
Scandinavian Brittlebread 116
Scones, Orange Griddle 161
Scottish Griddle Scones 161
Seed Butter, Sunflower 53

Index

Seeded Bagels 92
Seeded Biscuits 113
Seeded Bread 19
Sesame Butter 53
Sesame-Yeast Biscuits 87
Setting Dough to Rise 11
Shaping and Punching Down 13
Sherried Tea Biscuits 114-115
Shredded-Wheat Bread 21
Slashing and Topping 14
Soda Bread, Irish 127
Sour Cream Waffles 170
Sourdough
   Basic Sourdough Starter 24
   Potato Sourdough Starter 24
   Quick Sourdough Starter 25
   Rye Sourdough Starter 24
   San Francisco Sourdough Bread 22, 25
   Sourdough English Muffins 163
   Sourdough Pancakes 171
   Sourdough-Rye Bread 25
   Sourdough Waffles 170
   Sourdough-Wheat Bread 25
   Whole-Wheat Sourdough Starter 24
   Working with Sourdough 24
Special Flours, Meals & Grains 6
Special-Occasion Breads 141
Speedy Bread Sticks 32
Spice Biscuits, Sugar 'N 87
Spiced-Apple Filling 103
Spiced Crumpets 168
Spiced Doughnuts 166
Spiced Honey-Butter Syrup 172
Spiced Nut Waffles 170
Spicy Orange Pancakes 171
Spicy Raisin Doughnuts 167
Spiral Rolls 90
Spirited Butter 82
Spreads, also see Butters
   Cocktail-Bagel Spreads 93
   Creamy Maple Spread 43
   Ginger-Orange Spread 94
   Kaymak 52
   Lox & Cream-Cheese Spread 93
   Nutty Mushroom Spread 93
   Orange & Cream-Cheese Spread 94-95
   Prune-Cheese Spread 94
   Strawberry Devonshire Cream 161
   Whipped Ginger Cream 70
Sprouted Wheat-Berry Bread 38-39
Squaw Bread 42
Starter, Basic Sourdough 24
Sticks, Beer 98-99
Sticks, Crunchy Onion 113
Sticks, Speedy Bread 32
Sticky Buns, Maple-Pecan 89
Sticky Buns, Raisin-Nut 89
Stollen, Dresden 152-153
Storing & Freezing Bread 54

Storing & Freezing Unbaked Dough 55
Strawberries 'N Cream Bread 135
Strawberry Devonshire Cream 161
Streusel Bread, Dutch Apple- 135
Streusel Coffeecake, Chocolate- 134
Striezel, Viennese 72, 98
Strips, Cinnamon-Nut 65
Stuffing Bread, Braided 141
Stuffing Bread, Savory 141
Sugar 'N Spice Biscuits 87
Sunflower Cornbread, Cheesy 126
Sunflower-Seed & Yogurt Bread 48
Sunflower-Seed Biscuits 113
Sunflower-Seed Butter 53
Sunflower-Seed Pancakes 171
Sunflower-Wheat Loaf 126
Sunshine Popovers 112
Swedish Limpa 54, 152
Sweet Bread, Hawaiian 75
Sweet Cheese Filling 103
Sweet Cornbread 126
Sweet Dough, Overnight 59
Sweet Langos 164
Sweet Quick Breads & Coffeecakes 128-139
Sweet Yeast Breads & Coffeecakes 58-73
Sweet Yeast Dough, Basic 59
Swirl Loaves, Poppy- 66-67
Swiss Onion Bread 33
Syrups
   Cranberry-Orange Syrup 170
   Honey-Almond Syrup 172
   Hot Buttered Rum Syrup 169
   Spiced Honey-Butter Syrup 172

T
Tea Biscuits, Sherried 114-115
Techniques for Making Yeast Breads 9-14
The Upper Crust 15
Toast Baskets 56-57
Toast, French, see Pain Perdu
Toast, Melba 23
Toasted Wheat-Germ Bread 81
Toasted-Oat Crisps 117
Topping, Slashing and 14
Traditional Cornbread 126
Triticale Bread 36
Twice Gingerbread 139

V
Valentine Bread, Cherry 142-143
Viennese Striezel 72, 98

W
Waffles
   Bran 170
   Cornmeal 170
   Gingerbread 170
   Ham & Cheese 170
   Luau 170
   Sour Cream 170
   Sourdough 170

   Spiced Nut 170
   Whole-Wheat 170
Waldorf Bread, Wheaty 76
Water Bagels 92
What Went Wrong? 16-17
Wheat & Oatmeal Bread 47
Wheat-Berry Sprouts 38-39
Wheat-Bran Buns 94-95
Wheat Bread, Cracked- 36
Wheat Bread, Shredded- 21
Wheat French Bread 23
Wheat-Germ Bread, Toasted 81
Wheaty Carrot-Raisin Bread 50
Wheaty Popovers 112
Wheaty Rais'n-Shine Bread 68
Wheaty Waldorf Bread 76
Whipped Ginger Cream 70
White-Flour Yeast Breads 18-34
Whole-Earth Date Bread 44-46
Whole-Grain & Rye Breads 35-57
Whole-Wheat Breads
   All-Wheat 39
   Banana 130
   Biscuits 113
   Buttermilk-Wheat 43
   Croissants 102
   Crumpets 168
   English Muffins 163
   French 23
   Fruited-Wheat 69
   Irish Soda 127
   Pancakes 171
   Popovers 112
   Sprouted Wheat-Berry 38-39
   Sunflower-Wheat Loaf 126
   Waffles 170
   Wheat French 23
Whole-Wheat Sourdough Starter 24
Working with Sourdough 24
Wreath, Gumdrop-Holly 150-151

Y
Yam Bread, Savory Yummy- 158
Yam Bread, Yummy- 158
Yeast Breads
   Batter Breads 74-85
   Festive & Holiday Breads
   Little Yeast Breads 86-106
   Sweet Yeast Breads & Coffeecakes 58-73
   White-Flour Yeast Breads 18-34
   Whole-Grain & Rye Breads 35-57
Yeast Biscuits, Buttermilk 87
Yeast Biscuits, Sesame 87
Yogurt Bread, Blueberry- 75
Yogurt Bread, Sunflower-Seed & 48
Yummy-Yam Bread 158

Z
Zucchini-Cheese Bread 120
Zucchini-Cheese Pancakes 171

8.7 2 3 0 9 3 8 1 2 0 6 8 7 4